# *Fifteen*

# *Thousand*

# USEFUL PHRASES

Grenville Kleiser

IAP © 20009

Printed in Scotts Valley, CA – USA.

Kleiser, Grenville.

Fifteen Thousand Useful Phrases / Greenville Kleiser – 1st ed.

1. English language

Book Image:

© IAP

*One cannot always live in the palaces and state apartments of language, but we can refuse to spend our days in searching for its vilest slums.* William Watson

*Words without thought are dead sounds; thoughts without words are nothing. To think is to speak low; to speak is to think aloud.* Max Muller

*The first merit which attracts in the pages of a good writer, or the talk of a brilliant conversationalist, is the apt choice and contrast of the words employed. It is indeed a strange art to take these blocks rudely conceived for the purpose of the market or the bar, and by tact of application touch them to the finest meanings and distinctions.* Robert Louis Stevenson

*It is with words as with sunbeams, the more they are condensed, the deeper they burn.* Southey

*No noble or right style was ever yet founded but out of a sincere heart.* Ruskin

*Words are things; and a small drop of ink, falling like dew upon a thought, produces that which makes thousands, perhaps millions, think.* Byron

*A good phrase may outweigh a poor library.* Thomas W. Higginson

# PLAN OF CLASSIFICATION

# INTRODUCTION

The most powerful and the most perfect expression of thought and feeling through the medium of oral language must be traced to the mastery of words. Nothing is better suited to lead speakers and readers of English into an easy control of this language than the command of the phrase that perfectly expresses the thought. Every speaker's aim is to be heard and understood. A clear, crisp articulation holds an audience as by the spell of some irresistible power. The choice word, the correct phrase, are instruments that may reach the heart, and awake the soul if they fall upon the ear in melodious cadence; but if the utterance be harsh and discordant they fail to interest, fall upon deaf ears, and are as barren as seed sown on fallow ground. In language, nothing conduces so emphatically to the harmony of sounds as perfect phrasing--that is, the emphasizing of the relation of clause to clause, and of sentence to sentence by the systematic grouping of words. The phrase consists usually of a few words which denote a single idea that forms a separate part of a sentence. In this respect it differs from the clause, which is a short sentence that forms a distinct part of a composition, paragraph, or discourse. Correct phrasing is regulated by rests, such rests as do not break the continuity of a thought or the progress of the sense.

GRENVILLE KLEISER, who has devoted years of his diligent life to imparting the art of correct expression in speech and writing, has provided many aids for those who would know not merely what to say, but how to say it. He has taught also what the great HOLMES taught, that language is a temple in which the human soul is enshrined, and that it grows out of life--out of its joys and its sorrows, its burdens and its necessities. To him, as well as to the writer, the deep strong voice of man and the low sweet voice of woman are never heard at finer advantage than in the earnest but mellow tones of familiar speech. In the present volume Mr. Kleiser furnishes an additional and an exceptional aid for those who would have a mint of phrases at their command from which to draw when in need of the golden mean for expressing thought. Few indeed are the books fitted to-day for the purpose of imparting this knowledge, yet two centuries ago phrase-books were esteemed as supplements to the dictionaries, and have not by any manner of means lost their value. The guide to familiar quotations, the index to similes, the grammars, the readers, the machine-made letter-writer of mechanically perfect letters of congratulation or condolence--none are sententious enough to supply the need. By the compilation of this praxis, Mr. Kleiser has not only supplied it, but has furnished a means for the increase of one's vocabulary by practical methods. There are thousands of persons who may profit by the systematic study of such a book as this if they will familiarize themselves with the author's purpose by a careful reading of the preliminary pages of his book. To speak in public pleasingly and readily and to read well are accomplishments acquired only after many days, weeks even, of practice.

Foreigners sometimes reproach us for the asperity and discordance of our speech, and in general, this reproach is just, for there are many persons who do scanty justice to the vowel-elements of our language. Although these elements constitute its music they are continually mistreated. We flirt with and pirouette around them constantly. If it were not so, English would be found full of beauty and harmony of sound. Familiar with the maxim, "Take care of the vowels and the consonants will take care of themselves," a maxim that when put into practice has frequently led to the breaking-down of vowel values--the writer feels that the common custom of allowing "the consonants to take care of themselves" is pernicious. It leads to suppression or to imperfect utterance, and thus produces indistinct articulation.

The English language is so complex in character that it can scarcely be learned by rule, and can best be mastered by the study of such idioms and phrases as are provided in this book; but just as care must be taken to place every accent or stress on the proper syllable in the pronouncing of every word it contains, so must the stress or emphasis be placed on the proper word in every sentence spoken. To read or speak pleasingly one should resort to constant practice by doing so aloud in private, or preferably, in the presence of such persons as know good reading when they hear it and are masters of the melody of sounds. It was Dean Swift's belief that the common fluency of speech in many men and most women was due to scarcity of matter and scarcity of words. He claimed that a master of language possessed a mind full of ideas, and that before speaking, such a mind paused to select the choice word--the phrase best suited to the occasion. "Common speakers," he said, "have only one set of ideas, and one set of words to clothe them in," and these are always ready on the lips. Because he holds the Dean's view sound to-day, the writer will venture to warn the readers of this book against a habit that, growing far too common among us, should be checked, and this is the iteration and reiteration in conversation of "the battered, stale, and trite" phrases, the like of which were credited by the worthy Dean to the women of his time.

Human thought elaborates itself with the progress of intelligence. Speech is the harvest of thought, and the relation which exists between words and the mouths that speak them must be carefully observed. Just as nothing is more beautiful than a word fitly spoken, so nothing is rarer than the use of a word in its exact meaning. There is a tendency to overwork both words and phrases that is not restricted to any particular class. The learned sin in this respect even as do the ignorant, and the practice spreads until it becomes an epidemic. The epidemic word with us yesterday was unquestionably "conscription"; several months ago it was "preparedness." Before then "efficiency" was heard on every side and succeeded in superseding "vocational teaching," only to be displaced in turn by "life extension" activities. "Safety-first" had a long run which was brought almost to abrupt end by "strict accountability," but these are mere reflections of our cosmopolitan life and activities. There are others that stand out as indicators of brain-weariness. These are most frequently met in the work of our novelists.

English authors and journalists are abusing and overworking the word intrigue to-day. Sir Arthur Quillercouch on page 81 of his book "On the Art of Writing" uses it: "We are intrigued by the process of manufacture instead of being wearied by a description of the ready-made article." Mrs. Sidgwick in "Salt and Savor," page 232, wrote: "But what intrigued her was Little Mamma's remark at breakfast," From the Parliamentary news, one learns that "Mr. Harcourt intrigued the House of Commons by his sustained silence for two years" and that "London is interested in, and not a little intrigued, by the statement."

This use of intrigue in the sense of "perplex, puzzle, trick, or deceive" dates from 1600. Then it fell into a state of somnolence, and after an existence of innocuous desuetude lasting till 1794 it was revived, only to hibernate again until 1894. It owes its new lease of life to a writer on The Westminster Gazette, a London journal famous for its competitions in aid of the restoring of the dead meanings of words.

One is almost exasperated by the repeated use and abuse of the word "intimate" in a recently published work of fiction, by an author who aspires to the first rank in his profession. He writes of "the intimate dimness of the room;" "a fierce intimate whispering;" "a look that was intimate;" "the noise of the city was intimate," etc. Who has not heard, "The idea!" "What's the idea?" "Is that the idea?" "Yes, that's the idea," with increased inflection at each repetition. And who is without a friend who at some time or another has not sprung "meticulous" upon him? Another example is afforded by the endemic use of "of sorts" which struck London while the writer was in that city a few years ago. Whence it came no one knew, but it was heard on every side. "She was a woman of sorts;" "he is a Tory of sorts;" "he had a religion of sorts;" "he was a critic of sorts." While it originally meant "of different or various kinds," as hats of sorts; offices of sorts; cheeses of sorts, etc., it is now used disparagingly, and implies something of a kind that is not satisfactory, or of a character that is rather poor. This, as Shakespeare might have said, is "Sodden business! There's a stewed phrase indeed!"[1]

The abuse of phrases and the misuse of words rife among us can be checked by diligent exercises in good English, such as this book provides. These exercises, in conjunction with others to be found in different volumes by the same author, will serve to correct careless diction and slovenly speech, and lead to the art of speaking and writing correctly; for, after all, accuracy in the use of words is more a matter of habit than of theory, and once it is acquired it becomes just as easy to speak or to write good English as bad English. It was Chesterfield's resolution not to speak a word in conversation which was not the fittest he could recall. All persons should avoid using words whose meanings they do not know, and with the correct application of which they are unfamiliar. The best spoken and the best written English is that which conforms to the language as used by men and women of culture--a high standard, it is true, but one not so high that it is unattainable by any earnest student of the English tongue.

FRANK H. VIZETELLY.

---

[1] Troilus and Cressida, act iii, sc. 1.

# HOW TO USE THIS BOOK

The study of words, phrases, and literary expressions is a highly interesting pursuit. There is a reciprocal influence between thought and language. What we think molds the words we use, and the words we use react upon our thoughts. Hence a study of words is a study of ideas, and a stimulant to deep and original thinking.

We should not, however, study "sparkling words and sonorous phrases" with the object of introducing them consciously into our speech. To do so would inevitably lead to stiltedness and superficiality. Words and phrases should be studied as symbols of ideas, and as we become thoroughly familiar with them they will play an unconscious but effective part in our daily expression.

We acquire our vocabulary largely from our reading and our personal associates. The words we use are an unmistakable indication of our thought habits, tastes, ideals, and interests in life. In like manner, the habitual language of a people is a barometer of their intellectual, civil, moral, and spiritual ideals. A great and noble people express themselves in great and noble words.

Ruskin earnestly counsels us to form the habit of looking intensely at words. We should scrutinize them closely and endeavor to grasp their innermost meaning. There is an indefinable satisfaction in knowing how to choose and use words with accuracy and precision. As Fox once said, "I am never at a loss for a word, but Pitt always has the word."

All the great writers and orators have been diligent students of words. Demosthenes and Cicero were indefatigable in their study of language. Shakespeare, "infinite in faculty," took infinite pains to embody his thought in words of crystal clearness. Coleridge once said of him that one might as well try to dislodge a brick from a building with one's forefinger as to omit a single word from one of his finest passages.

Milton, master of majestic prose, under whose touch words became as living things; Flaubert, who believed there was one and one only best word with which to express a given thought; De Quincey, who exercised a weird-like power over words; Ruskin, whose rhythmic prose enchanted the ear; Keats, who brooded over phrases like a lover; Newman, of pure and melodious style; Stevenson, forever in quest of the scrupulously precise word; Tennyson, graceful and exquisite as the limpid stream; Emerson, of trenchant and epigrammatic style; Webster, whose virile words sometimes weighed a pound; and Lincoln, of simple, Saxon speech,--all these illustrious men were assiduous in their study of words.

Many persons of good education unconsciously circumscribe themselves within a small vocabulary. They have a knowledge of hundreds of desirable words which they do not put into practical use in their speech or writing. Many, too, are conscious of a poverty of language, which engenders in them a sense of timidity and self-depreciation. The method used for building a large vocabulary has usually been confined to the study of single words. This has produced good results, but it is believed that eminently better results can be obtained from a careful study of words and expressions, as furnished in this book, where words can be examined in their context.

It is intended and suggested that this study should be pursued in connection with, and as a supplement to, a good standard dictionary. Fifteen minutes a day devoted to this subject, in the manner outlined, will do more to improve and enlarge the vocabulary than an hour spent in desultory reading.

There is no better way in which to develop the mental qualities of clearness, accuracy, and precision, and to improve and enlarge the intellectual powers generally, than by regular and painstaking study of judiciously selected phrases and literary expressions.

# PLAN OF STUDY

First examine the book in a general way to grasp its character, scope, and purpose. Carefully note the following plan of classification of the various kinds of phrases, and choose for initial study a section which you think will be of the most immediate value to you.

1. USEFUL PHRASES 2. SIGNIFICANT PHRASES 3. FELICITOUS PHRASES 4. IMPRESSIVE PHRASES 5. PREPOSITIONAL PHRASES 6. BUSINESS PHRASES 7. LITERARY EXPRESSIONS 8. STRIKING SIMILES 9. CONVERSATIONAL PHRASES 10. PUBLIC SPEAKING PHRASES 11. MISCELLANEOUS PHRASES

There are many advantages in keeping before you a definite purpose in your study of this book. A well-defined plan will act as an incentive to regular and systematic effort, and incidentally develop your power of concentration.

It is desirable that you set apart a certain convenient time each day for this study. Regularity tends to produce maximum results. As you progress with this work your interest will be quickened and you will realize the desirability of giving more and more time to this important subject.

When you have chosen a section of the book which particularly appeals to you, begin your actual study by reading the phrases aloud. Read them slowly and understandingly. This tends to impress them more deeply upon your mind, and is in itself one of the best and most practical ways of acquiring a large and varied vocabulary. Moreover, the practice of fitting words to the mouth rapidly develops fluency and facility of speech.

Few persons realize the great value of reading aloud. Many of the foremost English stylists devoted a certain period regularly to this practice. Cardinal Newman read aloud each day a chapter from Cicero as a means of developing his ear for sentence-rhythm. Rufus Choate, in order to increase his command of language, and to avoid sinking into mere empty fluency, read aloud daily, during a large part of his life, a page or more from some great English author. As a writer has said, "The practice of storing the mind with choice passages from the best prose writers and poets, and thus flavoring it with the essence of good literatures, is one which is commended both by the best teachers and by the example of some of the most celebrated orators, who have adopted it with signal success."

This study should be pursued with pencil in hand, so that you may readily underscore phrases which make a special appeal to you. The free use of a pencil in marking significant parts of a book is good evidence of thoroughness. This, too, will facilitate your work of subsequent review.

The habit of regularly copying, in your own handwriting, one or more pages of phrases will be of immense practical value. This exercise is a great aid in developing a facile English style. The daily use of the pen has been recommended in all times as a valuable means of developing oral and literary expression.

A helpful exercise is to pronounce a phrase aloud and then fit it into a complete sentence of your own making. This practice gives added facility and resourcefulness in the use of words.

As an enthusiastic student of good English, you should carefully note striking and significant phrases or literary expressions which you find in your general reading. These should be set down in a note-book reserved for this exclusive purpose. In this way you can prepare many lists of your own, and thus greatly augment the value of this study.

The taste for beauty, truth, and harmony in language can be developed by careful study of well-selected phrases and literary expressions as furnished in this book. A good literary style is formed principally by daily study of great English writers, by careful examination of words in their context, and by a discriminating use of language at all times.

GRENVILLE KLEISER. New York City, July, 1917

# SECTION 1

# USEFUL PHRASES

A

abandoned hope
abated pride
abbreviated visit
abhorred thraldom [thraldom = enslaved
or in bondage]
abiding romance
abject submission
abjured ambition
able strategist
abnormal talents
abominably perverse
abounding happiness
abridged statement
abrogated law
abrupt transition
absolutely irrevocable
absorbed reverie
abstemious diet [abstemious = eating
and drinking in moderation]
abstract character
abstruse reasoning
absurdly dangerous
abundant opportunity
abusive epithet
abysmally apologetic
academic rigor
accelerated progress
accentuated playfulness
accepted littleness
accessible pleasures
accessory circumstances
accidental lapse
accommodating temper
accomplished ease
accredited agent
accumulated burden
accurate appraisement
accursed enemy
accusing glance
accustomed lucidity

aching desire
acknowledged authority
acoustical effects
acquired timidity
acrid controversy
acrimonious warfare
actively zealous
actualized ideals
acutely conscious
adamantine rigidity [adamantine =
unyielding; inflexible]
adaptive wit
adduced facts [adduce = cite as an
example]
adequate execution
adhesive quality
administered rebuke
admirable reserve
admissible evidence
admittedly inferior
admonitory gesture
adolescent youth
adorable vanity
adroit flatterer
adulated stranger
adventitious way [adventitious = not
inherent; added extrinsically]
adventurous mind
adverse experience
affably accommodating
affected indifference
affectionate approval
affianced lady
affirmative attitude
affluent language
affrighted slave
aggravated faults
aggregate body
aggressive selfishness
agile mind

agitated imagination
agonizing appeal
agreeable frankness
aimless confusion
airy splendor
alarming rapidity
alert acceptance
algebraic brevity
alien splendor
alleged reluctance
allegorical vein
allied subjects
alliterative suggestion
all-pervading influence
alluring idleness
alternating opinion
altogether dissimilar
altruistic ideal
amatory effusions [amatory = expressive
of sexual love]
amazing artifice
ambidextrous assistant
ambiguous grimace
ambitious project
ambling pedestrian
ambrosial essence [ambrosial = fragrant
or delicious; worthy of the gods; divine.]
amiable solicitude
amicable arrangement
amorous youth
ample culture
amusing artlessness
analogous example
analytical survey
ancestral creed
ancient garb
angelic softness
angry protestations
anguished entreaty
angular features
animated eloquence
annoying complications
anomalous appearance
anonymous benefactor
answering response
antagonistic views
antecedent facts

anticipated attention
antiquated prudery
anxious misgiving
apathetic greeting
aphoristic wit [aphoristic = Tersely
phrased statement]
apish agility
apocalyptic vision
apocryphal lodger [apocryphal =
questionable authenticity]
apologetic explanation
apostrophic dignity
appalling difficulties
apparent significance
appealing picture
appointed function
apposite illustration
appreciable relief
appreciative fervor
apprehensive dread
apprentice touch
appropriate designation
approving smile
approximately correct
aptly suggested
arbitrarily imposed
arch conspirator
arched embrasure [embrasure = flared
opening for a gun in a wall or parapet]
archeological pursuits
architectural grandeur
ardent protest
arduous quest
arid formula
aristocratic lineage
aromatic fragrance
arrant trifling
arrested development
arrogant imposition
artful adaptation
artificial suavity
artistic elegance
artless candor
ascending supremacy
ascetic devotion
ascribed productiveness
aspiring genius

assembled arguments
asserted activity
assiduously cultivated
assimilative power
assumed humiliation
assuredly enshrined
astonishing facility
astounding mistakes
astute observer
athletic prowess
atmospheric vagueness
atoning sacrifice
atrocious expression
atrophied view
attending circumstances
attentive deference
attenuated sound
attested loyalty
attractive exordium [exordium = introduction of a speech or treatise]
audacious mendicant [mendicant = depending on alms; beggar]
audible intimations

augmented force
august tribunal
auspicious moment
austere charm
authentic indications
authoritative critic
autobiographical pages
autocratic power
automatic termination
autumnal skies
auxiliary aids
available data
avaricious eyes
avenging fate
average excellence
averted calamity
avowed intention
awakened curiosity
awed devotion
awful dejection
awkward dilemma
axiomatic truth
azure sky

B

babbling gossip
bacchanalian desires
bachelor freedom
bad omen
baffled sagacity [sagacity = farsighted; wise]
balanced capacity
baldly described
baleful glances
balmy fragrance
bandying talk
baneful impression
banished silence
barbarous statecraft
barefaced appeal
barest commonplaces
barren opportunities
base intrigues
baseless assumptions
bashful modesty
basic principles
battered witticism
beaming countenance
bearish rudeness
beatific vision
beautiful modesty
beckoning horizon
becoming diffidence
bedraggled wretch
befitting honor
beggarly flimsiness
beguiling voice
belated acknowledgment
belittling fears
bellicose humanity
beneficent career
benevolent regard
benighted sense
benignant pity [benignant = favorable; beneficial; kind]
beseeching gesture
besetting heresy
besotted fanaticism
bestial ferocity
bewildering maze
bewitching airs

beyond peradventure [peradventure = perhaps]
bibulous diversions [bibulous = consumes alcoholic drink]
bigoted contempt
binding obligation
bitter recrimination
bizarre apparel
blackening west
blameless indolence
blanched desolation
bland confidence
blank misgivings
blasphemous hypocrisy
blatant discourse
blazing audacity
blazoned shield
bleak loneliness
blended impression
blessed condolence
blighted happiness
blind partizan
blissful consciousness
blistering satire
blithe disregard
bloated equivalent
bloodless creature
bloodthirsty malice
blundering discourtesy
blunt rusticity [rusticity = rustic; awkward or tactless]
blurred vision
blustering assertion
boastful positiveness
bodily activity
boisterous edification
bold generalization
bombastic prating [prating = idle talk]
bookish precision
boon companion
boorish abuse
bored demeanor
borrowed grace
bottomless abyss
boundless admiration
bountiful supply

16

boyish appreciation
braggart pretense
bravely vanquished
braying trumpet
brazen importunity [importunity = insistent request]
breathless eagerness
brief tenure
briefless barrister
bright interlude
brilliant embodiment
brisk energy
bristling temper
brittle sarcasm
broadening fame
broken murmurs

brooding peace
brutal composure
bubbling frivolities
bucolic cudgeling [bucolic = about shepherds or flocks; pastoral] [cudgeling = beat with a short heavy stick]
budding joy
bulky figure
buoyant pluck
burdensome business
burly strength
burning zeal
bursting laugh
busily engrossed
business acumen
bygone period

## C

cabalistic phrase [cabalistic = secret or hidden meaning]
cadaverous appearance
calamitous course
calculating admiration
callous indifference
calm resignation
calumnious suspicions [calumnious = harmful and often untrue; discredit]
cantankerous enemy
canting hypocrite [canting = monotonous platitudes; hypocritically pious]
capacious mind
capricious allurements
captivating speech
cardinal merit
careless parrying
caressing grasp
carping critic
castellated towers [castellated = with turrets and battlements like a castle]
casual violation
cataclysmic elements
causelessly frightened
caustic remark
cautious skepticism
cavernous gloom
ceaseless vigilance

celebrated instance
celestial joy
censorious critic
centralized wealth
ceremonious courtesy
cerulean blue [cerulean = azure; sky-blue]
challenge admiration
chance reflections
changing exigencies [exigencies = pressing or urgent situation]
chaotic plans
characteristic audacity
charitable allowance
charming radiance
chary instincts [chary = cautious; wary]
chastened hope
chatty familiarity
cheap resentment
cheery response
chequered career
cherished objects
childlike ingenuousness [ingenuous = frank; candid.]
chilled cynicism
chirpy familiarities
chivalrous spirit
choicest refinements
choleric temperament [choleric = easily

angered; bad-tempered]
choral chant
chronic frailties
churlish temper [churlish = boorish;
vulgar; rude]
circling eddyings
circuitous information
circumscribed purpose
civic consciousness
civilizing influence
clammy death
clamorous vibration
clangorous industry
clarion tone
class demarcations
classical objurgation [objurgation =
harsh rebuke]
clattering accents
clear insight
climactic revelation
clinching proof
cloaked nature
cloistered virtue
close condensation
cloudy magnificence
clownishly insensible
cloying sweetness [cloying = too filling,
rich, or sweet]
clumsy talk
clustering trees
coarse necessity
coaxing eloquence
coercive enactment
cogent statement
coherent thinking
coined metaphor
cold formalities
collateral duties
collective wisdom
colloquial display
colonial character
colossal failure
comatose state
combative tone
comforting reassurance
comic infelicity
commanding attitude

commendable purpose
commercial opulence
commingled emotion
commodiously arranged
common substratum
commonplace allusions
compact fitness
comparative scantiness
compassionate love
compelling force
compendious abstract
compensatory character
competent authority
competitive enterprise
complacent platitudes
complaining sea
complaisant observation
complete aloofness
complex notions
complicated maze
complimentary glance
component aspects
composed zeal
composite growth
compound idea
comprehensive design
compressed view
compromising rashness
compulsory repetition
compunctious visitings [compunctious =
feeling guilt]
concatenated pedantries [pedantries =
attention to detail or rules]
concealed advantage
conceivable comparison
concentrated vigor
concerted action
conciliating air
concomitant events
concrete realities
concurrent testimony
condemnable rashness
condescending badinage [badinage =
frivolous banter]
conditional approval
confessed ardor
confidently anticipated

confirmed misanthrope [misanthrope = one who dislikes people in general]
conflicting influences
confused mingling
conjectural estimate
conjugal felicity
connected series
connotative damage
connubial love
conquering intelligence
conscientious objection
conscious repugnance
consecrated endeavor
consequent retribution
conservative distrust
considerate hint
consistent friendliness
consoling consciousness
conspicuous ascendency
constant reiteration
constitutional reserve
constrained politeness
constructive idealists
consuming zeal
consummate mastery
contagious wit
contaminating influence
contemplative nature
contemporary fame
contemptuous disrespect
contented indolence
contingent reasons
continuous endeavor
contorted expression
contracted view
contradictory theories
contrary tendencies
contrasted types
controversial disputant
contumelious epithet [contumelious = Rudeness or contempt arising from arrogance]
convenient footing
conventional verbiage
conversational decorum
convincing forcefulness
convivial habits

convulsive agony
cool confidence
copious materials
coquettish advances
cordial approval
corporate selfishness
corporeal constituent
correct forecast
corresponding variation
corroborated truth
corrosive effect
corrupting tendency
cosmical changes
cosmopolitan position
costly advantages
counterbalancing power
countless barriers
courageous eagerness
courteous solicitude
courtly bearing
covert curiosity
coveted honors
cowardly concession
cowering agitation
coy reluctance
crackling laughter
crafty deception
craggy eminence
cramped energies
crass stolidity
craven determination
creative faculty
credibly informed
creditable performance
credulous superstition
creeping progress
criminal negligence
cringing smile
crisp dialogue
critical judgment
crouching culprit
crowning indiscretion
crucial instance
crucifying irony
crude affectation
cruel handicap
crumbling precipice

crunching jangle
crushing sorrow
cryptic saying
crystalline sky
crystallized conclusions
culinary myrmidons [myrmidon = one
who carries out orders without question]
culminating fascination
culpable behavior
cultivated ferocity
cultured idleness
cumbrous fragments [cumbrous =
cumbersome; difficult to handle or use]

cumulative tendency
cunningly contrived
curbed profligacy
curious coincidence
current gossip
curry favor
cursed inactivity
cursory acquaintance
curt formality
curtained embrasure
cutting directness
cycloramic sweep
cynical disregard

# D
damaging admission
damask cheek [damask = rich patterned
fabric; wavy pattern on Damascus steel]
dampened ardor
dancing sunshine
dangerous temerity
dappled shadows
daring candor
dark superstition
dashing gallantry
dastardly injustice
dauntless courage
dawning instinct
dazed brain
dazzling triumph
deadly virulence
deaf tribunal
deathless structure
debasing tendency
debatable point
debilitating features
decadent poets
deceiving mists
decided superiority
decisive manner
declamatory treatment [declamatory =
pretentiously rhetorical; bombastic]
declared brotherhood
decorously adorned
deepening dusk
deep-seated curiosity
deep-toned lamentations

defective construction
defenseless innocence
defensive alliance
deferential regard
defiant coldness
deficient vitality
definite conception
deformed visage
deft evasion
degrading tendencies
delectable speculations
delegated power
deliberate abnegation [abnegation = self-
denial]
delicate discrimination
delicious vagueness
delightful variation
delirious ecstasies
delusive charm
demagogic style
democratic institutions
demoniacal force
demonstrable conclusion
demoralizing luxury
demure composure
denunciatory terms
departed glories
deplorable decay
deprecatory shrug
depressing concomitants
depthless forest
derisive voice

derogatory denial
descriptive power
desecrated ideals
deserted desert
deserved approbation [approbation = warm approval; praise]
desirable distinction
desolating dread
despairing austerity
desperate defiance
despicable vices
despondent exaggeration
despotic rulers
destructive radicalism
desultory vacillation [desultory = disconnected; haphazard; random]
detailed portraiture
detected hypocrisies
determinate swing
detestable purpose
dethroned princes
detrimental result
devastating effect
devilish sophistries
deviously subtle
devitalized personality
devoted attachment
devouring ambition
devout thanksgiving
dewy coolness
dexterous impudence
diabolical passion
dialectic power
diametrically opposite
dictatorial manner
dictionary significance
didactic exposition [didactic = intended to be morally instructive]
different distortion
difficult portraiture
diffident civility [diffident = lacking self-confidence; shy; timid]
diffuse verbosity
dignified austerity
digressional adventure
dilettante mind [dilettante = dabbler in a field of knowledge]

diligently propagated
dim comprehension
diminished efficacy
diminutive stature
diplomatic skill
dire consummation
direct obligation
disappointing attitude
disarmed criticism
disastrous termination
discarded reminiscences
discerning critic
disciplined mind
disclosed insincerity
discomfited opponent
disconcerted conjecture
disconnected fancies
disconsolate opinions
discordant sounds
discredited statement
discretional opinion
discriminating homage
discursive staggerings
disdainful comment
diseased hallucinations
disembodied personality
disengaged air
disfiguring disguise
disgraceful plight
disgruntled pessimist
disguised contempt
disgusted protest
disheartening facts
dishonorable submission
disillusioned youth
disintegrating tendency
disinterested motive
disjoined reminiscences
dismal seclusion
dismantled appearance
disordered imagination
disparaging criticism
dispassionate judgment
dispelling fear
displeasing softness
disproportionate ideas
disputative philosopher

disquieting thrill
disreputable aspect
dissenting opinion
dissimilar laws
dissipated illusion
dissolute audacity
dissolving years
dissonant jargon
distant adherent
distasteful notion
distempered feeling
distinct desideratum
distorted vanity
distracting babble
distraught air
distressing laxity
disturbed equanimity
diurnal rotation
divergent calculations
diversified attributes
diverting interests
divine potentialities
dizzy precipice
documentary evidence
dogged determination
doggerel expressions [doggerel = crude, humorous verse]
dogmatic assurance
doleful forebodings

domestic endearment
dominating influence
domineering insolence
dormant capacities
doubly odious
doubtful authenticity
downright nonsense
downtrodden drudge
drab apology
dramatic liveliness
drastic action
dread presence
dreaming adventurer
dreamless rest
dreary disrelish
droll incongruity
droning world
drowsy tranquillity
dubious success
ductile language
dulcet tone
dull aversion
dumb surprise
dumbfounded amazement
durable impression
dusky obscurity
dutiful compliance
dynamic energy
dynastic insolence

E
eager animosity
early servitude
earnestly espoused
earthly splendor
easy garrulity [garrulity = excessive talkativeness]
eccentric casuists [casuistry = excessively subtle reasoning intended to mislead]
ecclesiastical rule
echoless silence
economic absurdity
ecstatically happy
edifying exhortation
educational enterprise
effective embellishment

effectual stimulus
effeminate grace
effervescent multitude
effete aristocracy
efficacious power
efficient education
efflorescent style [efflorescent = bursting into flower]
effulgent daybeams [effulgent = radiating light]
egoistic sentiment
egregious mistake [egregious = outrageously reprehensible]
ejaculatory prayer
elaborate composition
elastic ductility

electric effluvium [effluvium = invisible emanation; an aura]
elegant mediocrity
elemental emotions
elephantine footsteps
elevated enjoyment
elfish grace
eloquent refutation
elusive charm
emancipating labors
embarrassing variety
embellished truths
embittered gaze
emblazoned pinnacles
embryo enterprise
emerald scintillations
eminent nonentity
emotional warmth
emotive power
emphatic earnestness
empirical corroboration
empty phraseology
emulative zeal
enamored troubadour
enchanted garden
encircling embrace
endearing appellation [appellation = name, title; act of naming]
endless dissertation
enduring charm
energetic enthusiasm
enervating humility [enervating = weaken or destroy the strength]
enfeebled activity
enforced silence
engaging affability
engendered feelings
engrossing purpose
engulfing waters
enhanced reputation
enigmatical silence
enlightened solicitude
enlivened monotony
ennobling personality
enormously outbalanced
enraptured attention
enriched experience

entangled subject
enthralling charm
enthusiastic adherents
enticing odors
entire domain
entrancing sadness
enveloping presence
envenomed attacks
enviable superiority
environing conditions
ephemeral duration [ephemeral = markedly short-lived]
epicurean taste
epigrammatic sallies [epigrammatic = terse and witty]
equable composure
equally efficacious
equitably governed
equivocal compliment
erotic poem
errant thoughts
erratic flight
erroneous assumption
erudite labors [erudite = having or showing profound knowledge]
eruptive violence
esoteric doctrine
especial pleasure
essential prerequisite
estimable qualities
eternal hostility
ethereal azure
ethical wisdom
euphuistic affectations [euphuistic = affected elegance of language]
evanescent glances [evanescent = vanishing like vapor]
evangelic doctrine
evasive answer
eventful circumstance
eventual failure
everlasting mysteries
everyday reality
evident authority
evil necromancy [necromancy = communicating with the dead to predict the future; black magic; sorcery]

eviscerating shrieks
exact antithesis
exacting taskmaster
exaggerated estimate
exalted imagination
exasperating coolness
exceedingly acceptable
excellent discernment
exceptional magnitude
excessive zeal
excitable temperament
exclusive pursuit
excretory secretion
excruciating accents
excursive fancy
execrable villainy [execrable = hateful;
extremely inferior; very bad]
executive efficiency
exemplary conduct
exhaustless energy
exhilarating charm
exoteric scorn [exoteric = easily
comprehensible; popular; outside]

exotic appearance
expansive benevolence
expectant throng
expeditionary force
expeditiously secreted
experimental suggestion
expiatory sacrifices
explicit injunction
explosive violence
expressionless visage
expressive lineaments [lineaments =
distinctive shape, especially of the face]
exquisite tact
extemporaneous effusion
extended magnitude
extenuating circumstance
external cheerfulness
extraneous ideas
extraordinary vivacity
extravagant caprice
extremely picturesque
exuberant mirth
exultant condition

F
facetious mood
facile criticism
factitious propensity
faded magnificence
faintly sinister
faithfully perpetuated
fallacious hopes
false illusions
faltering tongue
familiar sacredness
famished voracity
fanatical admiration
fanciful alliance
fantastic display
farcical expedient
far-reaching influence
fascinating illusiveness
fashioned symmetrically
fastidious taste
fatal disclosure
fatalistic belief
fathomless powers

fatiguing assertion
fattening servitude
fatuous pedantry [pedantry = attention
to detail or rules]
faultless taste
favorable augury
fawning flatteries
fearful imprecations
fearless integrity
feasible mode
feeble dribble
feigned reluctance
felicitous expression
feminine capriciousness
ferocious foe
fertile fancy
fervent invocation
fervid enthusiasm
festive illuminations
fetid dampness
fettered tyranny
feverish bewilderment

fickle fancy
fictitious pretext
fidgety impatience
fierce resentment
fiery indignation
figurative eloquence
filial tenderness
final enthronement
fine sensibilities
finished artistry
fireside delights
fitful desire
fitting opportunity
fizzing flame
flaccid faith
flagging popularity
flagitious attack [flagitious = extremely brutal or cruel crimes; vicious; infamous]
flagrant boasting
flamboyant brilliancy
flaming zeal
flashing wit
flat denial
flattering aspect
flaunting insolence
flawless constitution
fleecy clouds
fleeting intimation
flickering conscience
flighty obstinacy
flimsy organization
flippant ease
floating blackness
florid oratory [florid = ornate; flowery]
flowery circumlocution
flowing imagery
fluctuating light
fluent sophist
fluffy indignation
fluid ideas
flushed embarrassment
fluttering laugh
focused attention
foggy notion
fond enthusiast
foolish frenzy

forbearing silence
forbidding air
forceful audacity
foregone conclusion
foremost opponent
forensic orator
forest stillness
forgotten graveyard
forlorn desolation
formal acquiescence
formidable barrier
formless jottings
formulated conclusions
fortified selfishness
fortuitous circumstance
foul calumny [calumny = maliciously lying to injure a reputation]
fragile form
fragmentary facts
fragrant reminiscence
frail craft
frank admiration
frantic ardor
fraternal pity
freakish humor
freeborn soul
freezing disdain
frenzied haste
frequent digression
fresh impetus
freshening breeze
fretful discontent
friendly familiarity
frightened sense
frightful apparition
frigid disdain
frisky lightness
frivolous expedient
frolicsome extravagance
frozen wonder
fructifying thought [fructifying = make fruitful or productive]
fruitful indignation
fruitless repining
fugitive thoughts
full plenitude
fulsome praise

fumbling endeavor
functional disparity
fundamental principles
funereal gloom
furious invective [invective = abusive
language]
furrowed cheeks
furtive glance
fussy enthusiasms
futile babble

G
gabbling reminiscences [gabbling =
speak rapidly or incoherently; jabber]
galling thought
galvanic jumpings
gaping chasm
garbled information
garish decorations
garnered experience
gathering gloom
gaudy embellishments
gaunt specter
gay defiance
general acclamation
generative influence
generic characteristics
generous abundance
genial tolerance
genteel parlance
gentle blandishments [blandishments =
coax by flattery]
gentlemanly personage
genuine cynicism
geological enigma
geometrical progression
germinal idea
ghastly loneliness
ghostly apparitions
giant height
giddy pleasure
gifted intelligence
gigantic sagacity [sagacity = discerning,
sound in judgment; wisdom.]
girlish sprightliness
gladdening influence
gladiatorial exercise
gladsome glow
glaring impropriety
glassy smoothness
gleaming escutcheon [escutcheon =
shield-shaped emblem bearing a coat of
arms]
gleeful spirit
glibly condoned
gliding measures
glimmering idea
glistening dewdrop
glittering epigram
gloomy musing
glorious freedom
glossed faults
glowering countenance
glowing anticipations
gnawing thoughts
godlike independence
golden opportunity
good-humored gibes
gorgeous splendor
gossiping opinion
governing impulse
graceful demeanor
gracious immunity
graduated sequence
grandiose nomenclature
graphic portrayal
grasping credulity
gratuitous rudeness
grave reticence
greedy grasp
gregarious humanity
grievously mistaken
grim swiftness
grinding despotism
grinning ghosts
griping fascination
grizzled warrior
gross exaggeration
grotesque perversion
groundless fear
groveling servility
growing tension

grudging thanks
grumbling monotone
guileless zeal
gullible humanity
gurgling brooks

gushing enthusiasm
gusty clamor
guttural incoherence
gymnastic agility

H
habitual deference
hackneyed statement
hairbreadth difference
halcyon innocence [halcyon = tranquil; prosperous; golden]
hallowed stillness
halting praise
hampered power
handsomely recompensed
haphazard ostentation
happy intuition
harassing anxiety
hardened indifference
harmless mirth
harmonious grace
harrowing details
harsh jarrings
hasty generalization
hateful malignity
haughty composure
haunting despair
hazardous enterprise
hazy recollection
headlong vehemence
healthful vitality
heartfelt amity
heartless perfidy [perfidy = breach of faith; treachery]
heartrending outcry
hearty contempt
heated discussion
heathen hordes
heavenly ecstasies
heavy handicap
hectic tittering
hectoring rant
heedless love
heightened charm
heinous enormity
helpless innocence

herculean monster
hereditary arrogance
heretical opinions
hermetically sealed
heroic fortitude
hesitating courage
heterogeneous mass
hidden pitfalls
hideous phantom
high-flying theories
highly meritorious
hilarious outburst
hillside mist
hissing murmur
historic edifice
hoarded vengeance
hoary antiquity
hollow joys
homebred virtues
homeless wind
homely pathos
homespun play
homicidal mania
homogeneous whole
honest admiration
honeyed eloquence
hooligan wind
hopelessly befogged
horrible swiftness
horrid significance
hortatory moonshine
hospitable courtesy
hostile partizan
hot frenzy
hovering presence
howling chaos
huddled faculties
huge aspiration
human derelict
humanitarian impulse

humbly propitiating [propitiating = appeasing]
humdrum inconsistencies
humid luster
humiliating discomfiture
humorless variety
humorous urbanity
hungry satisfaction
hurrying years

hurtful indulgence
hushed laughter
husky shrillness
hybrid emotions
hypnotic fascination
hypochondriacal terrors
hypocritical pretense
hysterical agitation

## I

iconoclastic attitude
icy smile
idealistic type
identical mode
idiomatic propriety
idiotic obstinacy
idle jesting
idolatrous fervor
idyllic nonsense
ignoble domination
ignominious retreat
ill-concealed impatience
illiberal superstition
illimitable progression
illiterate denizens
illogical interruption
illuminating insight
illusive touch
illustrative anecdote
illustrious era
imaginative warmth
imbittered controversy
immaterial connection
immature dissent
immeasurable scorn
immediate abjuration [abjuration = renounce under oath]
immemorial bulwark
immense complacency
imminent perplexities
immitigable contempt
immoderate grief
immortal creation
immovably silent
immutable law
impaired prestige

impalpable nothingness
impartial justice
impassable serenity
impassioned impulse
impatient yearning
impeccable felicity
impecunious exile
impelling movement
impending fate
impenetrable calmness
imperative necessity
imperceptible deviation
imperfect equipment
imperial authority
imperious mind [imperious = arrogantly domineering or overbearing]
imperishable renown
impersonal compliment
impertinent drollery
imperturbable gravity
impetuous zeal
impious defiance
impish humor
implacable resentment
implicit faith
implied concealment
implored pardon
imponderable air
important epoch
importunate questions [importunate = insistent request]
imposing mien [mien = manner revealing a state of mind; appearance or aspect]
impossible contingency
impotent desperation

impoverished age
impracticable obstinacy
impregnable fortress
impressionistic stroke
imprisoning limitations
improbable conjecture
impromptu utterance
improvising powers
imprudent indebtedness
impudent knowingness
impulsive gratitude
inaccessible dignity
inadequate appreciation
inadmissible expression
inadvertent remark
inalienable right
inanimate existence
inapposite blandness [inapposite = inappropriate or misapplied nature]
inaptly designated
inarticulate lispings
inaugural discourse
inborn refinement
inbred taste
incalculable mischief
incarnate hate
incendiary opinions
incessant volume
incidental duty
incipient fancy
incisive critic
incoherent loquacity [loquacity = very talkative]
incommunicable gift
incomparable excellence
incompletely apprehended
inconceivable absurdity
incongruous contrast
inconsiderable trifle
inconsistent conduct
inconsolable cares
incontestable inference
incontrovertible proof
incorrigible merriment
incorruptible constancy
increasing clamor
incredible swiftness

indecent saturnalia [saturnalia = unrestrained revelry; an orgy]
indecorously amused
indefatigable diligence [indefatigable = tireless]
indefeasible title [indefeasible = cannot be annulled]
indefinable reluctance
indefinite yearning
indelible obligation
indelicate impetuosity
indented outline
independent research
indescribably lugubriou [lugubriou = exaggerated gloom]
indestructible atoms
indeterminable value
indifferent promise
indigenous growth
indignant denunciation
indirect interrogation
indiscriminate censure
indispensable requisites
indisputable chronicler
indissoluble compact
indistinct association
individual valor
indivisible aspects
indolent neglect
indomitable pride
indubitable signs
indulgent construction
indwelling delight
ineffable disdain
ineffaceable incongruity [ineffaceable = indelible]
ineffectual blandishment
ineradicable coquetry
inestimable honor
inevitable corollary
inexcusable laughter
inexhaustible abundance
inexorable authority [inexorable = incapable of being persuaded]
inexplicable reluctance
inexpressible benignity
inextricable confusion

infallible judgment
infamous pretense
infantile simplicity
infectious hilarity
infelicitous arrangement
inferential method
infernal machinations
infinite deference
infinitesimal gradations
infirm purpose
inflamed curiosity
inflated optimism
inflexible integrity
influential voice
informing feature
infuriated demagogues
ingenious trick
inglorious victory
ingrained love
ingratiating exterior
inharmonious prelude
inherent dignity
inherited anxieties
inimitable felicity
iniquitous fortune
initiatory period
injudicious yielding
injured conceit
inky blackness
inmost recesses
innate forbearance
inner restlessness
innocent amenities
innocuous desuetude [desuetude = state
of disuse or inactivity]
innovating spirit
inoffensive copiousness
inopportune condition
inordinate ambition
inquisitional rack
inquisitive observer
insatiable vanity
inscrutable austerity
insecure truce
insensate barbarism
insensibly flattered
inseparably associated

insidious tendency
insignificant blot
insincere profession
insinuatingly pursued
insipid tameness
insistent babel
insolent placidity
insoluble riddles
inspiring achievement
inspiriting spectacle
instant readiness
instantaneous cessations
instinctive disapproval
insufferably dull
insufficient appeal
insular strength
insulting invectives [invective = abusive
language]
insuperable difficulty
insurmountable obstacles
intangible something
integral element
intellectual integrity
intelligent adaptation
intemperate scorn
intense perplexity
intensive cultivation
intentional garbling
interior spirit
interlocking directorate
intermediate link
interminable question
intermingled gloom
intermittent threats
internal dissension
interpolated speech
interpretative criticism
interwoven thread
intimately allied
intolerably tedious
intoxicating hum
intractable temper
intrenched privilege
intrepid dexterity
intricate interlacings
intriguing braggart
intrinsic fecundity [fecundity =

productive or creative power]
intrusive brightness
intuitive perception
invaluable composition
invariable kindness
inveighing incessantly [inveighing =
angry disapproval]
inventive jealousy
inveterate antipathy
invidious mention [invidious = rousing
ill will or resentment]
invigorating discipline
invincible optimism
inviolable confidence
involuntary yearnings
involuted sentences [involuted =
intricate; complex]
involved pomposity
invulnerable solemnity
inward disinclination
irascible doggedness
irate remonstrance
iridescent sheen
irksome task

iron resolution
ironic iciness
irradiating spirit
irrational awe
irreclaimable dead
irreconcilable parting
irrecoverably lost
irrefragable laws [irrefragable =
indisputable]
irrefutable argument
irregular constellations
irrelevant suggestion
irremediable sorrow
irreparable injury
irrepressible excitement
irreproachable exterior
irresistible will
irresponsible gossip
irretrievable blunder
irreverent audacity
irreversible facts
irrevocable verdict
irritable impatience
isolated splendor

J
jaded sensibility
jagged outline
jarring discord
jaundiced opinion
jaunty confidence
jealous animosity
jesting allusion
jingling alliteration
jocular mirth
jocund host [jocund = sprightly;

lighthearted]
jostling confusion
jovial fancy
joyful alacrity
joyous stagnation
jubilant antagonist
judicial impartiality
judicious candor
just rebuke
juvenile attempt

K
kaleidoscopic pictures
keen insight
kindled enthusiasm
kindly innocence
kindred sympathies

kingly generosity
knavish conduct
knightly achievement
known disingenuousness [ingenuous =
frank; candid.]

L
labored levity
labyrinthian windings

lacerated feelings
lachrymose monotony

31

lackadaisical manner
laconic force
lagging footsteps
lamentable helplessness
languid impertinence
large receptivity
lashing scorn
latent conviction
laudable zeal
laughable absurdity
lavish liberality
lawless freedom
lazy acquiescence
leaden steps
leaping ambition
learned gravity
leering smile
legal perspicacity [perspicacity =
perceptive, discerning]
legendary associations
legislative enactment
legitimate inference
leisurely composure
lengthening shadows
leonine powers
lethargic temperament
lettered coxcomb [coxcomb = conceited
dandy; jester's cap]
liberal contemplations
lifeless imbecility
lifelong adherence
lightless eyes
lightly disregard
lightning glare
limpid twilight
lingering tenderness
linguistic attainments
liquid eloquence
lisping utterance
listening reverence

listless apathy
literal exactness
literary research
lithe contortions
little idiosyncrasies
lively susceptibility
livid lightning
living manifestation
loathsome oppression
local busybody
loftiest aspirations
logical precision
lone magnificence
longing fancy
looming probabilities
loquacious assurances [loquacious =
very talkative]
lordly abhorrence
loud vociferation [vociferation = cry out
loudly, especially in protest]
lounging gait
loutish rudeness
lovingly quizzical
lowering aspects
lowest degradation
loyal adhesion
lucid treatment
lucrative profession
ludicrous incongruity
lugubrious question [lugubrious =
mournful, dismal, gloomy]
lukewarm repentance
lumbering gaiety
luminous interpretation
lurid picturesqueness
lurking suspicion
lustrous surface
luxuriant richness
lying equivocations

M
maddening monotony
magic fascination
magisterial emphasis
magnanimous concessions
magnetic fascination

magnificent florescence
magniloquent diction [magniloquent =
extravagant in speech]
maidenly timidity
main ramifications

32

majestic dignity
maladjusted marriages
malevolent ingenuity
malicious aspersions
malign influence
malodorous gentility
manageable proportions
mangled arguments
manifest reluctance
manifold functions
manly reticence
mantling smile [mantling = cover with a mantle; concealing]
manual dexterity
manufactured melancholy
marked individuality
marketable commodity
marshaled hosts
martial footsteps
marvelous lucidity
masculine power
masked expression
massive strength
master achievement
matchless charm
material misconception
maternal solicitude
mathematical precision
matrimonial alliance
matured reflection
maudlin sentimentalism [maudlin = tearfully sentimental]
mawkish insipidity
maximum intensity
meager evidence
mean trickeries
meaningless confusion
measured cadence
mechanical handicraft
meditatively silent
meek ambition
melancholy musing
mellifluous eloquence [mellifluous = flowing with sweetness or honey]
mellow refinement
melodious platitudes
melodramatic resource

melting mood
memorable experience
menacing attitude
mendacious tongue [mendacious = false; untrue]
mendicant pilgrim [mendicant = beggar]
mental metamorphosis
mercenary view
merchantable literature
merciful insensibility
merciless censor
mercurial temperament
mere generalization
meretricious allurements [meretricious = plausible but false]
meridian splendor
merited ridicule
merry jest
metallic immobility
metaphysical obscurity
meteoric splendors
methodical regularity
metrical exactness
microscopic minuteness
mighty animosity
mild rejoinder
militant struggles
military autocracy
millennial reign
mimic gestures
minatory shadow [minatory = menacing or threatening]
mincing precision
mingled decorousness
miniature imitations
minor impulses
minute consideration
miraculous profusion
mirroring lake
mirthful glance
mischievous effusion
miserable musings
misleading notion
misshapen oddities
misspent strength
mistaken assumption
mistrustful superiority

misty depression
mitigating circumstances
mobile countenance
mock seriousness
modest cheerfulness
modified sentiment
moldy doctrines
mollifying conditions [mollifying =
calming; soothing]
momentary discomfiture
momentous pause
monarchial institutions
monastic austerity
monotonous sameness
monstrous absurdity
monumental structure
moody silence
moonlight witchery
moral obliquity [obliquity = deviation or
aberration]
morbid imagination
mordant wit
moribund mediocrities
mortal affront
mortified coldness
motley appearance

N
naive manner
naked eye
nameless fear
narcotic effect
narrowing axioms
nasal drone
nascent intercourse
national shortcomings
native incompetence
natural sluggishness
nauseous dose
nautical venture
neat refutation
nebulous uncertainty
necessary adjuncts
necromantic power [necromancy =
communicating with the dead to predict
the future. Black magic; sorcery.]
needless depression

mountainous inequalities
mournful magnificence
mouthing amplitude
muddled opinion
muddy inefficiency
muffled detonations
mullioned windows [mullioned =
vertical member dividing a window]
multifarious activity
multiform truth
multiple needs
multitudinous details
mundane importance
mural decorations
murderous parody
murky recesses
musical diapason [diapason = full, rich
outpouring of harmonious sound]
mute insensibility
mutinous thoughts
muttered warning
mutual animosity
myriad lights
mysterious potency
mystic meaning
mythical kingdom

nefarious scheme
negative approbation [approbation =
warm approval; praise]
negligible quantity
neighboring mists
nerveless hand
nervous solicitude
nettled opponent
neutral eye
new perplexities
nice discrimination
niggardly allowance
nightmare fantasy
nimble faculty
noble condescension
nocturnal scene
nodding approval
noiseless reverie
noisy platitudes

nomadic life
nominal allegiance
nonchalant manner
non-committal way
nondescript garb
nonsense rhymes
noonday splendor
normal characteristics
notable circumstance

## O

obdurate courage [obdurate = hardened in wrongdoing]
obedient compliance
objectionably apologetic
obligatory force
obligingly expressed
oblique tribute
obscure intimation
obsequious homage [obsequious = servile compliance; fawning]
observant eye
obsolete phraseology
obstinate defiance
obstreperous summons [obstreperous = noisily and stubbornly defiant]
obtrusive neatness
obvious boredom
occasional flights
occult sympathy
ocean depth
odd makeshifts
odious tyranny
odorous spring
offensive hostility
official asperity [asperity = harshness; ill temper or irritability]
olfactory sense
olive grayness
ominous rumors
omnipotent decree
omniscient affirmation
oncoming horde
onerous cares
onflaming volume
opalescent sea
opaque mass

noteworthy friendship
noticeably begrimed
notoriously profligate
novel signification
nugatory cause [nugatory = little or no importance; trifling]
numbed stillness
numberless defeats
numerical majority

openly disseminated
opinionated truculence [truculence = ferociously cruel behavior]
opportunely contrived
oppressive emptiness
opprobrious epithet [opprobrious = contemptuous reproach; scornful]
oracular utterance [oracular = solemnly prophetic; enigmatic; obscure]
oratorical display
ordinary delinquencies
organic assimilation
oriental spicery
originally promulgated
oscillatory movement
ostensible occupation
ostentatious display
outlandish fashion
outrageously vehement
outspoken encouragement
outstanding feature
outstretching sympathies
outward pomp
outworn creed
overbearing style
overestimated importance
overflowing sympathy
overhanging darkness
overmastering potency
overpowering argument
overshadowing dread
overstrained enthusiasm
overt act
overvaulting clouds
overweening sense [overweening = presumptuously arrogant; overbearing]

P

pacific disposition
painful obstinacy
painstaking reticence
palatable advice
pallidly illumined
palpable originality
palpitating emotion
paltry hypocrisies
pampered darling
panic fear
panting eagerness
parabolic obscureness
paradoxical talker
paralyzing sentimentalism
paramount authority
parasitical magnificence
parental permission
paroxysmal outburst
particularly notable
partizan prejudice
passing panorama
passionate insistence
passive obedience
patchwork manner
patent example
paternal tenderness
pathetic helplessness
patient endurance
patriarchal visage
patriotic enthusiasm
peacefully propagated
peculiar piquancy [piquancy = appealingly provocative; charming]
pecuniary privation
pedantic ineptitude [pedantic = attention to detail or rules]
pedestrian vigor
peerless raconteur [raconteur = skilled storyteller]
peevish ingratitude
pending determination
penetrating warmth
penitential cries
penniless wanderer

pensive reflections
perceptible difference
peremptory punishment [peremptory = ending all debate or action]
perennial charm
perfect embodiment
perfunctory inquiries
perilous expedient
permanent significance
pernicious doctrine
perpetual oscillation
perplexing problem
persecuting zeal
persistent adherence
personal predilection [predilection = a preference]
persuasive eloquence
pert prig
pertinacious solemnity [pertinacious = stubbornly persistent]
pertinent question
perusing earnestness
pervading tendencies
perverse quaintness
pessimistic skepticism
pestiferous career [pestiferous = evil or deadly; pernicious]
pet aversion
petrified smile
petticoat diplomacy
pettifogging business
petty pedantries [pedantries = attention to detail or rules]
phantom show
philanthropic zeal
philosophical acuteness
phlegmatic temperament [phlegmatic = calm, sluggish; unemotional]
phosphorescent shimmer
photographic exactitude
physical convulsion
pictorial embellishments
picturesque details
piercing clearness

pinchbeck dignity [pinchbeck = cheap imitation]
pining melancholy
pioneering spirit
pious platitudes
piquant allusions [piquant = attracting or delighting]
pitiable frenzy
pitiless precision
pivotal point
placid stupidity
plainly expedient
plainspoken rebuke
plaintive cadence
plastic mind
plausible commonplaces
playful wit
pleasing reveries
pleasurable excitement
plenary argument
plentiful harvest
plighted word [plighted = promised by a solemn pledge]
poignant clearness
pointless tale
poisonous counsels
polished ease
polite indifference
political malcontent
polluting taints
pompous platitudes
ponderous research
pontifical manner
popular resentment
populous fertility
portentous gulf
positively deteriorating
posthumous glory
potential energy
powerful stimulant
practical helpfulness
precarious path
precautionary measure
precipitous flight
precise purpose
precocious wisdom
preconceived view

predatory writers
predestined spinster
predominant habit
pregnant hint
preliminary assumption
premature ripening
premonitory symptoms
preoccupied attention
prepossessing appearance
preposterous assertion
prescient reflection [prescient = perceiving the significance of events before they occur]
prescribed conditions
presiding genius
pressing necessity
pretended surprise
pretentious dignity
preternatural sagacity [preternatural = extraordinary] [sagacity = farsighted; wise]
pretty plaintiveness
prevailing misconception
priestly austerity
primal energy
prime factor [no integer factors; irreducible; 1,2,3,5,7,11...]
primeval silence
primordial conditions
princely courtesy
prismatic blush
pristine dignity
private contempt
privileged caste
prized possession
problematic age
prodigally lavished
prodigious variety
productive discipline
profane denunciation
professedly imitated
professional garrulity [garrulity = excessive talkativeness]
proffered service
profitable adventure
profligate expenditure
profound conviction

profuse generosity
projected visit
prolegomenous babbler [prolegomenous = preliminary discussion]
prolific outpouring
prolix narrative [prolix = wordy]
prolonged happiness
promiscuous multitude
promising scions [scions = descendants]
prompt courage
propagandist literature
propelling impulse
proper punctilio [punctilio = fine point of etiquette]
prophetic vision
propitious moment [propitious = auspicious, favorable]
proportionately vigilant
proprietary sense
prosaic excellence [prosaic = dull and lacking excitement]
prospective success
prosperity revival
prostrate servility
protoplasmic ancestors
protracted agony
proud destiny
proverbial situation

provincial prejudice
provoked hostility
prudential wisdom
prurient desire
prying criticism
psychic processes
public derision
puerile fickleness [puerile = immature; childish]
pugnacious defiance
pulsating life
punctilious care [punctilious = precise; scrupulous]
pungent epigram
puny dimensions
purblind brutality [purblind = partly blind; slow to understanding]
pure coincidence
purgatorial fires
puritanical primness
purplish shadows
purposed attempt
purposeful drama
pursuing fancies
pusillanimous desertion [pusillanimous = cowardly]
pyrotechnic outburst

Q

quailing culprit
quaint peculiarities
qualifying service
quavering voice
queer tolerance
quenchless despair
querulous disposition [querulous = habitually complaining]
questionable data

questioning gaze
quibbling speech
quick sensibility
quiescent melancholy
quiet cynicism
quivering excitement
quixotic impulse
quizzical expression
quondam foe [quondam = former]

R

racial prejudice
racy humor
radiant happiness
radical distinction
raging billows
rambling looseness

rampant wickedness
rancorous animosities
random preconceptions
rank luxuriance
ranting optimism
rapacious speculation [rapacious =

taking by force; plundering]
rapid transitions
rapturous adoration
rare endowment
rarefied humor
rashly overrated
rational discourse
ravenous eagerness
ravishing spectacle
raw composition
reactionary movement
ready sympathy
realistic portrayal
reanimating ideas
reasonably probable
rebellious thought
reciprocal influence
reckless lavishness
recognized authority
recondite description [recondite = not
easily understood; abstruse]
reconstructive era
recovered composure
recumbent figure
recurring doubt
reddening dawn
redoubled activity
refining influence
reflective habits
refractory temper
refreshing novelty
regal countenance
regretful melancholy
regular recurrence
relatively mild
relaxed discipline
relentless justice
religious scruples
reluctant tolerance
remarkable sagacity [sagacity = wisdom]
remedial measure
remorseless logic
remote epoch
renowned achievement
repeated falsification
repelling vices
repentant sense

reprehensible action
repressed ardor
reproachful misgiving
repulsive spectacle
reputed disposition
requisite expertness
resentful flame
resilient spirit
resistless might
resolute daring
resonant gaiety
resounding blare
resourceful wickedness
respectful condescension
resplendent brightness
responsive throb
restless inquisitiveness
restorative influence
restricted meaning
resultant limitation
retaliating blows
retarding influence
retreating footsteps
revengeful scowl
reverent enthusiasm
revolting cynicism
revolutionary tradition
rhapsodical eulogy
rhetorical amplification
rhythmical movements
richly emblazoned
righteous indignation
rightful distinction
rigid propriety
rigorous reservation
riotous clamor
ripe reflection
rising misgivings
riveted attention
robust sense
rollicking mirth
romantic solitudes
rooted habits
roseate tints
rough brutality
roundabout approach
rousing chorus

royal exultations
rubicund tinge [rubicund = healthy rosiness]
rude awakening
rudimentary effort
rueful conclusion
ruffled feelings
rugged austerity

ruling motive
rumbling hoarseness
ruminating mood
rural imagery
rustic simplicity
rustling forest
ruthless commercialism

S

sacerdotal preeminence [sacerdotal = priestly]
sacred tenderness
sacrilegious violence
sacrosanct fetish
sadly disconcerted
sagacious mind [sagacious = keen discernment, sound judgment]
sage reflections
saintly serenity
salient feature
salutary amusement
sanctimonious hypocrite [sanctimonious = feigning piety]
sane observer
sanguinary measures [sanguinary = eager for bloodshed; bloodthirsty]
sanguine expectations [sanguine = cheerfully confident; optimistic]
sarcastic incredulity
sardonic taciturnity [sardonic = cynically mocking] [taciturnity = habitually untalkative]
satirical critic
satisfying equipoise [equipoise = equilibrium]
savage satirist
scalding jests
scandalous falsehood
scant recognition
scathing satire
scattered distractions
scholarly attainments
scientific curiosity
scintillating wit
scoffing defiance
scorching criticism

scornful negligence
scriptural exegesis [exegesis = Critical explanation or analysis]
scrubby foreland
scrupulous fidelity
sculptured sphinx
scurrilous blustering [scurrilous = foul-mouthed]
searching eye
secluded byways
secret dismay
sectarian sternness
secure anchorage
sedentary occupation
seditious speaking [seditious = arousing to action or rebellion]
seductive whisperings
sedulously fostered [sedulously = persevering]
seeming artlessness
seething hate
selective instinct
self-conscious activity
self-deprecating irony
selfish vindictiveness
selfsame strain
senile sensualist
senseless gibberish
sensibly abated
sensitively courteous
sensuous music
sententious wisdom [sententious = terse and energetic; pithy]
sentimental twaddle
sepulchral quiet
sequestered nook
seraphic promiscuousness

serene triumph
serious resentment
serpentine curves
servile obedience
sesquipedalian words [sesquipedalian = long]
settled dislike
severe censure
shabby imitation
shadowy abstraction
shady retirements
shallow sophistry
sham enthusiasm
shambling gait
shamed demeanor
shameless injustice
shapeless conformations
shaping impulses
sharp rebuke
shattered reason
sheepish look
sheer boredom
sheltering hypocrisy
shifting panorama
shimmering gaiety
shining virtues
shivering soul
shocking rudeness
shoreless sea
shortening days
shrewd suspicion
shrewish look
shrill dissonance
shrunken wisp
shuddering reluctance
shuffling preliminaries
shy obeisance
sibilant oath [sibilant = producing a hissing sound]
sickening jealousy
sidelong glance
significant symbol
silent agony
silken filaments
silly escapades
silvery sea
similar amplitude

simple rectitude
simulated rapture
simultaneous acclamation
sincere hospitality
singular sensitiveness
sinister forebodings
sinuous movements
skeptical contempt
skillfully maintained
skulking look
slackened tension
slavish imitation
sledge-hammer blows
sleepless soul
sleepy enchantment
slender resource
slight acceleration
slovenly deportment
slow stupefaction
sluggish resolution
slumbering stream
smacking breeze
small aptitude
smiling repose
smirking commonplace
smoldering resentment
smothered sob
smug hypocrisy
snappish impertinence
sneering jibes
snowy whiteness
snug retreat
soaring ambition
sobbing wail
sober melancholy
social banalities
sociological bearing
soft allurement
solemn emptiness
solid knowledge
solidifying substance
solitary grandeur
somber relations
somewhat scandalized
somnolent state
sonorous simplicity [sonorous = full, deep, rich sound; impressive in style of

41

speech]
sophistical argument
soporific emanations [soporific = inducing sleep]
sordid selfishness
sorely beset
sorrowful resignation
soulless mechanism
sounding verbiage
sourly ascetic
sovereign panacea
spacious tracklessness
sparkling splendor
specialized skill
specific characteristics
specious artifice [specious = having the ring plausibility but actually fallacious]
spectral fears
speculative rubbish
speechless surprise
speedy extinction
spendthrift prodigality
spirited vindication
spiritual dazzlement
splendid irony
splenetic imagination [splenetic = ill humor or irritability]
spontaneous challenge
sporadic exception
sportive gaiety
spotless honor
sprightly talk
spurious enthusiasm
squalid distress [squalid = Dirty and wretched; morally repulsive; sordid]
squandered talent
squeamish taste
staggering surprise
stainless womanhood
stale sciolism [sciolism = superficial knowledge]
stalwart defiance
stammered apology
starched sterility
starlit eminence
startling eccentricity
starving proletariat

stately stride
statesmanlike person
statistical knowledge
statuesque immobility
staunch manhood
steadfast obedience
stentorian voice [stentorian = extremely loud]
stereotyped commonness
sterile hatred
sterling sense
stern defiance
stiff conceit
stifled convulsions
still solitudes
stilted bombast
stimulating impression
stinging reproach
stinted endowment
stipulated reward
stock pleasantries
stoic callousness
stolid obstinacy
stony stare
storied traditions
stormy passion
stout assertion
straggling association
straightforward logic
straightway vanished
strained interpretation
straitened circumstance
strange wistfulness
strenuous insistence
striking diversity
stringent statement
strong aversion
stubborn reality
studious reserve
stultified mind
stunning crash
stupendous magnitude
stupid bewilderment
sturdy genuineness
subaltern attitude [subaltern = secondary]
subconscious conviction

subduing influence
sublime anticipations
submissive behavior
subordinate pursuit
subsidiary advantage
substantial agreement
subterranean sunlessness
subtle sophistry
subversive accident
successfully dispelled
successive undulations
succinct phrase
sudden perturbation
sullen submission
summary vengeance
sumptuously decorated
superabundant energy
superannuated coquette [superannuated = retired] [coquette = flirt]
superb command
supercilious discontent [supercilious = haughty disdain]
superficial surliness
superfluous precaution
superhuman vigor
superior skill

superlative cleverness
supernatural incident
supine resignation
suppliant posture
suppressed excitement
supreme exaltation
surging multitude
surly tone
surpassing loveliness
surprising intimacy
surreptitious means [surreptitious = clandestine; stealthy]
sustained vigor
swaggering bully
swampy flatness
swarming population
sweeping assertion
sweet peaceableness
swelling magnitude
swift transition
swinging cadence
symmetrical brow
sympathetic insight
syncopated tune
synthetic judgment
systematic interaction

T
tacit assumption
taciturn magnanimity [taciturn = habitually untalkative]
tactical niceties
tameless energy
tangible realities
tangled network
tardy recognition
tarnished reputation
tart temper
tasteful gratification
tasteless insipidity
tattered mendicant [mendicant = beggar]
taunting accusation
tawdry pretentiousness
tearful sensibilities
tearing gallop
teasing persistency

technical precision
tedious formality
teeming population
temerarious assertion [temerarious = presumptuous; reckless]
temperamental complacency
tempered pathos
tempestuous breeze
temporary expedient
tenacious memory
tender solicitude
tense attention
tentative moment
tepid conviction
termagant wife [termagant = quarrelsome, scolding]
terrible sublimity
terrifying imprecations [imprecations = curses]

43

terse realism
testamentary document
thankless task
thawing laughter
theological complexities
thirsting ear
thorny pathway
thorough uprightness
thoughtful silence
thoughtless whim
threadbare sentiment
threatened wrath
thrilling eloquence
throbbing pride
throneless monarch
thronging images
thundering rage
thwarted impulse
tideless depth
tigerish stealth
tightened ominously
timid acquiescence
tingling expectation
tinkling cymbal
tipsy jocularity [jocularity = given to joking]
tip-toe curiosity
tireless egotism
tiresome braggadocio [braggadocio = pretentious bragging]
titanic force
toilsome pleasure
tolerably comprehensive
tolerant indifference
tormenting thought
torn asunder
torpid faculties
tortuous labyrinth
tortured innocence
totally engrossed
touching pathos

U
ubiquitous activity
ugly revelation
ulterior purpose
ultimate sanction

tousled head
towering pride
traceable consanguinity
trackless forest
traditional type
tragic intensity
trailing sweetness
tranquil grandeur
transcendent power
transfiguring tints
transient emotion
translucent cup
transmuting touch
transparent complement
treacherous intelligence
treasured possessions
trembling anxiety
tremendous domination
tremulous sense [tremulous = timid or fearful]
trenchant phrase [trenchant = forceful, effective, vigorous]
trifling superfluity
trite remark
triumphant boldness
trivial conventionality
tropical luxuriance
troubled inertness
trudging wayfarer
trustworthy source
tumultuous rapture
tuneful expression
turbulent times
turgid appeal [turgid = excessively ornate or complex]
twilight shadow
twittered sleepily
twofold bearing
typical excellence
tyrannical disposition

ultrafashionable world
unabashed insolence
unabated pleasure
unaccountable protervity [protervity =

peevishness; petulance]
unaccustomed toil
unadorned style
unaffected pathos
unaffrighted innocence
unagitated abstraction
unalloyed satisfaction
unalterable determination
unanimous acclamation
unanswerable argument
unapologetic air
unappeasable resentment
unapproached supremacy
unassailable position
unassuming dignity
unattainable perfection
unavailing consolation
unavoidable propensities
unballasted eloquence [unballasted = unsteady; wavering]
unbeaten track
unbecoming behavior
unbending reserve
unbiased judgment
unblemished character
unblinking observation
unblushing iteration
unbounded hospitality
unbridgeable chasm
unbridled fancy
unbroken continuity
uncanny fears
unceasing variation
unceremonious talk
uncertain tenure
unchallenged supremacy
unchanging affection
uncharitable ambition
uncharted depths
unchastised offense
unclouded splendor
uncomfortable doubt
uncommonly attractive
uncommunicable quality
uncomplaining endurance
uncomprehending smile
uncompromising dogmatism

unconcealed aversion
unconditioned freedom
uncongenial task
unconquerable patience
unconscious serenity
uncontrollable delight
unconventional demeanor
uncounted generations
uncouth gambols
uncritical position
unctuously belaud [unctuously = exaggerated, insincere] [belaud = praise greatly]
undaunted defender
undazzled eyes
undefined anticipations
undeniable charm
underlying assumption
undeviating consistency
undignified peccadilloes [peccadilloes = small sin or fault]
undiluted skepticism
undiminished relish
undimmed luster
undisciplined genius
undisguised amusement
undismayed expression
undisputed ascendency
undistracted attention
undisturbed silence
undivided energies
undoubted authenticity
undue predilection [predilection = preference]
undulating hills
unduly troublesome
undying friendship
unearthly gladness
uneasy craving
unembarrassed scrutiny
unembittered sweetness
unending exactions
unenlightened zealot
unenvied insipidity
unequaled skill
unequivocally resented
unerring fidelity

unessential details
unexampled sweetness
unexhausted kindliness
unexpected confidence
unfailing courtesy
unfaltering glance
unfamiliar garb
unfathomable indifference
unfeigned assent
unfettered liberty
unflagging zest
unflattering truth
unflecked confidence
unfledged novice [unfledged = young bird without feathers necessary to fly]
unflinching zeal
unfolding consciousness
unforced acquiescence
unforeseen vicissitudes [vicissitudes = sudden or unexpected changes]
unforgivable tragedy
unfounded conjecture
unfulfilled longing
ungainly figure
ungarnished reality
ungenerously resolved
ungenial temperament
ungovernable vehemence
ungracious temper
ungrudging tribute
unguessed riches
unhallowed threshold
unhampered expression
unhappy predecessor
unheeded beauties
unheroic measure
unhesitating faith
unhindered flight
unholy triumph
uniform blending
unimaginable bitterness
unimpassioned dignity
unimpeachable sentiment
unimpeded activity
uninstructed critic
uninterrupted process
unique personality

universal reprobation [reprobation = condemned to hell; severe disapproval]
unjust depreciation
unknown appellations [appellation = name, title, or designation]
unlettered laborer
unlikely contingency
unlimited opulence
unlucky dissembler
unmanly timidity
unmastered possibility.
unmeaning farce
unmeasured hostility
unmellowed dawn
unmelodious echoes
unmerciful plundering
unmingled consent
unmistakably fabulous
unmitigated gloom
unmixed astonishment
unmodified passion
unmurmuring sea
unnecessary platitudes
unnumbered thousands
unobtrusive deference
unostentatious display
unpalatable truth
unparalleled atrocities
unpardonable error
unphilosophical dreamer
unpleasant excrescence [excrescence = abnormal enlargement]
unprecedented advance
unprejudiced intelligence
unpretentious character
unprincipled violence
unprofitable craft
unpurchasable luxury
unqualified submission
unquenchable tenderness
unquestionable genius
unquestioning fate
unreasonable pretense
unreasoning distrust
unredeemable forfeit
unrefreshing sameness
unrelaxing emphasis

unrelenting spirit
unremembered winter
unremitting toil
unrepining sadness
unreproved admiration
unrequited love
unresentful disposition
unreserved assent
unresisted authority
unresolved exceptions
unresponsive gloom
unresting speed
unrestrained anger
unrestricted ease
unrivaled distinction
unruffled concord
unsatisfied yearning
unscrupulous adventurer
unseasonable apology
unseemly mirth
unselfish fidelity
unsettled trait
unshakable foundation
unshrinking determination
unslackened volubility [volubility = ready flow of speech; fluent]
unsophisticated youth
unsparing abuse
unspeakable delight
unspiritual tone
unspoiled goodness
unstinted praise
unsullied virtue
unsurpassed purity

unswerving integrity
untameable energy
unthinkable hypothesis
untiring energy
untold calamity
untoward circumstances [untoward = improper]
untrammeled expression
untrodden woodland
untroubled repose
untuneful phrase
untutored mind
unusual audacity
unutterable sadness
unvarnished feeling
unwarranted limitation
unwasting energies
unwavering allegiance
unwearied diligence
unwelcome alliance
unwieldy bulk
unwilling homage
unwittingly mingled
unwonted kindness [unwonted = unusual]
unworldly foolishness
unworthy alliance
unyielding nature
uproarious laughter
upstart pretensions
useless fripperies [fripperies = pretentious, showy]
utmost scorn

V
vacant stupidity
vacillating obedience
vacuous ease
vagabondish spirit
vagrant wandering
vaguely discursive
vain contemplation
vainglorious show
valid objection
valuable acquisition
valueless assertion

vampire tongue
vanished centuries
vantage ground
vapid generalities [vapid = lacking liveliness, interest; dull]
variable temperament
variegated career [variegated = varied]
vast advantage
veering purpose
vehement panting
veiled insolence

velvety lawn
venerable placidity
venomous passion
veracious journals [veracious = honest; truthful; accurate; precise]
verbal audacities
verbose manner
verdant hope
verifiable facts
veritable triumph
vernacular expression
vernal charm [vernal = resembling spring; fresh; youthful]
versatile grace
vexatious circumstances
vicarious virtue
vigilant sensibility
vigorous invective [invective = abusive language]
vile desecrater
villainous inconsistency
vindictive sentiment
violent agitation
virgin grace

virile leadership
virtual surrender
virtuous disdain
virulent prejudice
visible embarrassment
visionary dreamer
vital interpretation
vitiated taste [vitiated = reduce the value; corrupt morally]
vitriolic sneer
vivacious excitement
vivid portrayal
vociferous appeal
voiceless multitude
volatile fragrance
volcanic suddenness
voluble prose [voluble = ready flow of speech; fluent]
voluminous biography
voluntary relinquishment
voracious animosity
votive wreath
vulgar prosperity
vulnerable foe

W
wabbling enterprise [wabbling = wobbling]
waggishly sapient [sapient = wise]
wailing winds
wandering fancy
waning popularity
wanton butchery
warbling lute
warlike trappings
warning prophecy
warped purpose
warranted interference
wasteful prodigality
wavering courage
waxwork sex
wayward fancy
weakly imaginative
wearisome wordiness
wedded incompatibility
weighty argument
weird fascination

welcoming host
well-turned period
weltering current
whimsical touch
whirling confusion
whirring loom
whispering breeze
whistling winds
whited sepulcher
wholesome aspirations
wholly commendable
wicked ingratitude
wide signification
widespread acclaim
wild extravagance
willful waywardness
willing allegiance
willowy nothingness
wily antagonist
winding pilgrimage
windowless soul

winged fancies
winking stars
winning plaintiveness
winsome girlhood
wise dissertations
wistful entreaty
withering scorn
witnessing approval
witty expedient
wizard influence
woebegone countenance
woeful weariness

wolfish tendency
womanlike loveliness
wonderful affluence
wonted activity [wonted = usual]
wordy warfare
worthy achievement
wounded avarice
wrathful pugnacity
wretched effeminacy
wriggling disputant
writhing opponent

Y
yawning space
yearning tenderness

yielding disposition
youthful ambition

Z
zealous devotion
zigzag method

zoologically considered

# SECTION 2
# SIGNIFICANT PHRASES

A

abashed and ashamed
abhorrence and repulsion
abilities and attainments
abject and hopeless
ably and vigorously
abrupt and perilous
absolute and eternal
absorbed and occupied
abstinence and self-denial
abstract and metaphysical
absurd and impertinent
abundant and sustained
abuse and slander
accentual and rhythmic
accidental and temporary
accomplished and popular
accurate and illuminating
achievement and character
acquisition and possession
active and aggressive
actual and immediate
acute and painful
admirable and accomplished
adorned and amplified
adroitness and judgment
adventurous and prodigal
advice and assistance
affable and courteous
affectation and coquetry
affectionate and warm-hearted
affluent and exuberant
affright and abhorrence
agencies and influences
ages and generations
aggrandizement and plunder
agreeable and ingenuous
aggressive and sullen
aghast and incredulous
agility and briskness
agitate and control
agony and despair

aids and auxiliaries
aim and purpose
airy and frivolous
alarm and uneasiness
alert and unsparing
all and sundry
allegiance and fidelity
alone and undistracted
alterations and additions
amazement and admiration
ambiguity and disagreement
ambition and determination
amiable and unpretending
ample and admirable
amusing and clever
analytical and critical
anarchy and chaos
ancient and venerable
anecdote and reminiscence
anger and fury
anguish and hopelessness
animated and effective
anomalies and absurdities
antagonism and opposition
antipathies and distastes
antiquated and obsolete
anxiety and trepidation
apathy and torpor
apologetic and uneasy
appalling and devastating
apparent and palpable
appearance and surroundings
apprehensive and anxious
appropriate and eloquent
approve and admire
apt and novel
archness and vivacity [archness =
inappropriate playfulness]
ardent and aspiring
argument and inference
arid and unprofitable

50

arrangement and combination
arrogant and overbearing
artificial and elaborate
artistic and literary
artlessness and urbanity
ashamed and speechless
aspects and phases
aspiring and triumphal
assiduity and success
assimilated and combined
assuaged and pacified
astonished and curious
astound and perplex
athletic and nimble
atonement and forgiveness

atrocious and abominable
attacks and intrigues
attention and respect
attitudes and expressions
attractiveness and ability
audacity and skill
august and splendid
austere and icy
available and capable
avarice and cruelty
avidity and earnestness [avidity = desire; craving]
awake and active
awe and reverence
awkwardness and crudity

## B

babel and confusion
backbone and sinew
baffled and disappointed
balanced and forceful
barbarity and wickedness
bards and sages
base and unworthy
beam and blaze
bearing and address
beautiful and majestic
bedraggled and disappointed
befogged and stupefied
beliefs and practises
bellowing and shouting
benevolence and candor
benign and hopeful
bent and disposition
benumbed and powerless
bewildered and stupefied
bigots and blockheads
billing and cooing
birth and breeding
bite and sting
bits and scraps
bitter and disdainful
black and solitary
bland and ingenious
blasphemous and profane
bleak and unrelenting

blend and harmonize
blessing and benediction
blind and unreasoning
blundering and plundering
blurred and confused
bluster and vulgarity
boast and assertion
bold and haughty
bombast and egotism
bone and sinew
boundless and unlimited
bourgeois and snobbish
brag and chatter
bravado and cowardice
brave and chivalrous
breathless and reverential
brevity and condensation
bribery and corruption
brief and pithy
bright and vivacious
brilliancy and grace
brisk and enlivening
broad and deep
brooding and solemn
brutal and degrading
bulks and masses
bungling and trifling
businesslike and practicable
bustle and business

# C

cajoled and bullied
calamity and sorrow
callous and impervious
calmness and composure
calumny and exaggeration [calumny =
maliciously lying to injure a reputation]
candor and kindness
cant and hypocrisy [cant =
hypocritically pious language]
capable and efficient
capacity and ability
capricious and unreasonable
career and occupation
cares and anxieties
carping and ungenerous
casual and transient
causes and circumstances
cautious and reticent
celebrated and praised
celerity and violence [celerity = swiftness
of action]
ceremony and splendor
certain and verifiable
chafe and exasperate
chagrin and despondency
chance and opportunity
change and variety
chaos and confusion
character and temperament
characteristic and complete
charges and insinuations
charm and perfection
chaste and refined
cheap and convenient
checked and thwarted
cheerfulness and gaiety
cherish and guard
chief and paramount
chilled and stiffened
choleric and sanguine [choleric = easily
angered; bad-tempered] [sanguine =
cheerfully confident; optimistic]
churlishness and violence [churlish =
boorish or vulgar]
citation and allusion
civility and communicativeness

civilized and cultured
clamorous and wild
claptrap and platitude
clarity and straightforwardness
classical and perspicuous [perspicuous =
easy to understand]
clatter and clang
clear and decisive
cleverness and acuteness
clogged and dulled
clumsy and smudgy
coarse and grotesque
coaxed and threatened
coexistent and correlative
cogent and conclusive
cohesion and sequence
cold and unemotional
comely and vivacious
comfort and security
command and threaten
common and familiar
commotion and annoyance
compact and complete
comparison and discrimination
compass and power
competent and experienced
complaints and imprecations
[imprecation = a curse]
complaisance and readiness
complete and permanent
complex and various
composure and gracefulness
comprehensive and accurate
compression and pregnancy
conceal and deny
conceit and impertinence
conceived and consummated
concentrated and intensified
conception and treatment
concern and wonder
concise and emphatic
concrete and definite
condemned and upbraided
conditions and limitations
confession and doubt
confidence and loyalty

confusion and dismay
congratulations and welcomings
connection and interdependence
conquered and transformed
conquest and acquisition
consciously and purposely
consistent and harmonious
conspicuous and impressive
conspired and contrived
constant and intimate
constructive and vital
contemn and decry [contemn = despise]
contempt and indignation
contentment and serenity
continuous and undeviating
contorted and fantastic
contradictions and inconsistencies
contrast and comparison
contrivance and disguise
conventional and limited
cool and indifferent
copiousness and vivacity
cordial and cheerful
corruption and decay
costly and gorgeous
counselor and guide
countless and indescribable
courage and endurance

courted and feted
courteous and sympathetic
coveted and deserved
coy and furtive
cramped and distorted
creative and inventive
credulity and ignorance
creeds and dogmas
crime and misdemeanor
crippled and maimed
crises and struggles
crisp and sparkling
critical and skeptical
crowded and jostled
crowned and sceptered
crude and primitive
cruel and rapacious
crumbling and shapeless
crushed and bewildered
cultured and refined
cumbrous and diffuse [cumbrous = cumbersome]
cunning and cruelty
curious and inexpressible
curved and channeled
customs and manners
cynical and contemptuous

## D

dangers and pitfalls
daring and resolute
dark and starless
dart and quiver
dashing and careless
dates and details
dazzled and confounded
debased and demoralized
debilitating and futile
decencies and restraints
deception and cruelty
decided and definite
declamation and delivery
decline and decay
deductions and inferences
deep and subtle
deface and injure

defame and tarnish
deference and concession
defiant and antagonistic
deficient and unskilled
definite and memorable
deft and offensive
degraded and dishonored
deliberate and effective
delicate and lambent [lambent = effortlessly brilliant]
delight and consolation
delusion and trickery
demands and expectations
demeanor and conduct
demoralizing and enfeebling
denial and defense
dense and luminous

53

denunciations and censures
deplorable and baneful
depravity and frivolity
depressing and discouraging
depth and richness
derision and skepticism
described and classified
desecration and decay
designs and activities
desires and motives
desolation and wretchedness
despatch and resolution
desperation and defiance
despise and satirize
despoiled and destroyed
despondency and melancholy
despotism and coercion
destitution and misery
desultory and slipshod [desultory =
haphazardly; random]
detached and isolated
determined and courageous
detestable and intolerable
development and culture
devoted and unwavering
dictatorial and insolent
diction and pronunciation
differences and disputes
difficult and arduous
diffidence and constraint
diffuseness and warmth
dignified and austere
digressive and wanton
dilatory and hesitating [dilatory =
postpone or delay]
diligent and sedulous [sedulous =
persevering ]
dim and distant
din and traffic
directed and controlled
disagreeable and painful
disappointed and abashed
disapprobation and condemnation
[approbation = warm approval; praise]
disapproval and apprehension
discipline and development
discomfiture and degradation

disconcerted and dismayed
discontent and disquiet
discords and differences
discouraging and distressing
discovery and invention
discretion and moderation
disdain and mockery
disfigured and shapeless
disgrace and ruin
disgust and dismay
dishonor and ruin
disillusioned and ironical
disintegration and decay
disinterested and gracious
disjointed and voluble [voluble = fluent]
dislike and disdain
dislocation and chaos
dismay and apprehension
dispirit and discourage
disposition and power
disquietude and uneasiness
dissolute and hateful
dissolve and disappear
distant and diverse
distended and distorted
distinctive and appropriate
distinguishing and differentiating
distress and humiliation
distrust and aversion
disturbed and anxious
diverging and contracting
docile and obedient
dogma and ritual
dominant and permanent
dormant and subdued
doubt and trepidation
dramatic and sensational
drastic and revolutionary
dread and terror
dreams and ambitions
dreariness and desolation
dregs and sediments
drill and discipline
driveling and childish
drollery and ridicule
drooping and disconsolate
dubious and dangerous

dull and spiritless
dumb and nerveless
dupe and victim
duplicity and equivocation

E

eagerness and ecstasy
earnestness and animation
ease and lightness
ebb and flow
eclectic and assimilated
edifying and enchanting
education and skill
effective and competent
efficiency and success
egotism and bigotry
elaboration and display
elation and delight
elegance and gentility
elementary and simple
elevate and ennoble
eligibility and suitableness
elongated and narrow
eloquent and expressive
elusive and exquisite
embarrassed and concerned
embittered and despairing
embodiment and actualization
emerged and flowered
eminent and remarkable
emoluments and honors [emoluments =
compensation]
emotion and passion
emphasize and magnify
employment and profession
encouragement and stimulus
energy and activity
enfeebled and exhausted
enfold and enwrap
engulfed and buried
enjoyment and satisfaction
enlightenment and progress
enraptured and amazed
enriched and ennobled
enslave and dominate
enterprising and intelligent
entertaining and diverting

dust and oblivion
duties and difficulties
dwarfed and obscured
dwindle and disappear

enthusiasm and zeal
enticing and alluring
entire and complete
environment and training
envy and despair
ephemeral and feeble [ephemeral =
markedly short-lived]
episodes and interludes
epithet and description
equality and solidarity
equity and justice
erratic and confused
errors and infirmities
essential and predominating
estimable and agreeable
eternal and sublime
ethical and religious
ever and anon
evident and manifest
exactitude and completeness
exaggerate and distort
exaltation and enthusiasm
examination and comparison
examples and models
exasperations and paroxysms
[paroxysms = outbursts of emotion or
action]
excellent and worthy
exceptional and remarkable
excessive and unreasonable
excitable and irritable
exclusive and limited
excusable and justifiable
execration and defiance [execration =
curse]
exertion and excitement
exhaustion and fatigue
exhibition and display
exhilarating and beneficial
exigency and requirement [exigency =
urgent situation]

expansive and digressive
expediency and utility
expensive and unprofitable
experience and skill
experiment and explorations
expert and vigorous
explanation and elucidation
explore and examine

expressions and exclamations
expressive and effective
exquisite and powerful
extent and importance
extraordinary and unexpected
extravagant and grotesque
extreme and morbid
exuberant and infectious

F
fabulous and fabricated
facile and brilliant
facts and traditions
faculties and powers
faded and withered
failures and misadventures
faint and obscure
fair and impartial
faith and reverence
fallacy and danger
false and fugitive
fame and fortune
familiar and gracious
famous and foremost
fancies and sentiments
fanciful and chimerical [chimerical =
highly improbable]
fantastic and meretricious [meretricious
= plausible but false]
fascination and awe
fashion and frivolity
fastidious and exacting
fatigued and careworn
faults and delusions
favors and kindnesses
fear and bewilderment
feasible and practical
feebleness and folly
feeling and passion
felicitous and exquisite
ferocious and mercenary
fertility and vigor
fervor and simplicity
feverishly and furiously
fickle and uncertain
fidelity and zeal
fierce and menacing

fiery and controversial
final and irreversible
finish and completeness
firm and decisive
first and foremost
fitful and capricious
fitting and appropriate
fixity and finality
flaming and mendacious [mendacious =
lying; untruthful]
flare and flicker
flatness and insipidity
flattery and toadyism
flexible and spontaneous
flickering and ambiguous
flighty and impetuous
flippant and contemptuous
florid and healthy [florid = ornate;
flowery]
flotsam and jetsam
flow and fullness
flowery and figurative
fluctuating and transitory
fluency and flippancy
fluttering and restless
focus and concentrate
fogs and complications
foibles and follies
foiled and defeated
folly and indecorum
fools and underlings
force and effectiveness
formal and cold
formidable and profound
formlessness and exaggeration
fortitude and perseverance
foul and ominous

fragile and pale
fragments and morsels
fragrance and beauty
frailties and absurdities
frank and genial
free and independent
frequent and poignant
freshness and fragrance
fretful and timorous
friend and benefactor
frigid and pompous
frivolous and empty
froth and effervescence

frustrated and confounded
fuddled and contradictory
full and sonorous
fumbling and blundering
fuming and bustling
fun and satire
function and aim
fundamental and necessary
furrowed and ragged
furtive and illusive
fury and madness
fussing and fuming
futile and untrustworthy

G

gaiety and grace
gallant and proud
galling and humiliating
gaunt and ghastly
gay and genial
general and universal
generosity and prodigality
generous and humane
genial and refreshing
genius and reputation
gentle and amiable
genuine and infectious
germ and root
gesticulation and emphasis [gesticulation
= deliberate, vigorous motion or gesture]
ghastly and inconceivable
gifts and graces
gigantic and portentous
glamour and fascination
glare and pretension
glib and loquacious [loquacious = very
talkative]
glitter and glamour
gloomy and morose
glorious and gorgeous
glowing and exaggerated
glum and grim
goodness and rectitude
goodwill and merriment
gorgeousness and splendor

gossiping and grumbling
govern and overrule
grace and dignity
gracious and generous
gradual and progressive
graft and dishonesty
grand and sublime
grandeur and massiveness
grandiose and oracular [oracular =
solemnly prophetic; obscure]
graphic and gorgeous
gratification and enjoyment
gratitude and generosity
gratuitous and ungracious
grave and stately
graveyards and solitudes
greatness and stability
greed and covetousness
grief and remorse
grim and sullen
grimaces and gesticulations
grope and fumble
grossness and brutality
grotesque and monstrous
grouped and combined
growth and development
guesses and fancies
guidance and inspiration
gush and hysteria
gusto and effect

H

habits and humors
habitual and intuitive
hackneyed and tawdry
haggard and pale
handsome and amiable
haphazard and dangerous
happiness and pleasantness
harass and pursue
hard and unsparing
hardships and indignities
harmony and beauty
harsh and austere
hasty and unwarranted
hateful and loathsome
haughtiness and arrogance
hauteur and disdain [hauteur = arrogance]
hazard and peril
hazy and indefinite
headstrong and foolish
healthy and vigorous
hearth and shrine
heartless and hypocritical
heat and impatience
heaviness and weariness
hecklings and interruptions
hectic and pitiful
heretics and schismatics
heritage and privilege

heroism and wisdom
hesitation and irresolution
hideous and grotesque
high and conscientious
hilarity and mirth
hints and suggestions
history and tradition
hither and thither
hoarse and rumbling
hobbies and eccentricities
hollowness and unreality
holy and prayerful
homeliness and simplicity
honestly and confessedly
honors and emoluments [emoluments = compensation]
hooted and mobbed
hopes and prospects
horror and ghastliness
hospitality and magnificence
hubbub and confusion
huge and unwieldy
humane and sympathetic
humility and devoutness
humors and singularities
hurry and bustle
hushed and still
husks and phantoms
hypocrisy and impudence

I
ideas and achievements
idle and presumptuous
ignoble and shabby
ignominy and misfortune
ignorance and superstition
illiterate and unfit
ill-tempered and unjust
illuminative and suggestive
illustrative and typical
images and impressions
imagination and memory
imbitter and exasperate
imitators and disciples
immature and unpromising
immediate and instantaneous
immensity and intricacy
imminent and terrible

immovable and unchangeable
impalpable and spiritual
impassioned and energetic
impatient and restless
imperfection and fallibility
imperil and destroy
imperious and ruthless [imperious = arrogantly domineering]
impertinent and personal
impinging and inexorable
implacable and destructive
important and formidable
imposed and enforced
impossibilities and absurdities
impressible and plastic
improvement and progress
imprudent and thoughtless

impulse and indignation
inaccessible and audacious
inactive and supine
inadequate and misleading
inapplicable and alien
inarticulate and confused
inborn and native
incensed and alarmed
inchoate and tentative [inchoate = imperfectly formed]
incoherent and inconclusive
incompetence and ignorance
incomplete and erroneous
incongruity and absurdity
inconvenient and troublesome
incorrigible and irrepressible
incredulous and mortified
indefatigable and irresistible
indefinite and vague
independent and democratic
indifference and brevity
indigence and obscurity
indignation and chagrin
indirectly and unconsciously
indispensable and irreplaceable
indistinct and misty
indolence and indifference
indomitable and dogged
indorsed and applauded
indulge and cherish
industrious and vigilant
ineffective and bungling
inert and uncertain
inevitable and assured
inexhaustible and indomitable
inexperienced and timid
infallible and disdainful
inference and suggestion
infinite and eternal
inflexible and unchanging
influence and authority
informed and competent
ingenious and eloquent
ingratitude and cruelty
inharmonious and irregular
injustice and inhumanity
innocence and fidelity

innuendo and suggestion
inopportune and futile
insanely and blindly
inscrutable and perplexing
insecurity and precariousness
insensibly and graciously
insignificant and transitory
insincere and worthless
insipid and silly
insistent and incongruous
insolence and absurdity
inspiring and animating
instant and momentous
instinctive and rational
insulted and thwarted
intangible and indefinable
integral and indestructible
integrity and honor
intelligence and insight
intense and overpowering
intentness and interest
interesting and engrossing
intimate and familiar
intolerant and bumptious [bumptious = loudly assertive; pushy]
intractable and untameable
intricate and endless
intrusive and unmannerly
intuitive and axiomatic
invasion and aggression
invective and innuendo [invective = abusive language]
investigation and research
invidious and painful [invidious = rousing ill will, animosity]
inviolate and unscathed
invisible and silent
involuntary and automatic
irksome and distasteful
irrational and excessive
irregular and intermittent
irreligious and immoral
irremediable and eternal
irrepressible and insistent
irreverence and ingratitude
irritable and churlish [churlish = boorish or vulgar]

isolated and detached

## J

jabber and chatter
jagged and multifarious
jargon and absurdity
jaundiced and jealous
jeer and scoff
jeopardy and instability
jests and sarcasms
jocular and vivacious
jostle and stumble
joy and felicity

jubilant and boastful
judgment and discretion
judicious and acute
juggled and manipulated
jumble and confuse
juncture and circumstance
jurisdiction and authority
justice and virtue
juvenile and budding

## K

keen and pertinacious [pertinacious = stubbornly persistent]
kind and forbearing
kindle and intensify
kindred and analogous

kingly and autocratic
knavish and tyrannical
knowledge and conviction
known and recognized

## L

labor and drudgery
lame and impotent
lamentable and depressing
languid and indifferent
large and opulent
lassitude and languor [languor = dreamy, lazy mood]
latent and lifeless
latitude and scope
laudable and deserving
laughable and grotesque
lavish and wasteful
lawlessness and violence
laxity and forbearance
laziness and profligacy
leafage and fruitage
learning and austerity
legends and traditions
legitimate and logical
leisure and tranquillity
lengthy and diffuse
lenient and sympathetic
lethargy and sloth
levity and gaiety
liberal and ample

liberty and freedom
license and laxity
likely and plausible
limited and abbreviated
listless and inert
literal and exact
literary and artistic
lithe and sinewy
lively and poignant
loathsome and abject
lofty and sonorous [sonorous = producing a full, rich sound; impressive speech]
logical and consistent
loquacity and exuberance [loquacity = very talkative.]
loss and deterioration
loud and passionate
loving and reverential
low and groveling
loyal and devoted
lucidity and vividness
lucky and propitious [propitious = auspicious, favorable; kindly]
lucrative and advantageous

ludicrous and detestable
lugubrious and unfortunate [lugubrious = dismal, gloomy]
lukewarm and indifferent
lull and silence
luminous and keen

lure and captivate
lurid and fiery
luscious and lasting
luster and resplendence
lusty and big-sounding
luxury and pomp

## M

madness and folly
magical and secret
magnificent and luxurious
majestic and imposing
malice and revenge
malignity and spitefulness
manifold and complex
manly and powerful
manner and conduct
marvels and mysteries
massive and compact
masterly and convincing
materialistic and sordid
maternal and filial
maudlin and grotesque [maudlin = tearfully sentimental]
maxims and morals
meager and bare
mean and debasing
meaning and significance
means and materials
mechanical and monotonous
meddling and muddling
meditative and sympathetic
meek and manageable
melody and softness
memorable and glorious
menace and superciliousness [superciliousness = haughty disdain]
merciful and chivalrous
merciless and unpitying
merit and virtue
mighty and majestic
mild and virtuous
mince and temporize

minds and memories
minuteness and fidelity
mirth and joviality
misdemeanors and improprieties
misery and degradation
misrepresented and reviled
misty and indefinite
mobile and expressive
mockery and imposture
moderate and cautious
modes and methods
modest and retiring
molding and upbuilding
momentary and languid [languid = lacking energy; weak]
momentous and appalling
monopoly and injustice
monotony and indecorum
monstrous and insupportable
moody and brooding
moral and religious
morbid and irritable
motionless and commanding
motives and aims
mud and mire
muddled and incoherent
murmurs and reproaches
muscularity and morality
mutable and fleeting
mute and insensate
mutilated and disfigured
muttering and murmuring
mutual and friendly
mysterious and incomprehensible
mystic and wonderful

## N

nagging and squabbling
nameless and obscure

narrow and timorous
natural and spontaneous

nauseous and disgusting
neatness and propriety
necessarily and essentially
needs and demands
nefarious and malevolent
negations and contradictions
neglect and evade
negotiate and bargain
nerve and fiber
neutral and colorless
nicety and precision
nimble and airy
noble and powerful
nodding and blinking
noisy and scurrilous [scurrilous =
vulgar, coarse, abusive language]

nonsense and absurdity
nooks and corners
notable and conspicuous
noted and distinguished
noteworthy and intelligible
notoriety and prominence
nourish and foster
novelty and freshness
novice and ignoramus
nucleus and beginning
nugatory and ineffectual [nugatory = no
importance; trifling]
nullify and destroy
number and variety
numerous and important

## O
oaths and revilings
obdurate and impenitent [obdurate =
hardened in wrongdoing ] [impenitent =
without remorse for sins]
obedient and dutious
obeisance and submission
objectionable and inexpedient
obligation and dependence
obliquity and hypocrisy
oblivious and insensible
obloquy and detraction [obloquy =
abusive language]
obnoxious and odious
obscure and enigmatical
obsequies and panegyrics [obsequies =
funeral rite] [panegyrics = elaborate
praise]
obsequious and conciliating [obsequious
= servile compliance; fawning]
observations and reflections
obstacles and disasters
obstinate and stupid
obstreperous and noisy [obstreperous =
stubbornly defiant]
obtrusive and vulgar
obtuse and imbecile
obvious and palpable
occasional and contingent
occult and hidden

occupations and habits
odd and dismal
odious and oppressive
offensive and aggressive
official and authoritative
oily and servile
old and decrepit
ominous and untrustworthy
omnivorous and sordid
oneness and unity
onerous and perplexing
open and inviting
opinions and hypotheses
opportunism and inconsistency
opposite and discordant
oppressed and sullen
optimistic and reassuring
opulence and magnitude
oracular and occult [oracular = solemnly
prophetic; obscure]
order and uniformity
organic and rational
organization and system
origin and discovery
original and attractive
ornate and variegated
ostensible and explicit
ostentatiousness and gaiety
outlines and appearances

outrageous and scandalous
overburdened and confused
overcome and vanquish
overstep and contravene

overt and unmistakable
overwearied and outworn
overworked and fagged [fagged = worked to exhaustion]

## P

pains and penalties
painstaking and cumbersome
pale and anxious
palpable and plain
paltry and inglorious
pampered and petted
parade and display
parched and dry
partial and provisional
particularly and individually
parties and sects
passion and prejudice
passive and indifferent
pastimes and diversions
patent and pertinent
pathos and terror
patience and perseverance
patriotism and reverence
pattern and exemplar [exemplar = worthy of imitation]
peaks and pinnacles
pedagogue and pedant [pedant = exhibits learning or scholarship ostentatiously]
pedantries and affectations
pedigree and genealogy
peevishness and spleen
pellucid and crystal [pellucid = transparently clear]
penetrating and insidious
penned and planned
peppery and impetuous
perception and recognition
peremptorily and irrevocably [peremptorily = not allowing contradiction]
perilous and shifting
permanent and unchangeable
permeate and purify
pernicious and malign
perplexity and confusion

persistent and reiterated
personal and specific
perspicuous and flowing [perspicuous = clearly expressed]
perturbed and restless
perverted and prejudicial
pessimistic and disenchanted
pestilence and famine
petted and indulged
pettiness and prudence
petulance and acrimony
pharisaical and bitter [pharisaical = hypocritically self-righteous and condemnatory]
pictorial and dramatic
picturesque and illustrative
pilgrim and crusader
pillage and demolish
piquant and palatable [piquant = agreeable pungent taste]
pith and brevity
pitiful and destitute
place and power
plagued and persecuted
plainness and severity
plaintive and mournful
plans and projects
plastic and ductile
plausibility and humbug
pleasant and pungent
pleasurable and wholesome
pliant and submissive
plot and verisimilitude
plunder and sacrilege
poetical and pastoral
pointless and ineffective
polite and elegant
political and sociological
pomp and pageantry
ponderous and unwieldy
poor and barren

63

possession and dominion
potent and prevailing
power and luxury
praise and commend
precedence and usage
precision and efficiency
preference and prejudice
pregnant and suggestive
prejudice and predilection [predilection = preference]
presence and address
present and tangible
prestige and authority
presumptuous and futile
pretentious and inept
pretty and enchanting
pride and indignation
primary and essential
priority and predominance
probity and candor [probity = integrity; uprightness]
prodigal and careless
profile and outline
profound and philosophical
profuse and tearful
prolix and tedious [prolix = prolonged; wordy]
prominence and importance

promise and performance
promptitude and dispatch
proneness and readiness
pronounced and diversified
proof and illustration
propensity and desire
proportion and consistency
propriety and delicacy
prostration and loss
protection and safety
protesting and repelling
protracted and fruitless
provincialism and vulgarity
prudent and sagacious [sagacious = keenly discerning]
puerile and sickly [puerile = immature; childish]
puffy and dissipated
puissant and vigorous [puissant = with power, might]
punctilious and severe [punctilious = precise; scrupulous]
purity and simplicity
purpose and intention
pusillanimous and petty [pusillanimous = cowardly]
puzzled and affected

## Q
quackery and incompetence
quaintness and oddity
qualities and gifts
quarrel and wrangle
queer and affected
querulous and plaintive [querulous = complaining; peevish]
quibble and fabricate

quickness and agility
quiet and unobtrusive
quintessential and nuclear [quintessential = perfect example]
quips and cranks
quirks and graces
quivering and fearful
quizzical and whimsical

## R
racked and oppressed
racy and incisive
rage and apprehension
rank and learning
rant and gush
rapacity and villainy [rapacity = plundering]

rapidity and precision
rapt and silent
rapture and enthusiasm
rare and exquisite
rashness and heedlessness
ready and spontaneous
real and positive

realistic and effective
reasonable and practical
rebellion and disloyalty
rebuffs and anxieties
receptive and responsive
recognized and honored
recoil and reaction
reconciliation and peace
recondite and abstruse [recondite =
concealed; hidden] [abstruse = difficult
to understand]
reconnoiter and explore
recreation and amusement
rectitude and delicacy
redeeming and transforming
refined and dignified
refreshing and invigorating
regard and esteem
regret and remorse
regular and symmetrical
rejection and scorn
reliable and trustworthy
relief and redress [redress = set right;
remedy]
remarkable and interesting
remorseful and sullen
remote and distant
rend and devastate
repellent and ungracious
repetition and reiteration
repress and silence
repugnance and aversion
repulsive and loathsome
resentment and indignation
reserve and coyness
resistless and implacable

resolution and effort
resonant and tuneful
resourceful and unscrupulous
respected and obeyed
responsibilities and burdens
restive and bored
restless and impatient
retaliation and revenge
reticence and repose
revered and cherished
reverses and disasters
revised and corrected
revolution and sedition [sedition =
insurrection; rebellion]
rhapsodies and panegyrics [panegyrics =
elaborate praise]
richness and fertility
ridicule and censure
right and praiseworthy
rigid and inexpressive
ripeness and plenitude
rivals and antagonists
roar and ring
robust and rugged
rococo and affected [rococo = elaborate
ornamentation]
romantic and pathetic
rough and barren
roundabout and complicated
roused and stimulated
rude and fiery
rugged and inaccessible
rumors and impressions
rushing and gurgling
rust and disuse

S
sad and melancholy
sagacity and virtue [sagacity =
farsighted; wise]
sane and simple
sarcastic and cruel
sayings and quibbles
scant and incidental
scattered and desultory [desultory =
haphazard; random]

scenes and associations
scholastic and erudite [erudite =
learned]
scientific and exact
scintillating and brilliant
scoffing and unbelief
scope and significance
scorched and shriveled
scorn and loathing

65

scrupulous and anxious
scrutiny and investigation
searching and irresistible
seared and scorched
secondary and subsidiary
secretive and furtive
sedate and serious
selfish and overbearing
sensational and trivial
senseless and unreasoning
sensibilities and emotions
sensitive and capricious
sententious and tiresome [sententious =
pompous moralizing; terse and
energetic]
sentiment and passion
serene and quiet
serious and studious
severe and saturnine [saturnine =
melancholy or sullen]
shabbiness and vulgarity
shadowy and confused
shame and mortification
shams and hypocrisies
shaped and sculptured
sharp and vigorous
shelter and safeguard
shifts and compromises
shivering and chattering
shocked and astonished
short and precarious
shreds and tatters
shrewd and diligent
shrill and piercing
shrinking and nervous
shy and subdued
significant and sinister
signs and tokens
silence and obscurity
similarities and resemblances
simple and straightforward
simpletons and nincompoops
sincerity and frankness
sinewy and active
skill and coolness
skulk and shirk
sleek and languid [languid = lacking

energy or vitality; weak]
slight and precarious
slipshod and untidy
slothfulness and perversity
slow and sluggish
slumbering and unsuspected
small and hampered
smirched and tarnished
smoothness and artifice
sneering and sentimental
soberly and truthfully
softness and effeminacy
solemn and dramatic
solitary and idle
solitude and depression
sonorous and musical
sons and scions [scions = descendant or
heir]
soporific and sodden [soporific =
inducing sleep]
sordid and stupid
sorrow and lamentation
soulless and mindless
sovereign and independent
spacious and lofty
sparkling and spontaneous
spasmodic and hysterical
speedy and inevitable
spicy and pungent
spiritual and invisible
spiteful and sordid
splash and dash
splendor and glory
spontaneity and intensity
sportive and playful
sprightly and vigorous
spur and impulse
spurious and misleading
squalid and dismal [squalid = wretched,
dirty, repulsive]
stare and gasp
stately and ponderous
statesmanship and character
staunch and influential
stay and solace
steadfast and resolute
steadily and patiently

stealthy and hostile
stern and unbending
stiff and cumbersome
stifling and venomous
still and translucent
stimulating and wholesome
stings and stimulants
stir and tumult
stolid and soulless
strain and struggle
strange and incomprehensible
stratagems and plots
strenuous and energetic
strictly and absolutely
strife and contention
striking and picturesque
strong and youthful
structure and organization
struggles and misgivings
studied and artificial
stunned and insensible
stupor and despair
sturdy and manly
style and temperament
suave and winning
sublime and aspiring
submission and patience
subordinate and dependent
substance and basis

subtle and elusive
suddenness and vehemence
suffering and desperation
suffused and transfigured
suggestions and stimulations
sullen and fierce
summarize and epitomize
sumptuous and aromatic
sunshine and smiles
superb and showy
supercilious and obstinate [supercilious = haughty disdain]
superficial and obvious
superfluous and impertinent
suppressed and restrained
surmises and suggestions
surprise and wonder
susceptibility and vulnerability
suspense and excitement
suspicion and innuendo [innuendo = indirect derogatory implication]
sustained and measured
sweet and wholesome
swelled and bloated
swift and stealthy
swoop and range
symbolism and imagery
sympathetic and consoling

T

taciturn and laconic [taciturn = untalkative] [laconic = terse]
tactful and conciliatory
talkative and effusive
tame and insipid
tangible and sufficient
tangled and shapeless
tardy and belated
tartness and contradiction
taste and elegance
tattle and babble
taunt and reproach
tawdry and penurious [tawdry = gaudy, cheap] [penurious = stingy]
tears and lamentations
tedious and trivial

temperament and taste
temperately and judiciously
tempest and violence
temporal and evanescent [evanescent = vanishing like vapor]
tenacity and coherence
tender and emotional
tense and straining
tentative and experimental
terrible and satanical
testiness and crabbedness
thankfulness and acknowledgment
theories and speculations
thorough and effective
threatening and formidable
thriftless and unenterprising

67

thrilling and vitalizing
ties and associations
time and opportunity
timid and vacillating
tiresome and laborious
tolerant and kindly
tone and treatment
topics and instances
tormented and tantalized
tortuous and twisted
tottering and hopeless
touched and thrilled
tractable and gracious
traditions and practises
training and temperament
tranquillity and benevolence
transfuse and irradiate
transitory and temporary
transparent and comprehensible
treacherous and cowardly

tremble and oscillate
trenchant and straightforward
[trenchant = effective, and vigorous]
trials and tribulations
tricks and stratagems
trifling and doubtful
trite and commonplace
trivial and ridiculous
troublous and menacing
truisms and trivialities
trust and confidence
truth and righteousness
turbid and noise some
turgid and bombastic [turgid =
excessively complex] [bombastic =
pompous]
turmoil and shouting
twisted and perverted
type and forerunner
tyrant and oppressor

U
unaccountable and grotesque
unaffected and undaunted
unapproached and unapproachable
unassuming and unpretending
unchangeable and enduring
unconsciously and innocently
uncouth and barbarous
unctuous and irresistible [trenchant =
insincere earnestness]
undeveloped and ignorant
undignified and futile
uneasiness and apprehension
uneducated and inexperienced
unfamiliar and distant
unfettered and vigorous
unforced and unchecked
unfortunate and unparalleled
unfounded and incredible
ungracious and reluctant
unhappiness and discomfort
unique and original
unity and completeness
unjust and ungrateful
unlimited and absolute
unnatural and harmful

unobserved and unsuspected
unobtrusive and tactful
unparalleled and inexhaustible
unpleasant and bewildering
unpopular and unimpressive
unprecedented and objectionable
unpremeditated and heartfelt
unpromising and scanty
unprotected and friendless
unreal and unsubstantial
unreasoning and uncompromising
unrecognized and unrewarded
unseemly and insufferable
unseen and unsuspected
unsmiling and critical
unswerving and unfaltering
unthinking and careless
untutored and infantine
unusual and unexpected
unuttered and unutterable
unwholesome and vile
upright and credible
uproar and confusion
upstart and braggart
urbanity and unction [unction =

exaggerated earnestness]

utter and disastrous

**V**

vacillation and uncertainty
vague and indistinct
vain and profitless
validity and value
vanities and vices
vapory and chaotic
varied and animated
varnish and falsehood
vassals and inferiors
vast and superlative
vehement and clamorous
veiled and unreadable
venality and corruption
venerable and interesting
veracity and fidelity
verbally and literally
versatility and sympathy
vexation and anxiety
vibrating and sonorous
views and experiences
vigilant and inflexible
vigorous and graphic

violent and ill-balanced
virtuous and wise
virulence and invective [invective = abusive language]
visible and apparent
visionary and obscure
vistas and backgrounds
vital and vigorous
vitiate and poison [vitiate = reduce the value]
vituperation and abuse [vituperation = abusive language]
vivacious and agreeable
vivid and varied
void and nothingness
volatile and fiery
volubly and exuberantly [volubly = ready flow of speech]
volume and impetus
voluminous and varied
voluntarily and habitually
vulgar and artificial

**W**

wandering and erratic
wanton and unnecessary
war and revelry
warp and woof [warp = lengthwise threads] [woof = crosswise threads]
wasteful and circuitous
waxing and waning
weak and perfidious
wealth and distinction
wearisome and dull
weighed and winnowed
weighty and dominant
weird and fantastic
wheezing and puffing
whims and inconsistencies
wholesome and beautiful
wholly and solely
wicked and malicious

widened and amplified
wild and irregular
wily and observant
winking and blinking
winning and unforced
wise and beneficent
wistful and dreamy
wit and jocularity [jocularity = given to joking]
withered and wan
woe and lamentation
wonder and delight
work and utility
worldly and ambitious
worth and excellence
wrath and menace
wretched and suppliant

**Y**

yearning and eagerness
yielding and obedience
yoke and bondage

Z
zeal and vehemence
zenith and climax

young and fragile
youthful and callow [callow =
immature]

zest and freshness
zigzag and deviating

# SECTION 3
# FELICITOUS PHRASES

## A

ability, humor, and perspicacity
[perspicacity = perceptive]
abrupt, rough, and immoderate
abstruse, metaphysical, and idealistic
abundant, varied, and vigorous
accessible, knowable, and demonstrable
accomplished, inventive, and deft-
fingered
accuracy, ease, and grace
acquire, classify, and arrange
action, incident, and interest
active, learned, and liberal
acts, activities, and aims
actual, stern, and pathetic
acuteness, honesty, and, fearlessness
addition, correction, and amplification
adventurous, eager, and afraid
affected, pedantic, and vain [pedantic =
attention to detail or rules]
affluent, genial, and frank
aggressive, envious, and arrogant
agreeable, engaging, and delightful
air, woodland, and water
alarmed, anxious, and uneasy
alert, hopeful, and practical
amazement, resentment, and indignation
ambiguous, strange, and sinister

amiable, genial, and charitable
amusing, sympathetic, and interesting
ancient, subtle, and treacherous
annoyances, shifts, and inconveniences
anxious, fearful, and anticipative
appearance, conversation, and bearing
approbation, wealth, and power
[approbation = warm approval; praise]
apt, explicit, and communicative
ardent, undisciplined, and undirected
arrogance, conceit, and disdain
artificial, rhetorical, and mundane
artistic, progressive, and popular
aspirations, dreams, and devotions
assured, stern, and judicial
astonishment, apprehension, and horror
attainments, possessions, and character
attention, forbearance, and patience
attract, interest, and persuade
augmenting, furthering, and reenforcing
austere, calm, and somber
authority, leadership, and command
avarice, pride, and revenge
awakened, girded, and active
awe, reverence, and adoration
awkwardness, narrowness, and self-
consciousness

## B

barbarous, shapeless, and irregular
beautiful, graceful, and accomplished
beggar, thief, and impostor
belittling, personal, and selfish
birth, rank, and fortune
bitter, baleful, and venomous
bland, patient, and methodical
blessing, bestowing, and welcoming
blind, partial, and prejudiced
blithe, innocent, and free
bluster, swagger, and might
body, soul, and mind

boisterous, undignified, and vulgar
bold, original, and ingenious
bombastic, incongruous, and
unsymmetrical
bountiful, exuberant, and luxurious
brain, energy, and enterprise
brave, authoritative, and confident
breadth, richness, and freshness
breathless, confused, and exhilarated
brief, isolated, and fragmentary
brilliancy, energy, and zeal
broad, spare, and athletic

broken, apologetic, and confused
brotherhood, humanity, and chivalry
brusqueness, rudeness, and self-assertion

brutish, repulsive, and terrible
busy, active, and toiling

C

calculated, logical, and dispassionate
calm, earnest, and genial
candor, integrity, and
straightforwardness
capricious, perverse, and prejudiced
careful, reasoned, and courteous
cautious, prudent, and decisive
caviling, petulance, and discontent
[caviling = finding trivial objections]
censured, slighted, and despised
certain, swift, and final
chance, doubt, and mutability
character, life, and aims
charitable, just, and true
charm, grace, and glory
cheerful, modest, and delicate
childish, discordant, and superfluous
chill, harden, and repel
circumstances, properties, and
characteristics
civilized, mild, and humane
clear, cloudless, and serene
cleverness, independence, and originality
coarseness, violence, and cunning
coherent, interdependent, and logical
cold, cynical, and relentless
color, intensity, and vivacity
comfort, virtue, and happiness
comments, criticisms, and judgments
common, dull, and threadbare
compact, determinate, and engaging

conceited, commonplace, and
uninspiring
conception, direction, and organization
confident, inflexible, and uncontrollable
conflict, confusion, and disintegration
confused, broken, and fragmentary
conscience, heart, and life
conscientious, clear-headed, and
accurate
consistent, thoughtful, and steadfast
consoling, pacifying, and benign
constant, wise, and sympathetic
constitution, temperament, and habits
convince, convert, and reconstruct
copious, redundant, and involved
corroding, venomous, and malignant
corrupt, self-seeking, and dishonest
countenance, voice, and manner
country, lake, and mountain
courage, patience, and honesty
courteous, patient, and indefatigable
covetousness, selfishness, and ignorance
credulous, weak, and superstitious
crimes, follies, and misfortunes
crisp, emphatic, and powerful
crude, warped, and barren
cruelty, violence, and injustice
culture, growth, and progress
cunning, cruelty, and treachery
curious, fantastic, and charming

D

danger, difficulty, and hardship
darkness, doubt, and difficulty
dazzle, amaze, and overpower
deadly, silent, and inaccessible
deceitful, lazy, and dishonest
decent, respectable, and sensible
decisions, affirmations, and denials
deep, flexible, and melodious
defeated, discredited, and despised

deferential, conciliatory, and courteous
definite, tangible, and practicable
deftness, delicacy, and veracity
degraded, defeated, and emasculated
dejected, discouraged, and disappointed
deliberately, coolly, and methodically
delicate, mobile, and complex
delightful, witty, and sensible
denounced, persecuted, and reviled

dependent, subsidiary, and allied
depth, tenderness, and sublimity
desolated, impoverished, and embittered
despair, finality, and hopelessness
detailed, described, and explained
devastating, horrible, and irremediable
devout, gentle, and kindly
difficult, painful, and slow
digestion, circulation, and assimilation
dignity, solemnity, and responsibility
diligent, cautious, and painstaking
dingy, cumbersome, and depressing
directness, spontaneity, and simplicity
disciplined, drilled, and trained
discontent, revolt, and despair
discordant, coarse, and unpleasing
discourses, lectures, and harangues
disheveled, wild, and distracted
disinterested, patient, and exact
dislikes, jealousies, and ambitions
dismal, cold, and dead
dismay, remorse, and anguish

disordered, wild, and incoherent
dispassionate, wise, and intelligent
disposition, taste, and temperament
dissension, discord, and rebellion
distracted, hopeless, and bankrupt
disturbed, shaken, and distressed
diversified, animated, and rapid
division, prejudice, and antagonism
doctrine, life, and destiny
dogmatic, scientific, and philosophic
doubt, cynicism, and indifference
draggled, dirty, and slouching
dramatic, picturesque, and vigorous
dream, speculate, and philosophize
drunkenness, licentiousness, and
profanity
dry, inane, and droll
dull, hideous, and arid
dullards, hypocrites, and cowards
dust, turmoil, and smoke
duties, labors, and anxieties
dwarfed, scant, and wretched

E

eagerness, heartiness, and vehemence
earnestness, zeal, and intelligence
ease, power, and self-confidence
easy, natural, and unembarrassed
effluent, radiating, and fructifying
[fructifying = Make fruitful or
productive]
egotistic, disdainful, and proud
elegant, convincing, and irresistible
emotion, affection, and desire
empty, noisy, and blundering
end, aim, and purpose
energies, capacities, and opportunities
enlighten, uplift, and strengthen
enmity, suspicion, and hatred
enrich, discipline, and embellish

enthusiasm, vehemence, and spirit
envy, jealousy, and malice
equable, animated, and alert
erect, elastic, and graceful
error, ignorance, and strife
essence, existence, and identity
esteem, confidence, and affection
evil, disease, and death
exact, logical, and convincing
examine, compare, and decide
excessive, inaccurate, and unliterary
excitements, interests, and
responsibilities
experience, knowledge, and conduct
exposure, ruin, and flight
exterior, formal, and imposing

F

faded, dusty, and unread
failures, experiences, and ambitions
fair, proud, and handsome
fairies, sprites, and angels
faith, hope, and love

false, wicked, and disloyal
fantastic, absurd, and impossible
fear, dread, and apprehension
features, form, and height
feeble, illogical, and vicious

73

feelings, motives, and desires
fertility, ingenuity, and resource
fervently, patiently, and persistently
fibs, myths, and fables
fierce, dogmatic, and bigoted
figure, face, and attitude
fire, force, and passion
flit, change, and vary
flushed, trembling, and unstrung
foibles, tricks, and fads
foliage, color, and symmetry
follies, fashions, and infatuations
foolish, ignorant, and unscrupulous
force, grace, and symmetry
forcible, extraordinary, and sublime
foremost, preeminent, and incomparable
foresight, prudence, and economy
form, color, and distance

formless, silent, and awful
forward, onward, and upward
frank, kindly, and unfaltering
free, equal, and just
freedom, honor, and dignity
fresh, vigorous, and telling
fretfulness, irritability, and petulance
friendly, amiable, and sincere
frigid, austere, and splendid
fruitful, luminous, and progressive
full, animated, and varied
fullness, force, and precision
furious, sanguinary, and disorganizing
[sanguinary = Accompanied by
bloodshed]
fustian, padding, and irrelevancy
[fustian = pompous, bombastic, and
ranting]

G
gaunt, desolate, and despoiled
gay, easy, and cordial
generous, large-hearted, and
magnanimous
genial, frank, and confiding
genius, learning, and virtue
gentle, firm, and loving
genuineness, disinterestedness, and
strength
germinate, develop, and radiate
gesture, accent, and attitude
ghastly, hateful, and ugly
gibes, sneers, and anger
gifts, graces, and accomplishments
gladness, exaltation, and triumph
glean, gather, and digest
gloomy, silent, and tranquil

glow, grace, and pleasantness
good, gentle, and affectionate
gorgeous, still, and warm
grace, simplicity, and sweetness
gracious, mild, and good
gradual, cautious, and well-reasoned
gratitude, happiness, and affection
grave, disastrous, and wanton
gravity, sweetness, and patience
gray, monotonous, and uninteresting
great, grand, and mighty
greed, lust, and cruelty
grim, lean, and hungry
gross, ignorant, and impudent
growth, progress, and extension
guide, philosopher, and friend

H
habits, tastes, and opinions
hard, stern, and inexorable
harmony, peace, and happiness
harsh, intolerant, and austere
health, character, and efficiency
helpful, suggestive, and inspiring
helpless, hopeless, and downtrodden
high, lofty, and noble

high-spirited, confident, and genial
history, philosophy, and eloquence
homage, ability, and culture
honesty, probity, and justice [probity =
integrity; uprightness]
honors, riches, and power
hopes, aspirations, and longings
hot, swift, and impatient

humanity, freedom, and justice
humble, submissive, and serviceable

humor, fancy, and susceptibility

I
idle, profuse, and profligate
ignorance, fear, and selfishness
illuminating, chastening, and transforming
images, events, and incidents
imagination, judgment, and reason
immediate, sure, and easy
immethodical, irregular, and inconsecutive
impatient, inconsiderate, and self-willed
impetuous, fierce, and irresistible
impracticable, chimerical, and contemptible
impulse, energy, and activity
inclinations, habits, and interests
incoherent, loud, and confusing
incomparable, matchless, and immortal
inconsiderate, irritable, and insolent
indignation, surprise, and reproach

indirect, obscure, and ambiguous
indolent, dreamy, and frolicsome
inert, torpid, and lethargic
ingenuity, force, and originality
innocence, intelligence, and youth
inordinate, excessive, and extravagant
insight, knowledge, and capacity
insincere, partial, and arbitrary
insipid, commonplace, and chattering
insolence, injustice, and imposture
intelligence, taste, and manners
intense, weighty, and philosophical
inventions, sciences, and discoveries
irksome, painful, and depressing
irresolute, procrastinating, and unenterprising
irritable, sulky, and furious
issues, hopes, and interests

J
jealousy, exclusiveness, and taciturnity
[taciturnity = habitually untalkative]
jovial, ready-witted, and broad-gaged

joyous, delightful, and gay
justice, mercy, and peace

K
keen, clear, and accurate
knowing, feeling, and willing

knowledge, skill, and foresight

L
labors, anxieties, and trials
large, rhythmical, and pleasing
laughter, ridicule, and sneers
lead, attack, and conquer
learning, profundity, and imagination
legislation, education, and religion
levity, indolence, and procrastination
libelers, reviewers, and rivals
liberating, vitalizing, and cheering
liberty, justice, and humanity
light, easy, and playful
literature, history, and legend

lively, careless, and joyous
lofty, serene, and impregnable
logical, clear, and consistent
loitering, heart-sick, and reluctant
lonely, sad, and enslaved
long, wailing, and passionate
lost, ruined, and deserted
loud, deep, and distinct
love, veneration, and gratitude
lucid, lively, and effective
luxurious, whimsical, and selfish

# M

magnificent, sumptuous, and stately
magnitude, duration, and scope
majesty, beauty, and truth
malevolence, vanity, and falsehood
manly, refined, and unaffected
mean, pitiful, and sordid
meek, humane, and temperate
melancholy, grave, and serious
mercy, truth, and righteousness
methodical, sensible, and conscientious
might, majesty, and power
mild, sweet, and peaceable
mischief, cruelty, and futility

moans, shrieks, and curses
mobile, quick, and sensitive
modest, sympathetic, and kind
molding, controlling, and conforming
monstrous, incredible, and inhuman
moral, material, and social
motionless, staring, and appalled
motives, purposes, and intentions
mountains, seas, and vineyards
moved, swayed, and ruled
murder, destruction, and agony
mystery, vagueness, and jargon

# N

narrow, precise, and formal
natural, innocent, and laudable
neatness, order, and comfort
necessary, just, and logical
neglect, rashness, and incompetence
new, strange, and unusual

niggardly, sordid, and parsimonious
[grudging, wretched and frugal]
noble, laudable, and good
noise, clatter, and clamor
null, void, and useless

# O

obscure, difficult, and subtle
observation, discrimination, and comparison
obsolete, artificial, and inadequate
obstinacy, stupidity, and wilfulness
officious, fidgety, and talkative
old, absurd, and meaningless
one, individual, and integral

openly, frankly, and legitimately
opposition, bitterness, and defiance
oppressive, grasping, and slanderous
opulent, powerful, and prosperous
organization, monopoly, and pressure
origin, character, and aim
original, terse, and vigorous
overriding, arrogant, and quarrelsome

# P

pain, toil, and privation
pale, ugly, and sinister
parable, precept, and practise
partial, false, and disastrous
passion, tenderness, and reverence
patient, gentle, and kind
peace, order, and civilization
pellucid, animated, and varied [pellucid = transparently clear]
permanent, true, and real
perplexed, tedious, and obscure
personal, sharp, and pointed
perspicuity, vivacity, and grace

[perspicuity = clearness and lucidity]
pert, smirking, and conceited
pervading, searching, and saturating
petty, unsuccessful, and unamiable
philosophy, morals, and discoveries
picturesque, daring, and potent
piety, charity, and humility
pillage, arson, and bloodshed
pious, patient, and trustful
pity, sympathy, and compassion
placable, reasonable, and willing
[placable = easily calmed; tolerant]
place, fame, and fortune

placid, clear, and mellow
plague, pestilence, and famine
plan, purpose, and work
pleasant, friendly, and amiable
pleased, interested, and delighted
pleasure, enjoyment, and satisfaction
plenty, content, and tranquillity
plodding, sedentary, and laborious
poise, dignity, and reserve
polished, elegant, and sumptuous
politics, business, and religion
pompous, affected, and unreal
poor, miserable, and helpless
pose, gesture, and expression
powerful, dazzling, and daring
practical, visible, and tangible
precious, massive, and splendid
precise, formal, and cynical
prejudice, dulness, and spite
prepossessions, opinions, and prejudices
presiding, directing, and controlling

pride, passion, and conceit
princely, picturesque, and pathetic
principles, conduct, and habits
progress, order, and happiness
prolonged, obstinate, and continued
prompt, fiery, and resolute
propriety, perspicacity, and accuracy
[perspicacity = perceptive]
prosaic, dull, and unattractive
protective, propitiatory, and
accommodating [propitiatory =
conciliatory]
protests, criticisms, and rebukes
proud, reserved, and disagreeable
prudence, mildness, and firmness
puckered, winking, and doddering
pure, honorable, and just
purge, brace, and strengthen
purpose, intention, and meaning
puzzles, tangles, and questionings

## Q

quarrels, misunderstandings, and
enmities
questions, disputes, and controversies

quicken, sharpen, and intensify
quiet, unaffected, and unostentatious

## R

raise, refine, and elevate
rapid, robust, and effective
rapt, emotional, and mystic
raptures, transports, and fancies
rash, violent, and indefinite
readiness, skill, and accuracy
reading, reflection, and observation
reaffirmed, amplified, and maintained
real, earnest, and energetic
regard, esteem, and affection
relaxation, recreation, and pleasure
religion, politics, and literature
reminiscences, associations, and
impressions
remote, careless, and indifferent
reparations, restitutions, and guarantees
repress, curb, and correct
reproach, shame, and remorse
reproof, correction, and instruction

resentment, hatred, and despair
resolute, patient, and fervent
resourceful, steadfast, and skilful
respect, admiration, and homage
rest, respite, and peace
restless, discontented, and rebellious
restraint, self-denial, and austerity
reticent, restrained, and reserved
reverie, contemplation, and loneliness
rich, thoughtful, and glowing
ridicule, sarcasm, and invective
[invective = abusive language]
rights, powers, and privileges
rise, flourish, and decay
robustness, elasticity, and firmness
romance, adventure, and passion
rough, barren, and unsightly
rude, sulky, and overbearing
rush, roar, and shriek

## S

sacredness, dignity, and loveliness
sad, gloomy, and suspicious
safe, sensible, and sane
sanguine, impulsive, and irrepressible
[sanguine = cheerfully confident; optimistic]
sarcasm, satire, and ridicule
satiety, surfeit, and tedium
savage, fierce, and intractable
scheming, contriving, and dishonesty
self-absorbed, conceited, and contemptuous
self-conscious, artificial, and affected
self-exacting, laborious, and inexhaustible
selfishness, coarseness, and mendacity [mendacity = untruthfulness]
sense, grace, and good-will
sensibility, harmony, and energy
sensitive, ardent, and conscientious
serene, ineffable, and flawless [ineffable = indescribable]
serious, calm, and searching
settled, adjusted, and balanced
shallow, false, and petty
shapes, forms, and artifices
sharpness, bitterness, and sarcasm
shivering, moaning, and weeping
shrewd, artful, and designing
shy, wild, and provocative
sick, ashamed, and disillusioned
silent, cold, and motionless
simple, full, and impressive
sin, selfishness, and luxury
sincere, placable, and generous [placable = easily calmed; tolerant]
skill, sagacity, and firmness [sagacity = farsighted; wise]
sleekness, stealth, and savagery
slovenly, base, and untrue
slow, reluctant, and unwelcome

smirking, garrulous, and pretentious [garrulous = excessive and trivial talk]
smooth, sentimental, and harmonious
smug, fat, and complacent
sneers, innuendoes, and insinuations
social, esthetic, and intellectual
solitary, sedentary, and lifeless
sound, human, and healthy
sour, malignant, and envious
spacious, clean, and comfortable
speechless, motionless, and amazed
spirit, vigor, and variety
spitefulness, dishonesty, and cruelty
splendid, powerful, and enduring
startling, alarming, and vehement
statesmen, philosophers, and divines
steadiness, self-control, and serenity
stern, forbidding, and unfeeling
stiff, decorous, and formal
strained, worn, and haggard
strange, dark, and mysterious
strengthen, invigorate, and discipline
strenuous, intelligent, and alive
striking, bold, and magnificent
stripped, swept, and bare
strong, cool, and inflexible
studied, discussed, and debated
sturdy, energetic, and high-minded
style, manner, and disposition
subtle, delicate, and refined
successful, energetic, and ingenious
sudden, vehement, and unfamed
suggestive, stimulating, and inspiring
sullen, silent, and disconsolate
suppliant, gentle, and submissive [suppliant = asking humbly]
surprise, admiration, and wonder
suspicious, restive, and untractable
swiftness, mobility, and penetrativeness
sympathy, service, and compassion

## T

talent, scholarship, and refinement
tameness, monotony, and reserve
taste, feeling, and sentiment

tedious, painful, and distressing
temper, pride, and sensuality
temperament, character, and

circumstance
temperate, sweet, and venerable
tenderness, loyalty, and devotion
terror, remorse, and shame
terseness, simplicity, and quaintness
theatrical, sensational, and
demonstrative
thought, utterance, and action
threats, cries, and prayers
thrilling, dramatic, and picturesque
thwart, criticize, and embarrass
time, thought, and consideration

touched, strengthened, and transformed
tradition, prejudice, and stupidity
tragic, tremendous, and horrible
transparent, theatric, and insincere
treachery, envy, and selfishness
tremulous, soft, and bright [tremulous =
trembling, quivering, shaking]
trial, discipline, and temptation
tricks, shufflings, and frauds
trivial, labored, and wearisome
true, lasting, and beneficial
tyranny, injustice, and extortion

## U

ugly, scowling, and offensive
unbending, contemptuous, and scornful
unclean, shameful, and degrading
undecided, wavering, and cautious
unearthly, horrible, and obnoxious
uneasy, overstrained, and melancholy
unity, emphasis, and coherence
unmodulated, cold, and expressionless
unphilosophical, unsystematic, and

discursive
unscrupulous, heartless, and hypocritical
unwholesome, bewildering, and
unprofitable
unworldly, peaceable, and philosophical
upright, kind-hearted, and blameless
urgent, tumultuous, and
incomprehensible

## V

vague, impalpable, and incongruous
vanities, stupidities, and falsehoods
venerable, patriotic, and virtuous
verities, certainties, and realities
vigilant, inveterate, and unresting
[inveterate = long established]
vigorous, subtle, and comprehensive

violent, sinister, and rebellious
virtue, genius, and charm
visionary, fraudulent, and empirical
vital, formidable, and dominant
vivid, comprehensible, and striking
vulgarity, ignorance, and
misapprehension

## W

waddling, perspiring, and breathless
want, worry, and woe
wasteful, indolent, and evasive
watchful, suspicious, and timid
wealth, position, and influence
wearied, despondent, and bewildered
weight, size, and solidity
well-proportioned, logical, and sane
whimsical, fantastic, and impracticable
wholesome, beautiful, and righteous

wicked, pernicious, and degrading
wild, confused, and dizzy
wilful, wanton, and deliberate
will, energy, and self-control
wisdom, patriotism, and justice
wit, fancy, and imagination
worthless, broken, and defeated
wretchedness, deformity, and malice
wrinkled, careworn, and pale

# SECTION 4
# IMPRESSIVE PHRASES

## A

able, skilful, thorough, and genuine
absolute, complete, unqualified, and final
accurate, precise, exact, and truthful
active, alert, vigorous, and industrious
actual, positive, certain, and genuine
adequate, uniform, proportionate, and equitable
adventurous, fine, active, and gossipy
adverse, antagonistic, unfriendly, and hostile
advisable, advantageous, acceptable, and expedient
affable, diffident, humble, and mild
affectionate, tender, loving, and attached
affluent, opulent, abundant, and ample
allurements, pits, snares, and torments
anger, indignation, resentment, and rage
animate, impel, instigate, and embolden
animosity, malice, enmity, and hatred
annul, frustrate, reverse, and destroy
anxiety, caution, watchfulness, and solicitude
apparent, ostensible, plausible, and specious
appropriate, use, arrogate, and usurp [arrogate = claim without right; appropriate]
approval, enthusiasm, sympathy, and applause

aptitude, capacity, efficiency, and power
arbitrary, dictatorial, domineering, and imperious [imperious = arrogantly domineering or overbearing]
architecture, sculpture, painting, and poetry
ardent, impatient, keen, and vehement
argue, discuss, dispute, and prove
arrangement, place, time, and circumstance
art, science, knowledge, and culture
artful, wily, insincere, and disingenuous
artificial, soulless, hectic, and unreal
assemble, amass, accumulate, and acquire
assiduity, tenderness, industry, and vigilance [assiduity = persistent application]
assurance, persuasion, fidelity, and loyalty
attention, effort, diligence, and assiduity [assiduity = persistent application]
august, magnanimous, important, and distinguished
authoritative, independent, arbitrary, and supreme
avaricious, grasping, miserly, and parsimonious [parsimonious = excessively frugal]
aversion, dislike, hatred, and repugnance

## B

bad, vicious, unwholesome, and distressing
babble, prate, chatter, and prattle
barbarous, brutal, inhuman, and cruel
base, cowardly, abject, and hideous
battle, defeat, frustrate, and ruin
bearing, deportment, manner, and behavior
beg, entreat, implore, and supplicate

beliefs, doctrines, ceremonies, and practices
boorish, clownish, rude, and uncultivated
boundless, immeasurable, unlimited, and infinite
bravery, courage, fearlessness, and confidence
breadth, knowledge, vision, and power

brilliant, beautiful, elegant, and faithful
broaden, enlarge, extend, and augment

C
candid, sincere, familiar, and ingenuous
captious, petulant, peevish, and splenetic
[captious = point out trivial faults]
cautious, discreet, considerate, and
provident
certain, confident, positive, and
unquestionable
chagrin, vexation, irritation, and
mortification
character, disposition, temperament, and
reputation
charm, fascinate, bewitch, and captivate
cheap, inexpensive, inferior, and
common
cheer, animate, vivify, and exhilarate
[vivify = bring life to]
chiefly, particularly, principally, and
especially
childhood, youth, manhood, and age
circumstance, condition, environment,
and surroundings
claim, grab, trick, and compel
clean, fastidious, frugal, and refined
clear, distinct, obvious, and intelligible
clumsy, crawling, snobbish, and

D
daring, cordial, discerning, and
optimistic
darkness, dimness, dulness, and
blackness
deadly, destructive, fatal, and implacable
deceit, delusion, treachery, and sham
deep, abstruse, learned, and profound
deficient, inadequate, scanty, and
incomplete
define, explain, determine, and
circumscribe
degrade, defame, humble, and debase
delicacy, daintiness, tact, and refinement
delicious, sweet, palatable, and delightful
democracy, equality, justice, and
freedom

business, profession, occupation, and
vocation

comfort-loving
coarse, gross, offensive, and nauseous
coax, flatter, wheedle, and persuade
cogitate, contemplate, meditate, and
ponder
cold, frigid, unfeeling, and stoical
commanding, authoritative, imperative,
and peremptory [peremptory = ending
all debate or action]
compassion, goodwill, admiration, and
enthusiasm
confirm, establish, sustain, and
strengthen
conform, submit, obey, and satisfy
confuse, distort, involve, and
misinterpret
consistent, congruous, firm, and
harmonious
cool, collected, calm, and self-possessed
copious, commanding, sonorous, and
emotional
cowardly, timid, shrinking, and timorous
crazy, absurd, nonsensical, and
preposterous
crude, rough, jagged, and pitiless

deny, dismiss, exclude, and repudiate
deprive, dispossess, divest, and despoil
describe, delineate, depict, and
characterize
designed, contrived, planned, and
executed
desperate, extreme, wreckless, and
irremediable
despicable, abject, servile, and worthless
destructive, detrimental, deleterious, and
subversive
desultory, discursive, loose, and
unmethodical [desultory = disconnected:
haphazard]
detestable, abominable, horrible, and
hideous

developed, revealed, measured, and tested

difference, disagreement, discord, and estrangement

difficult, arduous, intricate, and perplexing

diffuse, discursive, rambling, and wordy

diligence, attention, industry, and assiduity [assiduity = persistent application]

disagreement, discrepancy, difference, and divergence

disconsolate, desolate, pessimistic, and impossible

discrimination, acuteness, insight, and judgment

disgust, distaste, loathing, and abhorrence

dissatisfied, rebellious, unsettled, and satirical

distinct, definite, clear, and obvious

distinguished, glorious, illustrious, and eminent

disturbed, shaken, distressed, and bewildered

docile, tractable, compliant, and teachable

dogmatic, bigoted, libelous, and unsympathizing

doubt, indecision, suspense, and perplexity

dread, disgust, repugnance, and dreariness

dreary, dispirited, unhappy, and peevish

dry, lifeless, tiresome, and uninteresting

dubious, equivocal, fluctuating, and uncertain

dull, heavy, painstaking, and conscientious

E

earth, air, stars, and sea

efficient, forcible, adequate, and potent

emaciated, scraggy, meager, and attenuated

endless, ceaseless, immutable, and imperishable

energy, eagerness, earnestness, and enthusiasm

enhance, exalt, elevate, and intensify

enormous, base, prodigious, and colossal

enrage, incense, infuriate, and exasperate

enthusiasm, devotion, intensity, and zeal

envy, discontent, deception, and ignorance

equitable, reasonable, just, and honest

equivocal, uncertain, cloudy, and ambiguous

eradicate, extirpate, exterminate, and annihilate [extirpate = pull up by the

roots]

erroneous, faulty, inaccurate, and inexact

eternal, unchangeable, unerring, and intelligent

evil, misfortune, corruption, and disaster

exacting, suspicious, irritable, and wayward

exalt, dignify, elevate, and extol

examination, inquiry, scrutiny, and research

exceed, outdo, surpass, and transcend

exceptional, uncommon, abnormal, and extraordinary

excitement, distraction, diversion, and stimulation

exhaustive, thorough, radical, and complete

expend, dissipate, waste, and squander

F

facile, showy, cheap, and superficial

faithful, truthful, loyal, and trustworthy

fame, distinction, dignity, and honor

fanatic, enthusiast, visionary, and zealot

fanciful, unreal, fantastic, and grotesque

fancy, humor, vagary, and caprice

[vagary = extravagant or erratic notion or action]
fashion, practise, habit, and usage
fastidious, proud, gracious, and poised
fate, fortune, contingency, and opportunity
fatuous, dreamy, moony, and impracticable
fear, timidity, cowardice, and pusillanimity
feeble, languid, timid, and irresolute
ferocious, restive, savage, and uncultivated
fervent, enthusiastic, anxious, and zealous
fiction, fancy, falsehood, and fabrication
fine, fragile, delicate, and dainty
firmness, steadfastness, stability, and tenacity
flash, flame, flare, and glare
flat, insipid, tame, and monotonous
fluctuating, hesitating, vacillating, and oscillating
folly, foolishness, imbecility, and fatuity
foolhardy, hasty, adventurous, and reckless
fop, coxcomb, puppy, and jackanapes [jackanapes = conceited person]
force, vigor, power, and energy
formal, precise, stiff, and methodical
fortunate, happy, prosperous, and successful
fragile, frail, brittle, and delicate
freedom, familiarity, liberty, and independence
frightful, fearful, direful, and dreadful
frivolous, trifling, petty, and childish
fruitful, fertile, prolific, and productive
fruitless, vain, trivial, and foolish
frustrate, defeat, disappoint, and thwart
fully, completely, abundantly, and perfectly
furious, impetuous, boisterous, and vehement

G
gaiety, merriment, joy, and hilarity
gallant, ardent, fearless, and self-sacrificing
garnish, embellish, beautify, and decorate
generous, candid, easy, and independent
genius, intellect, aptitude, and capacity
genteel, refined, polished, and well-bred
gentle, persuasive, affective, and simple
genuine, true, unaffected, and sincere
ghastly, grim, shocking, and hideous
gibe, mock, taunt, and jeer
giddy, fickle, flighty, and thoughtless
gleam, glimmer, glance, and glitter
gloomy, dismal, dark, and dejected
glorious, noble, exalted, and resplendent
glut, gorge, cloy, and satiate [cloy = too filling, rich, or sweet]
good, safe, venerable, and solid
government, law, order, and organization
grand, stately, dignified, and pompous
grave, contemplative, reserved, and profound
great, joyous, strong, and triumphant
greed, avarice, covetousness, and cupidity
gross, academic, vulgar, and indiscriminate

H
habit, custom, method, and fashion
handsome, exquisite, brilliant, and accomplished
harmless, innocent, innocuous, and inoffensive
harmony, order, sublimity, and beauty
harsh, discordant, disagreeable, and ungracious
hasty, superficial, impatient, and desultory [desultory = disconnected: haphazard]
healed, soothed, consoled, and assuaged

healthy, hale, sound, and wholesome
heavy, sluggish, dejected, and crushing
high-minded, truthful, honest, and
courageous
holy, hallowed, sacred, and consecrated
homely, hideous, horrid, and unsightly
honor, obedience, virtue, and loyalty
hopefulness, peace, sweetness, and
strength
hopes, dreams, programs, and ideals
hospitable, generous, tolerant, and
kindly
hot, hasty, fervent, and fiery
humane, gentle, kind, and generous
humble, simple, submissive, and
unostentatious

I

idea, imagination, conception, and ideal
idleness, recreation, repose, and rest
ignominious, infamous, despicable, and
contemptible
illumine, instruct, enlighten, and inform
imaginative, sensitive, nervous, and
highly-strung
impatience, indolence, wastefulness, and
inconclusiveness
impel, stimulate, animate, and inspirit
imperious, wayward, empirical, and
impatient [imperious = arrogantly
domineering or overbearing]
improvident, incautious, prodigal, and
thriftless
impudent, insolent, irrelevant, and
officious
inadvertency, carelessness, negligence,
and oversight
indecision, doubt, fear, and lassitude
indifference, caution, coldness, and
weariness
indolent, passive, sluggish, and slothful
ineffectual, powerless, useless, and
unavailing
infamy, shame, dishonor, and disgrace
infantile, childish, boyish, and dutiful
informal, natural, unconventional, and
careless
insolent, impudent, impertinent, and
flippant
integrity, frankness, sincerity, and
truthfulness
intellectual, moral, emotional, and
esthetic
intense, earnest, violent, and extreme
invent, discover, design, and contrive
inveterate, confirmed, chronic, and
obstinate
invidious, envious, odious, and offensive
invincible, unconquerable,
insurmountable, and insuperable
irksome, tiresome, tedious, and annoying
irregular, uncertain, devious, and
unsystematic
irritable, choleric, petulant, and
susceptible

J

jangle, wrangle, squabble, and quarrel
jealousy, suspicion, envy, and
watchfulness
joyful, lively, happy, and hilarious
judgment, discrimination, penetration,
and sagacity [sagacity = farsighted; wise]
just, impartial, equitable, and unbiased
juvenile, childish, trifling, and puerile
[puerile = immature; childish]

K

keen, intelligent, penetrating, and severe
keep, protect, support, and sustain
kind, sympathetic, ready, and
appreciative
kingly, noble, imperial, and august
knowledge, learning, enlightenment, and
understanding

## L

lapses, makeshifts, delays, and irregularities
lawful, legitimate, allowable, and just
lazy, listless, drowsy, and indifferent
lightly, freely, unscrupulously, and irresponsibly
lively, vivacious, vigorous, and forcible

loss, deprivation, forfeiture, and waste
loud, noisy, showy, and clamorous
loutish, prankish, selfish, and cunning
love, depth, loyalty, and faithfulness
lucidity, impressiveness, incisiveness, and pungency [pungency = to the point]

## M

malice, anger, uncharitableness, and indignation
malignity, brutality, malevolence, and inhumanity
manners, morals, habits, and behavior
marvelous, wonderful, extraordinary, and incredible
massive, ponderous, solid, and substantial
mastery, proficiency, dexterity, and superiority
matchless, unrivaled, inimitable, and incomparable
maxim, proverb, truism, and apothegm [apothegm = terse, witty, instructive saying]
medley, mixture, jumble, and hodge-podge

meekness, inwardness, patience, and self-denial
merciless, remorseless, relentless, and ruthless
mild, gentle, humble, and submissive
mismanagement, indecision, obstinacy, and hardihood
mixture, medley, variety, and diversification
modesty, fineness, sensitiveness, and fastidiousness
money, position, power, and consequence
mood, temper, humor, and caprice
motive, impulse, incentive, and intimation
mysterious, dark, secret, and enigmatical

## N

narrow, limited, selfish, and bigoted
necessary, expedient, indispensable, and unavoidable
necessity, emergency, exigency, and crisis [exigency = urgent situation]
neglect, overlook, disregard, and contemn [contemn = despise]
nice, finical, effeminate, and silly [finical = Finicky]

niggardly, close, miserly, and parsimonious [parsimonious = Excessively frugal]
noble, pure, exalted, and worthy
nonsense, trash, twaddle, and rubbish
novel, recent, rare, and unusual
noxious, unwholesome, mischievous, and destructive

## O

obdurate, unfeeling, callous, and obstinate
obedient, respectful, dutiful, and submissive
object, propose, protest, and decline
obliging, kind, helpful, and courteous

obscure, shadowy, intricate, and mysterious
obsequious, cringing, fawning, and servile [obsequious = fawning.]
observations, sentiments, ideas, and theories

obstinacy, pertinacity, stubbornness, and inflexibility [pertinacity = persistent]
offensive, disagreeable, distasteful, and

obnoxious
officious, impertinent, insolent, and meddlesome

## P
particular, precise, formal, and punctilious [punctilious = scrupulous]
passions, weaknesses, uglinesses, and deformities
patient, loyal, hard-working, and true
peace, quiet, tranquillity, and harmony
peculiar, individual, specific, and appropriate
perplex, embarrass, confuse, and mystify
phrases, figures, metaphors, and quotations
piteous, woebegone, dismal, and dolorous
placid, meek, gentle, and moderate
plain, transparent, simple, and obvious
play, diversion, pastime, and amusement
pleasant, jocular, witty, and facetious
pliable, ductile, supple, and yielding
poetry, sentiment, morality, and religion
polished, deft, superficial, and conventional
polite, polished, cultured, and refined
positive, direct, explicit, and dogmatic
powerful, efficient, vivid, and forcible
precise, delicate, discriminating, and fastidious
prejudicial, injurious, noxious, and pernicious
preposterous, irrational, unreasonable,

and nonsensical
pretense, subterfuge, simulation, and disguise
prevent, restrain, dissuade, and dishearten
primary, foremost, leading, and principal
probity, directness, simplicity, and sincerity [probity = integrity]
profession, business, trade, and vocation
profit, advantage, benefit, and emolument [emolument = compensation]
profuse, excessive, copious, and extravagant
progress, prosperity, peace, and happiness
prolix, prosaic, prolonged, and wordy [prolix = excessive length]
property, comforts, habits, and conveniences
prudence, judgment, wisdom, and discretion
pulsing, coursing, throbbing, and beating
pure, kind, sweet-tempered, and unselfish
purified, exalted, fortified, and illumined
purpose, meaning, scope, and tendency

## Q
quack, imposture, charlatan, and mountebank [mountebank = flamboyant charlatan]
qualified, powerful, vigorous, and effective
quality, property, attribute, and character

quarrels, misunderstandings, enmities, and disapprovals
queries, echoes, reactions, and after-thoughts
quick, impetuous, sweeping, and expeditious
quiet, peaceful, sane, and normal

## R
racy, smart, spicy, and pungent
rational, sane, sound, and sensible

ravenous, greedy, voracious, and grasping

recreation, sport, pastime, and amusement

relation, work, duty, and pleasure

reliable, accurate, truthful, and duty-loving

reports, stories, rumors, and suspicions

reproach, dishonor, disgrace, and ignominy

restrained, calm, quiet, and placid

reverential, disciplined, self-controlling, and devoted

rigid, inelastic, stiff, and unbending

rough, rude, gruff, and surly

rude, curt, insolent, and unpleasant

## S

sad, despondent, melancholy, and depressed

sane, sober, sound, and rational

scandalize, vilify, traduce, and offend [traduce = humiliate with false statements]

scanty, pinched, slender, and insufficient

science, art, religion, and philosophy

scope, design, purpose, and judgment

sensual, cruel, selfish, and unscrupulous

sentence, judgment, verdict, and doom

serene, composed, conservative, and orderly

several, sundry, many, and various

severe, stern, stiff, and stringent

shameless, corrupt, depraved, and vicious

shock, surprise, terror, and forlornness

simple, hearty, joyous, and affectionate

sin, injustice, grievance, and crime

skill, courage, prowess, and attractiveness

sleepy, soporific, sluggish, and dull [soporific = induces sleep]

slim, slender, slight, and scraggy

slow, dilatory, slack, and procrastinating [dilatory = postpone]

solemn, profound, serious, and difficult

solicit, urge, implore, and importune [importune = insistent requests]

sorrow, disaster, unhappiness, and bereavement

spontaneity, freedom, ease, and adequacy

stately, stern, august, and implacable

steady, reliable, dependable, and well-balanced

stern, severe, abrupt, and unreasonable

stories, pictures, shows and representations

strength, agility, violence, and activity

strong, inventive, daring, and resourceful

sublime, consoling, inspiring, and beautiful

substantial, solid, strong, and durable

suffering, regret, bitterness, and fatigue

superficial, shallow, flimsy, and untrustworthy

superfluous, excessive, unnecessary, and redundant

suspicious, cynical, crafty, and timid

symmetry, proportion, harmony, and regularity

## T

tact, courtesy, adroitness, and skill

talents, opportunities, influence, and power

talkative, selfish, superstitious, and inquisitive

tastes, appetites, passions, and desires

tease, tantalize, worry, and provoke

tenacious, stubborn, pertinacious, and obstinate [pertinacious = perversely persistent]

tendency, drift, scope, and disposition

tests, trials, temptations, and toils

theatrical, ceremonious, meretricious, and ostentatious [meretricious = plausible but insincere]

theory, assumption, speculation, and conjecture

think, reflect, weigh, and ponder

tortuous, twisted, sinuous, and circuitous
tractable, gentle, pliant, and submissive
traditional, uncertain, legendary, and
unverified
traffic, trade, commerce, and intercourse
tricky, insincere, wily, and shifty

trite, ordinary, commonplace, and
hackneyed
trivial, petty, frivolous, and insignificant
true, upright, real, and authentic
tumultuous, riotous, disorderly, and
turbulent

U
ugly, evil, hateful, and base
uncertain, questionable, erroneous, and
mistaken
unctuous, shrill, brisk, and
demonstrative [unctuous = exaggerated,
insincere]
unhappy, unfortunate, distressed, and
disastrous
uninteresting, lifeless, obscure, and
commonplace
unity, aggressiveness, efficiency, and

force
unkind, severe, oppressive, and callous
unpractical, childish, slipshod, and silly
unreasonable, foolish, excessive, and
absurd
unrivaled, unequaled, incomparable,
and matchless
upright, high-minded, brave, and liberal
urgent, important, immediate, and
imperative
usage, custom, habit, and practise

V
vain, useless, unproductive, and
unavailing
vanities, envies, devices, and jealousies
vast, scattered, various, and incalculable
versatile, eloquent, sagacious, and
talented [sagacious = wise]
vigorous, upright, dignified, and

imperative
vile, mean, debased, and sordid
violent, impetuous, intense, and
ungovernable
virtuous, upright, honest, and moral
visionary, dreamy, pensive, and sensitive
vulgar, heavy, narrow, and obtuse

W
want, lack, poverty, and paucity
warm, soft, clear, and serene
waste, devastate, pillage, and destroy
watched, tendered, fostered, and pruned
weak, inefficient, stupid, and futile
wealth, position, influence, and
reputation
well-being, happiness, prosperity, and
distress

wild, restless, aimless, and erring
wisdom, judgment, understanding, and
far-sightedness
wit, purity, energy, and simplicity
wonderful, interesting, active, and
delightful
works, sorrows, visions, and experiences
worry, annoyance, awkwardness, and
difficulty

# SECTION 5
# PREPOSITIONAL PHRASES

Preposition "of"

A

abandon of spontaneity
abatement of misery
aberrations of judgment
abhorrence of meanness
absence of vainglory
abyss of ignominy
accent of conviction
accretions of time
accumulation of ages
accuracy of aim
acquisition of knowledge
activity of attention
acuteness of sensibility
admixture of fear
affectation of content
affinity of events
age of ignorance
agility of brain
agony of despair
air of assumption

ambitious of success
amiability of disposition
amplitude of space
anachronisms of thought
anchor of moderation
angle of vision
annulment of influence
aping of manners
apostle of culture
ardor of life
arrogance of opinion
aspect of grandeur
assumption of sternness
atmosphere of obscurity
attitude of mind
attribute of weakness
austerities of fanaticism
authority of manner
avalanche of scorn
avenues of dissemination

B

babel of tongues
ban of exclusion
barren of enthusiasm
barriers of reticence
bars of sunlight
basis of fact
beam of moonlight
beast of prey
beauty of imagery
beggared of faith
bent of mind
betrayal of trust
bevy of maidens
bewilderment of feeling
birds of prey
bit of portraiture
bitterness of anguish
blackness of spirit

blandishments of society
blast of adversity
blaze of fury
blend of dignity
bliss of solitude
bloom of earth
blow of fate
boldness of conception
bond of alliance
bone of contention
bouts of civility
breach of law
breath of life
breeze of anxiety
brilliancy of wit
brimful of fun
broil of politics
brood of emotions

89

brow of expectation
brunt of disgrace
bulk of mankind
bundle of conceptions

buoyancy of youth
burden of proof
burst of confidence
business of life

## C

cadences of delirium
calmness of manner
calumny of passion [calumny =
maliciously lying to injure a reputation]
caprice of inclination
careless of opinion
catholicity of spirit [catholicity =
universality]
cause of solicitude
celerity of movement [celerity =
swiftness; speed]
chain of evidence
change of habitude
chaos of confusion
chill of indifference
chimera of superstition [chimera =
fanciful illusion]
chorus of approbation [approbation =
warm approval; praise]
circle of hills
clamor of envy
clap of thunder
clarity of thinking
clash of arms
cloak of ecclesiasticism
code of morals
cogency of argument
combination of calamities
command of wit

community of interest
compass of imagination
complexity of life
confidence of genius
conflict of will
conquest of difficulty
consciousness of peril
constellation of luminaries
contagion of conflict
continuity of life
contradiction of terms
contrariety of opinion
convulsion of laughter
copiousness of diction
cord of sympathy
countenance of authority
courage of conviction
course of existence
courtliness of manner
cover of hospitality
crash of thunder
creature of circumstance
criteria of feeling
crown of civilization
crudity of thought
cry of despair
curl of contempt
current of thought

## D

darkness of calamity
dash of eccentricity
dawning of recognition
day of reckoning
daylight of faith
decay of authority
declaration of indifference
deeds of prowess
defects of temper
degree of hostility

delicacy of thought
delirium of wonder
depth of despair
dereliction of duty
derogation of character
despoiled of riches
destitute of power
desultoriness of detail [desultoriness =
haphazard; random]
device of secrecy

devoid of merit
devoutness of faith
dexterity of phrase
diapason of motives [diapason = full,
rich, harmonious sound]
dictates of conscience
difference of opinion
difficult of attainment
dignity of thought
dilapidations of time
diminution of brutality
disabilities of age
display of prowess

distinctness of vision
distortion of symmetry
diversity of aspect
divinity of tradition
domain of imagination
drama of action
dream of vengeance
drop of comfort
ductility of expression
dull of comprehension
duplicities of might
dust of defeat

E

earnestness of enthusiasm
easy of access
ebullitions of anger [ebullitions =
sudden, violent outpouring; boiling]
eccentricity of judgment
ecstasy of despair
effect of loveliness
efficacy of change
effusion of sentiment
elasticity of mind
element of compulsion
elevation of sentiment
eloquence of passion
emotions of joy
emulous of truth [emulous = prompted
by a spirit of rivalry]
encroachments of time
encumbrance of mystery
energy of youth

enigma of life
equanimity of mind
era of fads
error of judgment
essence of eloquence
excellence of vision
excess of candor
excitation of purpose
excursiveness of thought
exhibition of joy
exhilaration of spirits
expenditure of energy
explosion of rage
expression of sternness
extension of experience
extravagance of eulogy
extremity of fortune
exuberance of wit

F

fabric of fact
facility of expression
faculty of perception
failure of coordination
feast of reason
feats of strength
feebleness of purpose
feeling of uneasiness
felicities of expression
fertility of invention
fervor of devotion

fickleness of fortune
field of activity
fierceness of jealousy
fineness of vision
fire of imagination
firmament of literature
firmness of purpose
fit of laughter
fitness of circumstance
fixity of purpose
flag of truce

flash of humor
flashlight of introspection
fleetness of foot
flexibility of spirit
flicker of recognition
flight of fancy
flood of hatred
flourish of manner
flower of life
fluctuation of fortune
flush of youth
flutter of expectation
fog of sentimentalism
force of conviction
forest of faces
form of captiousness [captiousness =

point out trivial faults]
fountain of learning
fragment of conversation
frame of mind
frankness of manner
freak of fancy
freedom of enterprise
frenzy of pursuit
freshness of feeling
frigidity of address
frivolity of tone
frown of meditation
fulfilment of purpose
fulness of time
fury of resentment
futility of pride

G
gaiety of spirit
gales of laughter
garb of thought
garlands of roses
gateway of fancy
gem of truth
genuineness of sentiment
gesture of despair
gift of repartee
glamor of sensationalism
glare of scrutiny
gleam of light
glib of speech
glimmer of suspicion
glory of salvation
glow of enthusiasm

gorgeousness of coloring
grace of simplicity
gradations of outrage
grandeur of outline
grasp of comprehension
gravity of manner
greatness of nature
greed of office
grimace of disappointment
grimness of spirit
grip of attention
groundwork of melancholy
growth of experience
guide of aspiration
gulf of incongruity
gust of laughter

H
harbor of refuge
harvest of regrets
haven of rest
haze of distance
heat of enthusiasm
height of absurdity
hint of bitterness

hopeful of success
horizon of life
horror of solitude
hubbub of talk
hue of divinity
hum of pleasure
hush of suspense

I
ideals of excellence
idol of society

illusion of youth
immensity of extent

immolation of genius
impatient of restraint
impetuosity of youth
implacability of resentment
impotent of ideas
impress of individuality
impulse of enthusiasm
imputation of eccentricity
incapable of veracity
independence of mind
index of character
indolence of temperament
indulgence of vanity
inequality of treatment
infinity of height
infirmity of temper

infusion of hatred
inheritance of honor
insensibility of danger
insolence of office
inspiration of genius
instability of purpose
instrument of expression
integrity of mind
intensity of faith
interchange of ideas
interval of leisure
intoxication of vanity
intrepidity of youth
intuition of immortality
invasion of thought
irony of life

## J

jangle of sounds
jargon of philosophy

jumble of facts
justness of decision

## K

keenness of intellect
kernel of truth
key of knowledge

keynote of success
king of finance
kinship of humanity

## L

lack of restraint
languor of nature [languor = dreamy,
lazy mood ]
lapse of time
laws of decorum
laxity of mind
legacy of thought
liberty of conscience
light of experience
limit of endurance

link of sequence
loftiness of spirit
look of dominance
loophole of escape
love of approbation [approbation =
warm approval; praise]
lust of conquest
lustihood of youth
luxuriance of expression

## M

magnanimity of mind
majesty of despair
man of iron
mantle of verdure [verdure = lush
greenness of flourishing vegetation]
martyrdom of ambition
marvel of competency
mask of flippancy
mass of mediocrity

master of phrasing
maze of words
measure of absurdity
minister of vengeance
minuteness of description
miracle of miracles
mists of criticism
modesty of reserve
moment of lassitude

monster of ingratitude
monstrosities of character
mood of tranquillity
muddle of motives
multitude of details
mummery of words [mummery =
N
narrowness of range
nebulae of romance
nectar of enjoyment
neglect of duty

O
obduracy of mind [obduracy =
intractable; hardened]
object of contempt
obligation of loyalty
obliquity of vision [obliquity = mental
deviation or aberration]
obscurity of twilight
ocean of eloquence
omission of fact
onrush of life

P
page of desolation
pageant of life
pang of regret
parade of erudition [erudition =
extensive learning]
passion of patriotism
passivity of mind
pattern of virtue
peals of laughter
pendulum of opinion
pensiveness of feeling
perils of fortune
period of lassitude
perturbation of mind
perversity of chance
pests of society
petrifaction of egoism [petrifaction =
fossilization; paralyzed with fear]
phantom of delight
phase of belief
physiognomy of nature
piece of pedantry [pedantry = attention

meaningless ceremonies and flattery]
murmur of satisfaction
mutations of time
myriads of stars
mysteries of taste

niceties of difference
nightingale of affection
nobility of purpose
note of triumph

onsets of temptation
openness of mind
opulence of detail
orgy of lying
ornaments of eloquence
outbreak of hostilities
outburst of tears
outflow of sympathy
outposts of morality
overflow of vitality

to detail]
pinions of eloquence [pinions = primary
feather of a bird]
pinnacle of favor
pit of oblivion
plainness of speech
play of fancy
plea of urgency
plenitude of power
point of view
poise of mind
policy of severity
portent of danger
power of imagination
precipice of stupefaction
precision of phrase
prerogative of age
presence of mind
pressure of expediency
presumption of doubt
prey of fancy
pride of life

process of effacement
profundity of thought
profusion of argument
progress of events
promptings of reason
propriety of action

provocative of scorn
puff of applause
pulse of life
purity of diction
pursuit of knowledge
puzzledom of life

## Q

quagmire of distrust
qualities of leadership
qualm of conscience

question of honor
quickness of apprehension
quivering of pain

## R

radiance of morning
range of experience
rashness of intention
ravages of time
ray of hope
reaches of achievement
realities of life
realm of peace
rebound of fascination
rectitude of soul
redress of grievances
redundance of words
refinement of style
reins of life
relish of beauty
remorse of guilt
residue of truth
resoluteness of conviction

resource of expression
restraint of speech
revel of imagination
revulsion of feeling
richness of outline
riddle of existence
ridicule of ignorance
riot of words
ripeness of wisdom
roars of exultation
robe of humility
robustness of mind
root of individuality
round of platitudes
rush of agony
rust of neglect
ruts of conventionality

## S

sadness of soul
sanguine of success [sanguine =
cheerfully confident; optimistic]
sanity of judgment
savoring of quackery
scantiness of resources
scarves of smoke
school of adversity
scrap of knowledge
scruple of conscience
searchlight of truth
semblance of composure
sensation of pity
sense of urgency

sentiment of disapprobation
[approbation = warm approval; praise]
sequence of events
serenity of mind
severity of style
shackles of civilization
shade of doubt
shadow of truth
shallowness of thought
shock of apprehension
shouts of approval
shower of abuse
shriek of wrath
shuttle of life

95

sigh of wind
singleness of purpose
slave of malice
slough of ignorance
slumber of death
smile of raillery [raillery = good-natured
teasing; banter]
solace of adversity
soul of generosity
source of renown
spark of perception
species of despotism
spell of emotion
sphere of influence
spice of caricature
splendor of imagination
spur of necessity
start of uneasiness
stateliness of movement
sting of satire
stolidity of sensation
storehouse of facts

storm of criticism
stream of humanity
stress of life
string of episodes
stroke of fate
substratum of belief
subtlety of intellect
succession of events
suggestion of fancy
sum of happiness
summit of misery
sunshine of life
supremacy of good
surface of events
surfeit of verbiage [surfeit = supply to
excess]
surge of pathos
suspense of judgment
suspicion of flattery
sweep of landscape
symbol of admiration
system of aspersion

T
taint of megalomania
tardiness of speech
task of conciliation
tempest of passion
tenacity of execution
tenderness of sentiment
term of reproach
threshold of consciousness
thrift of time
thrill of delight
throb of compunction
throng of sensations
tide of humanitarianism
timid of innovation
tincture of depreciation
tinge of mockery
tissue of misrepresentations
tolerant of folly
tone of severity
top of ambition

torrent of fervor
totality of effect
touch of severity
touchstone of genius
trace of bitterness
tradition of mankind
train of disasters
trait of cynicism
trance of delight
transport of enthusiasm
trappings of wisdom
trend of consciousness
tribute of admiration
trick of fancy
tumult of applause
turmoil of controversy
turn of events
twilight of elderliness
twinge of envy

U
unity of purpose

universality of experience

## V

vagrancy of thought
valley of misfortune
vanguard of progress
vehemence of manner
vehicle of intercourse
veil of futurity
vein of snobbishness
velocity of movement
vestige of regard

vicissitudes of life [vicissitudes = sudden or unexpected changes]
vision of splendor
vividness of memory
voice of ambition
void of authority
volume of trade
vow of allegiance

## W

warmth of temperament
waste of opportunity
wave of depression
wealth of meaning
weariness of sorrow
web of villainy
weight of argument
whiff of irritation
whirl of delight
whirligig of life

whirlwind of words
wilderness of perplexities
wiles of innocence
word of opprobrium [opprobrium = disgrace from shameful conduct]
work of supererogation [supererogation = to do more than is required]
world of fantasy
worthy of mention

Y
yoke of convention

Z
zest of enjoyment                          zone of delusion

Preposition "by"
A
affected by externals                      assailed by conscience
allayed by sympathy                        attained by effort
animated by victory                        avert by prayer
appraised by fashion

B
ballasted by brains                        bound by opinion
beset by difficulties                      branded by defeat

C
characterized by discretion                condemned by posterity
chastened by sorrow                        confirmed by habit
cheek by jowl                              consoled by prayer
circulated by malice                       convinced by argument
clogged by insincerity                     convulsed by divisions
colored by environment

D
darkened by shadows                        devoured by curiosity
dazzled by fame                            disgusted by servility
depraved by pain                           driven by remorse

E
embarrassed by timidity                    enjoined by religion
encouraged by success                      enriched by gifts
enfeebled by age                           established by convention
enforced by action                         evoked by shame

F
fascinated, by mystery                     fired by wrath
favored by fortune                         forbid by authority
fettered by systems                        fortified by faith

G
governed by precedent                      guided by instinct

H
haunted by visions                         hushed by denial

98

I
impelled by duty
inculcated by practise
induced by misrepresentation

influenced by caution
inspired by love

L
learned by rote

M
marked by acuteness

measured by years

N
narrowed by custom

O
occasioned by irritation

oppressed by destiny

p
parched by disuse
persuaded by appeal
portray by words
prescribed by custom

prevented by chance
prompted by coquetry
purged by sorrow

R
racked by suffering
refuted by reason
repelled by censure

restrained by violence
rising by industry

S
sanctioned by experience
shaped by tradition
soured by misfortune

stung by derision
supplanted by others
supported by evidence

T
thwarted by fortune
tempered by charity

tormented by jealousy
tortured by doubt

U
unadorned by artifice
undaunted by failure
undetermined by sorrow

undone by treachery
unfettered by fear
urged by curiosity

V
vitalized by thought

W

won by aggression
worn by time

wrenched by emotions

Preposition "in"
A
absorbed in meditation
affable in manner [affable = gentle and
gracious]
atone in measure

B
barren in intellect
basking in sunshine

buried in solitude

C
call in question
clothed in truth
cloying in sweetness [cloying = too
filling, rich, or sweet]
confident in opinion

confute in argument
contemplative in aspect
cumbrous in style [cumbrous =
cumbersome; difficult to use]

D
deficient in insight
delight in learning
deterioration in quality
difference in detail

diligent in application
diminish in respect
dwarfed in numbers

E
end in smoke
enumerate in detail

experienced in duplicity

F
feeble in influence
fertile in consequence

flourish in luxuriance
founded in truth

G
gaze in astonishment
go in pursuit

graceful in proportion
grievously in error

H
hold in bondage

I
immersed in thought
indulge in reverie
inferior in character
influential in society

ingenuity in planning
instance in point
involved in obscurity

K
kept in abeyance

L
landmarks in memory
languish in obscurity
lie in wait
limited in scope
linger in expectation

listen in amazement
lost in awe
lower in estimation
luxuriant in fancy

M
monstrous in dulness

mysterious in origin

N
noble in amplitude

nursed in luxury

O
organized in thought

P
petulant in expression
plead in vain
pleasing in outline
plunged in darkness
positive in judgment

practical in application
pride in success
protest in vain
pursued in leisure

Q
quick in suggestion

R
ready in resource
recoiling in terror
remote in character

revel in danger
rich in variety
rooted in prejudice

S
schooled in self-restraint
scrupulous in conduct
set in motion
skilled in controversy
sound in theory

stammer in confusion
stricken in years
strides in civilization
striking in character
stunted in growth

T
tender in sentiment

U
unique in literature
unity in diversity

unprecedented in kind

V

versed in knowledge

W
wallow in idolatry
wanting in dignity

waver in purpose
weak in conception

Preposition "into"
A
abashed into silence

B
beguile into reading
betray into speech
blending into harmony
bring into disrepute

bullied into silence
burn into memory
burst into view

C
call into question
carry into conflict
chill into apathy
coming into vogue

cringe into favor
crumbled into dust
crystallized into action

D
dash into fragments
deepen into confusion
degenerate into monotony
deluded into believing
descent into death
dissolve into nothingness

dragged into pursuit
drawn into controversy
dribbling into words
driven into servitude
dulled into acquiescence

E
electrify into activity
elevated into importance
enquire into precedents

enter into controversy
expand into weakness

F
fade into insignificance
fall into decay
fashion into festoons
flame into war

flower into sympathy
forced into action
frozen into form
fuse into unity

G
galvanize into life
go into raptures

goaded into action

H
hushed into silence

I
incursions into controversy
insight into truth

inveigled into dispute [inveigled =
convince by coaxing, flattery]

K
kindle into action

L
lapse into pedantry [pedantries =
attention to detail or rules]
lash into silence
launch into disapproval

lead into captivity
leap into currency
lulled into indifference

M
melt into space

merge into character

p
pass into oblivion
plunge into despair

pour into print

Q
quicken into life

R
relapse into savagery
rendered into music
resolve into nothingness

retreat into silence
ripened into love
rush into print

S
shocked into attention
sink into insignificance
smitten into ice
snubbed into quiescence

stricken into silence
summoned into being
swollen into torrents

T
take into account
thrown into disorder

transform into beauty
translated into fact

U
usher into society

V
vanish into mystery

W
wander into digression

wheedled into acquiescence

withdraw into solitude

Preposition "to"

A

addicted to flattery

adherence to principle

affect to believe

akin to truth

alive to opportunity

allied to virtue

amenable to reason

aspire to rule

attempt to suppress

aversion to publicity

B

blind to demonstration

brought to repentance

C

claim to perpetuity

come to nothing

committed to righteousness

common to humanity

conducive to happiness

conformable to fact

consigned to oblivion

constrained to speak

contribution to knowledge

D

deaf to entreaty

dedicated to friendship

deference to custom

devoted to ideals

disposed to cavil [cavil = raise trivial

objections]

doomed to destruction

driven to despair

dwarf to unimportance

E

empowered to act

endeared to all

excite to pity

exposed to derision

F

fly to platitudes

foredoomed to failure

G

given to extravagance

ground to atoms

H

harassed to death

hostile to progress

I

impervious to suggestion

impossible to reconcile

impotent to save

incentive to devotion

incitement to anger

inclined to vascillate

indifference to truth

intent to deceive

intolerable to society

inured to fatigue [inured = habituate to

something undesirable]

invocation to sleep

**L**
laugh to scorn

lost to remembrance

left to conjecture

**O**
obedience to conscience

open to reason

oblivious to criticism

opposed to innovation

offensive to modesty

**p**
pander to prejudice

propose to undertake

pertaining to fashion

provoke to laughter

prone to melancholy

put to confusion

**R**
recourse to falsehood

repugnant to justice

reduced to impotence

requisite to success

related to eternity

resort to violence

repeat to satiety

run to seed

**S**
seek to overawe

subject to scrutiny

serve to embitter

succumb to fascination

spur to action

superior to circumstances

stimulus to ambition

susceptible to argument

stirred to remonstrance

**T**
temptation to doubt

trust to chance

tend to frustrate

**U**
utilize to advantage

**V**
venture to say

vital to success

**W**
wedded to antiquity

**Y**
yield to reason

Preposition "with"
**A**
abounding with plenty

accord with nature

act with deliberation
adorn with beauty
afflict with ugliness
aflame with life

allied with economy
anticipate with delight
ascertain with exactness
attended with danger

B
beam with self-approval
behave with servility
big with fate
blinded with tears

blush with shame
branded with cowardice
bubbling with laughter
burn with indignation

C
cling with tenacity
clothe with authority
compatible with freedom
comply with tradition

conceal with difficulty
consistent with facts
covered with ignominy
crush with sorrow

D
deny with emphasis
depressed with fear

dispense with formality
distort with passion

E
echo with merriment
endow with intelligence
endued with faith [endued = provide

with a quality; put on]
endure with fortitude
examine with curiosity

F
face with indifference
flushed with pride

fraught with peril
furious with indignation

G
glowing with delight

I
imbued with courage
incompatible with reason
inconsistent with beauty

inflamed with rage
inspired with patriotism
intoxicated with joy

K
kindle with enthusiasm

L
laugh with glee

M
meet with rebuke
mingled with curiosity

move with alacrity

106

## O

oppressed with hardship
overcome with shyness

overflowing with love
overhung with gloom

## P

performed with regularity
pervaded with grandeur

proceed with alertness
punish with severity

## Q

quicken with pride

quiver with anxiety

## R

radiant with victory
regard with loathing

relate with zest
repel with indignation

## S

saddle with responsibility
scream with terror
scrutinize with care
seething with sedition [sedition =
conduct or language inciting rebellion]

sick with dread
sob with anguish
squirm with delight
suffuse with spirituality

## T

tainted with fraud
teeming with life
tense with expectancy
thrill with excitement
throb with vitality

tinged with romance
touched with feeling
treat with contempt
tremble with fear

## U

unmixed with emotion

utter with sarcasm

## V

vibrant with feeling

view with awe

## W

wield with power

work with zeal

# SECTION 6
# BUSINESS PHRASES

## A

A request for further particulars will not involve any obligation

A telegram is enclosed for your use, as this matter is urgent

Accept our thanks for your recent remittance

Acknowledging the receipt of your recent inquiry

After examination we can confidently say

After very carefully considering

Again thanking you for the inquiry

Agreeable to our conversation

An addressed envelope is enclosed for your convenience

An early reply will greatly oblige

Answering your recent inquiry

Any information you may give us will be appreciated

Any time that may suit your convenience

As a matter of convenience and economy

As a special favor we ask

As directed in your letter, we are shipping to you

As explained in our previous letter

As it will give us an opportunity to demonstrate our ability

As stated in our previous letter

As we have received no response from you

As you, doubtless, are aware

As you probably have been told

As your experience has probably shown you

Assuring you of every courtesy

Assuring you of our entire willingness to comply with your request

Assuring you of prompt and careful cooperation

At the present writing

At the suggestion of one of our patrons

At your earliest opportunity

Awaiting the favor of your prompt attention

Awaiting the pleasure of serving you

Awaiting your early communication

Awaiting your further commands

Awaiting your pleasure

## B

Believing you will answer this promptly

## C

Complying with your request

Conditions make it obligatory for us

## D

Do not hesitate to let us know

Do not overlook this opportunity

Do you realize that you can

## E

Enclosed please find a memorandum

Enclosed we beg to hand you

Enclosed you will find a circular which will fully explain

## F

For some years past
For your convenience we enclose a
stamped envelope
For your further information we take

H
Here is a complete answer to
Here is your opportunity
Hoping for a continuance of your
interest
Hoping for a definite reply
Hoping that our relations may prove

I
I am compelled to inform you
I am confident that you will be
thoroughly satisfied
I am directed to say to you
I am, gentlemen, yours faithfully
I am giving the matter my personal
attention
I am, my dear sir, yours faithfully
I am still holding this offer open to you
I ask that you be good enough
I beg to request that you give me some
information
I believe I understand perfectly just how
you feel about
I have been favorably impressed by your
I have now much pleasure in confirming
I have pleasure in acknowledging
I have the honor to acknowledge the
receipt
I have the honor to remain
I herewith submit my application
I highly appreciate this mark of
confidence
I look forward to pleasant personal
relations in the future
I regret exceedingly to inform you
I remain, my dear sir, yours faithfully
I shall be pleased to forward descriptive
circulars
I shall esteem it a personal favor
I should welcome an interview at your
convenience
I sincerely hope that you will give the
subject your earnest consideration

pleasure in sending to you
Frankly, we believe it is extremely worth
while for you
From the standpoint of serviceability

mutually satisfactory
Hoping to be favored with your order
How may we serve you further?
However, because of the special
circumstances attached

I take pleasure in replying to your
inquiry concerning
I trust I shall hear from you soon
I want to express the hope that our
pleasant business relations will continue
I want to interest you
I want to thank you for your reply
I wish to confirm my letter
If I can be of further service, please
address me
If it is not convenient for you
If there is any valid reason why you are
unable
If we can be of service to you
If we can help you in any way
If we have not made everything perfectly
clear, please let us know
If you accommodate us, the favor will be
greatly appreciated
If you are interested, please let us hear
from you
If you are thinking about ordering
If you desire, our representative will call
If you have any cause for dissatisfaction
If you give this matter your prompt
attention
In accordance with the terms of our offer
In accordance with your request
In answering your inquiry regarding
In any event, a reply to this will be very
much appreciated
In closing we can only assure you
In compliance with your favor
In compliance with your request, we are

pleased to send to you

In conclusion, we can assure you

In order to facilitate our future transactions

In reference to your application

In regard to your proposition

In reply thereto, we wish to inform you

In reply to your valued favor

In response to your recent request

In spite of our best efforts it is not probable

In thanking you for the patronage with which you have favored us

In view of all these facts, we feel justified in claiming

Information has just reached me

It gives us pleasure to recommend

It has consistently been our aim to help our customers

It is a matter of great regret to us

It is a pleasure for me to answer your inquiry

It is a well known fact

It is interesting to note

It is our very great pleasure to advise you

It is the policy of our house

It seems clear that our letter must have miscarried

It was purely an oversight on our part

It will be entirely satisfactory to us

It will be our aim to interest you

It will be readily appreciated

It will be to your advantage

It will doubtless be more convenient for you

It will interest you to know

It will receive the same careful attention

## J
Just mail the enclosed card

## K
Kindly endorse your reply on the enclosed sheet

Kindly let us have your confirmation at your earliest convenience

Kindly let us know your pleasure concerning

Kindly read the enclosed list

## L
Let me thank you for the opportunity to give this matter my personal attention

Let us assure you of our desire to cooperate with you

Let us assure you that we are very much pleased

Let us know if there is any further attention

Let us thank you again for opening an account with us

Looking forward to the early receipt of some of your orders

## M
May I ask you to do us a great favor by

May we be favored with a reply

Meantime soliciting your forbearance

Meanwhile permit me to thank you for your kind attention

## O
On referring to your account we notice

Our letter must have gone astray

Our relations with your house must have hitherto been very pleasant

Our services are at your command

Our stock has been temporarily exhausted

Owing to our inability to collect outstanding debts

## P
Permit me to add
Permit us to express our sincere
appreciation
Please accept the thanks of the writer
Please consider this letter an
acknowledgment
Please favor us with a personal

communication
Please feel assured that we shall use
every endeavor
Possibly the enclosure may suggest to
you
Promptly on receipt of your telegram
Pursuant to your letter

## R
Recently we had occasion
Referring to your esteemed favor
Regretting our inability to serve you in
the present instance

Reluctant as we are to believe
Requesting your kind attention to this
matter

## S
Should you decide to act upon this latter
suggestion
So many requests of a similar nature

come to us
Soliciting a continuance of your
patronage

## T
Thank you for your expression of
confidence
Thanking you for your inquiry
Thanking you for your past patronage
Thanking you for your promptness.
Thanking you in advance for an early
reply
Thanking you in anticipation
The causes for the delay were beyond
our control
The margin of profit which we allow
ourselves
The proof is in this fact
The proposition appeals to us as a good
one
Therefore we are able to make you this
offer
Therefore we trust you will write to us

promptly
These points should be most carefully
considered
This arrangement will help us over the
present difficulty
This is according to our discussion
This matter has been considered very
seriously
This personal guarantee I look upon as a
service to you
This privileged communication is for the
exclusive use
This will amply repay you
Trusting that we may have the pleasure
of serving you
Trusting to receive your best
consideration

## U
Under no circumstances can we
entertain such an arrangement
Under separate cover we are mailing to
you

Under these circumstances we are
willing to extend the terms
Unfortunately we are compelled at
certain times

Unless you can give us reasonable assurance

Upon being advised that these terms are satisfactory

Upon receiving your letter of

# W

We acknowledge with pleasure the receipt of your order

We admit that you are justified in your complaint

We again solicit an opportunity

We again thank you for your inquiry

We always endeavor to please

We appreciate the order you were kind enough to send to us

We appreciate your patronage very much

We are always glad to furnish information

We are anxious to make satisfactory adjustment

We are at a loss to understand why

We are at your service at all times

We are confident that you will have no further trouble

We are extremely desirous of pleasing our patrons

We are in a position to give you considerable help

We are in receipt of your communication regarding

We are indeed sorry to learn

We are perfectly willing to make concessions

We are pleased to receive your request for information

We are pleased to send you descriptive circulars

We are reluctant to adopt such severe measures

We are satisfied regarding your statement

We are sending to you by mail

We are sorry to learn from your letter

We are thoroughly convinced of the need

We are totally at a loss to understand

We are very anxious to have you try

We are very glad to testify to the merit of

We ask for a continuance of your confidence

We ask that you kindly let us hear from you

We assume that you are considering

We assure you of our confidence in the reliability

We assure you of our desire to be of service

We await an early, and we trust, a favorable reply

We await the courtesy of an early answer

We beg a moment of your attention and serious consideration

We believe that if you will carefully consider the matter

We believe you will readily understand our position

We can assure you that any order with which you favor us

We desire information pertaining to your financial condition

We desire to effect a settlement

We desire to express our appreciation of your patronage

We desire to impress upon you

We expect to be in the market soon

We feel assured that you will appreciate

We feel sure that you will approve of our action in this matter

We frankly apologize to you

We hasten to acknowledge the receipt

We have anticipated a heavy demand

We have, as yet, no definite understanding

We have come to the conclusion

We have endeavored to serve the needs of your organization

We have found it impossible

We have much pleasure in answering

112

your inquiry
We have no desire to adopt harsh measures
We have not had the pleasure of placing your name on our ledgers
We have not, however, had the pleasure of hearing from you
We have not yet had time to sift the matter thoroughly
We have the honor to be, gentlemen
We have the honor to inform you
We have thought it best to forward
We have your request for information regarding
We hesitated for a while to pursue the matter
We hope that an understanding can be reached
We hope that we shall have many opportunities to demonstrate our ability
We hope that you will find the enclosed booklet very interesting
We hope to hear favorably from you
We hope you will appreciate
We hope you will excuse the unavoidable delay
We invite your attention to
We must insist upon a prompt settlement
We must, therefore, insist on the terms of the agreement
We note that the time is at hand
We offer you the services of an expert
We particularly want to interest you
We realize that this matter has escaped your attention
We realize that this is simply an oversight on your part
We regret exceedingly that you have been inconvenienced
We regret our inability to meet your wishes
We regret that owing to the press of business
We regret that this misunderstanding has occurred
We regret that we are not in a position
We regret that we are unable to grant

your request
We regret the necessity of calling your attention
We regret to be compelled for this reason to withdraw the privilege
We regret to learn that you are disappointed
We remain, dear sir, yours faithfully
We remain, gentlemen, with thanks
We shall await your early commands with interest
We shall await your reply with interest
We shall be glad to fill your order
We shall be glad to have you tell us frankly
We shall be glad to render you any assistance in our power
We shall be happy to meet your requirements
We shall be indebted to you for your courtesy
We shall be pleased to receive the remittance
We shall be pleased to take the matter up further
We shall do everything in our power
We shall do our best to correct the mistake
We shall feel compelled
We shall heartily appreciate any information
We shall use every endeavor
We suggest that this is an opportune time
We suggest that you consider
We take pleasure in enclosing herewith
We take pleasure in explaining the matter you asked about
We take the liberty of deviating from your instructions
We take the liberty of writing to you.
We thank you for calling our attention
We thank you for your courteous letter
We thank you for your kind inquiry of recent date
We thank you very gratefully for your polite and friendly letter

We thank you very much for the frank
statement of your affairs
We thank you very sincerely for your
assistance
We think you will agree
We trust our explanation will meet with
your approval
We trust that we may hear favorably
from you
We trust that you will give this matter
your immediate attention
We trust you may secure some of the
exceptional values
We trust you will find it correct
We trust you will not consider us unduly
strict
We trust you will promptly comply with
our previous suggestions
We understand your position
We urge that you write to us by early
mail
We venture to enclose herewith
We very much wish you to examine
We want every opportunity to
demonstrate our willingness
We want particularly to impress upon
you this fact
We want to please you in every respect
We want to remind you again
We want you to read the booklet
carefully
We will at once enter your order
We will be compelled to take the
necessary steps
We will be glad to lay before you the
fullest details
We will be pleased to give it careful

consideration
We will gladly accommodate you
We will gladly extend to you similar
courtesies whenever we can do so
We will make it a point to give your
correspondence close attention
We would appreciate a remittance
We would consider it a great favor
We would draw your attention to the
fact
We would request, as a special favor
We write to suggest to you
We write to urge upon you the necessity
We wrote to you at length
While we appreciate the peculiar
circumstances
While we feel that we are in no way
responsible
Why not allow us this opportunity to
satisfy you
Will you give us, in confidence, your
opinion
Will you give us the benefit of your
experience
Will you kindly advise us in order that
we may adjust our records
Will you please give us your immediate
attention
With our best respects and hoping to
hear from you
With reference to your favor of
yesterday
With regard to your inquiry
With the fullest assurance that we are
considering
With the greatest esteem and respect

Y
You are certainly justified in
complaining
You are evidently aware that there is a
growing demand
You are quite right in your statement
You cannot regret more than I the
necessity
You undoubtedly are aware

You will find interest, we believe, in this
advance announcement
You will get the benefit of this liberal
offer
You will have particular interest in the
new and attractive policy
Your early attention to this matter will
oblige

Your further orders will be esteemed
Your inquiry has just been received, and
we are glad to send to you
Your orders and commands will always

have our prompt and best attention
Your satisfaction will dictate our course
Your trial order is respectfully solicited
Your usual attention will oblige

# SECTION 7
# LITERARY EXPRESSIONS

A

A bitterness crept into her face

A blazing blue sky poured down torrents of light

A book to beguile the tedious hours

A brave but turbulent aristocracy

A broad, complacent, admiring imbecility breathed from his nose and lips

A burlesque feint of evading a blow

A callous and conscienceless brute

A calm and premeditated prudence

A calmness settled on his spirit

A campaign of unbridled ferocity

A carefully appraising eye

A ceaselessly fleeting sky

A certain implication of admiring confidence

A charming air of vigor and vitality

A childish belief in his own impeccability

A cold, hard, frosty penuriousness was his prevalent characteristic
[penuriousness = stingy; barren; poverty-stricken]

A compassion perfectly angelic

A constant stream of rhythmic memories

A covertly triumphant voice

A creature of the most delicate and rapid responses

A crop of disappointments

A cunning intellect patiently diverting every circumstance to its design

A curious and inexplicable uneasiness

A curious vexation fretted her

A daily avalanche of vituperation
[vituperation = harshly abusive language]

A dandified, pretty-boy-looking sort of figure

A dark and relentless fate

A day monotonous and colorless

A dazzling completeness of beauty

A deep and brooding resentment

A delicious throng of sensations

A deliciously tantalizing sense

A detached segment of life

A dire monotony of bookish idiom

A disheveled and distraught figure

A face singularly acute and intelligent

A faint accent of reproach

A faint sense of compunction moved her

A faint, transient, wistful smile lightened her brooding face

A faint tremor of amusement was on his lips

A faintly quizzical look came into his incisive stare

A fawn-colored sea streaked here and there with tints of deepest orange

A fever of enthusiasm

A few tears came to soften her seared vision

A fiery exclamation of wrath and disdain

A figure full of decision and dignity

A firm and balanced manhood

A first faint trace of irritation

A fitful boy full of dreams and hopes

A flame of scarlet crept in a swift diagonal across his cheeks

A fleeting and furtive air of triumph

A flood of pride rose in him

A foreboding of some destined change

A fortuitous series of happy thoughts

A frigid touch of the hand

A fugitive intangible charm

A gay exuberance of ambition

A generation of men lavishly endowed with genius

A gentle sarcasm ruffled her anger

A ghastly whiteness overspread the cheek

A glance of extraordinary meaning

A glassy expression of inattention

A glassy stare of deprecating horror
A glittering infectious smile
A gloom overcame him
A golden haze of pensive light
A golden summer of marvelous fertility
A graceful readiness and vigor
A grave man of pretending exterior
A great pang gripped her heart
A great process of searching and shifting
A great sickness of heart smote him
A great soul smitten and scourged, but still invested with the dignity of immortality
A grim and shuddering fascination
A gush of entrancing melody
A gusty breeze blew her hair about unheeded
A half-breathless murmur of amazement and incredulity
A half-uneasy, half-laughing compunction
A harassing anxiety of sorrow
A harvest of barren regrets
A haunting and horrible sense of insecurity
A heavy oppression seemed to brood upon the air
A helpless anger simmered in him
A hint of death in the icy breath of the gale
A hot and virulent skirmish
A hot uprush of hatred and loathing
A kind of ineffable splendor crowns the day
A lapse from the well-ordered decencies of civilization
A large, rich, copious human endowment
A late star lingered, remotely burning
A laugh of jovial significance
A light of unwonted pleasure in her eyes [unwonted = unusual]
A little jaded by gastronomical exertions
A lukewarm and selfish love
A man of imperious will [imperious = arrogantly domineering]
A man of matchless modesty and refinement
A manner bright with interest and interrogation
A manner nervously anxious to please
A melancholy monotone beat on one's heart
A mere exhibition of fussy diffuseness
A mere figment of a poet's fancy
A mien and aspect singularly majestic [mien = bearing or manner]
A mild and deprecating air
A mind singularly practical and sagacious [sagacious = wise]
A mouth of inflexible decision
A murmur of complacency
A mystery everlastingly impenetrable
A nameless sadness which is always born of moonlight
A new and overmastering impulse
A new doubt assailed her
A new marvel of the sky
A new trouble was dawning on his thickening mental horizon
A nimble-witted opponent
A painful thought was flooding his mind
A pang of jealousy not unmingled with scorn
A patience worthy of admiration
A perfect carnival of fun
A perfect crime of clumsiness
A piteous aspect of woe
A portent full of possible danger
A potion to be delicately supped at leisure
A powerful agitation oppressed him
A prevailing sentiment of uneasy discontent
A prey to listless uneasiness
A profound and absorbing interest
A profound and eager hopefulness
A profound and rather irritating egotist by nature
A prop for my faint heart
A propitious sky, marbled with pearly white [propitious = favorable; kindly; gracious]
A protest wavered on her lip

A puissant and brilliant family [puissant = powerful; mighty]

A queer, uncomfortable perplexity began to invade her

A quick flame leaped in his eyes

A quick shiver ruffled the brooding stillness of the water

A quiver of resistance ran through her

A remarkable fusion of morality and art

A random gleam of light

A rare and dazzling order of beauty

A rhythmical torrent of eloquent prophecy

A river of shame swept over him

A sad inquiry seemed to dwell in her gaze

A satisfied sense of completeness

A secret sweeter than the sea or sky can whisper

A sensation of golden sweetness and delight

A sense of desolation and disillusionment overwhelmed me

A sense of infinite peace brooded over the place

A sense of meditative content

A sense of repression was upon her

A sentiment of distrust in its worth had crept into her thoughts

A sheaf of letters

A shimmer of golden sun shaking through the trees

A shiver of apprehension crisped her skin

A shuffling compromise between defiance and prostration

A sigh of large contentment

A sight for the angels to weep over

A skepticism which prompted rebellion

A slight movement of incredulous dissent

A smile full of subtle charm

A smile of exquisite urbanity

A soft insidious plea

A soft intonation of profound sorrow

A soft suspicion of ulterior motives

A solemn glee possessed my mind

A solemn gray expanse that lost itself far away in the gray of the sea

A solemn utterance of destiny

A somber and breathless calm hung over the deepening eve

A somewhat melancholy indolence

A somewhat sharp and incisive voice

A sonorous voice bade me enter

A soothing and quieting touch was gently laid upon her soul

A sort of eager, almost appealing amiability

A sort of stolid despairing acquiescence

A sort of stunned incredulity

A soundless breeze that was little more than a whisper

A spacious sense of the amplitude of life's possibilities

A staccato cough interrupted the flow of speech

A state of sullen self-absorption

A steady babble of talk and laughter

A step was at her heels

A stifling sensation of pain and suspense

A stinging wind swept the woods

A strange compound of contradictory elements

A stream of easy talk

A strong convulsion shook the vague indefinite form

A strong susceptibility to the ridiculous

A subtle emphasis of scorn

A sudden and stinging delight

A sudden gleam of insight

A sudden uncontrollable outburst of feeling

A super-abundance of boisterous animal spirits

A supercilious scorn and pity [supercilious = haughty disdain]

A super-refinement of taste

A swaggering air of braggadocio [braggadocio = pretentious bragging]

A sweet bewilderment of tremulous apprehension [tremulous = fearful]

A sweet, quiet, sacred, stately seclusion

A swift knowledge came to her

A swift unformulated fear

A swiftly unrolling panorama of dreams
A tangle of ugly words
A thousand evanescent memories of happy days [evanescent = vanishing like vapor]
A thousand unutterable fears bore irresistible despotism over her thoughts
A time of disillusion followed
A tiny stream meandering amiably
A tone of arduous admiration
A torn and tumultuous sky
A total impression ineffable and indescribable
A tragic futility
A treacherous throb of her voice
A true similitude of what befalls many men and women
A tumult of vehement feeling
A tumultuous rush of sensations
A twinge of embarrassment
A vague and wistful melancholy
A vast sweet silence crept through the trees
A veritable spring-cleaning of the soul
A very practised and somewhat fastidious critic
A violent and mendacious tongue [mendacious = false; untrue]
A vivid and arresting presentation
A waking dream overshadowed her
A weird world of morbid horrors
A well-bred mixture of boldness and courtesy
A wild vivacity was in her face and manner
A wile of the devil's [wile = trick intended to deceive or ensnare]
A wind strayed through the gardens
A withering sensation of ineffable boredom
A wordless farewell
Absolutely vulgarized by too perpetual a parroting
Absorbed in a stream of thoughts and reminiscences
Absorbed in the scent and murmur of the night

Accidents which perpetually deflect our vagrant attention
Across the gulf of years
Administering a little deft though veiled castigation
Affected an ironic incredulity
Affecting a tone of gayety
After a first moment of reluctance
After an eternity of resolutions, doubts, and indecisions
Aghast at his own helplessness
Agitated and enthralled by day-dreams
Agitated with violent and contending emotions
Alien paths and irrelevant junketings
All embrowned and mossed with age
All her gift of serene immobility brought into play
All hope of discreet reticence was ripped to shreds
All the lesser lights paled into insignificance
All the magic of youth and joy of life was there
All the place is peopled with sweet airs
All the sky was mother-of-pearl and tender
All the unknown of the night and of the universe was pressing upon him
All the world was flooded with a soft golden light
All was a vague jumble of chaotic impressions
All was incomprehensible
All was instinctive and spontaneous
Aloof from the motley throng
Ambition shivered into fragments
Amid distress and humiliation
Amid the direful calamities of the time
An acute note of distress in her voice
An agreeably grave vacuity
An air half quizzical and half deferential
An air of affected civility
An air of being meticulously explicit
An air of inimitable, scrutinizing, superb impertinence
An air of stern, deep, and irredeemable

gloom hung over and pervaded all

An air of uncanny familiarity

An air which was distinctly critical

An almost pathetic appearance of ephemeral fragility [ephemeral = markedly short-lived]

An almost riotous prodigality of energy

An answering glow of gratitude

An antagonist worth her steel

An artful stroke of policy

An assumption of hostile intent

An assurance of good-nature that forestalled hostility

An atmosphere of extraordinary languor [languor = dreamy, lazy mood ]

An atmosphere thick with flattery and toadyism

An attack of peculiar virulence and malevolence

An audacious challenge of ridicule

An avidity that bespoke at once the restlessness, [avidity = eagerness] and the genius of her mind

An awe crept over me

An eager and thirsty ear

An easy prey to the powers of folly

An effusive air of welcome

An equal degree of well-bred worldly cynicism

An erect, martial, majestic, and imposing personage

An eternity of silence oppressed him

An expression of mildly humorous surprise

An expression of rare and inexplicable personal energy

An exquisite perception of things beautiful and rare

An iciness, a sinking, a sickening of the heart

An ignoring eye

An impenetrable screen of foliage

An impersonal and slightly ironic interest

An impervious beckoning motion

An inarticulate echo of his longing

An increased gentleness of aspect

An incursion of the loud, the vulgar and meretricious [meretricious = plausible but false]

An inexplicable and uselessly cruel caprice of fate

An inexpressible fervor of serenity

An ingratiating, awkward and, wistful grace

An inspired ray was in his eyes

An instant she stared unbelievingly

An intense and insatiable hunger for light and truth

An intense travail of mind

An obscure thrill of alarm

An odd little air of penitent self-depreciation

An open wit and recklessness of bearing

An oppressive sense of strange sweet odor

An optimistic after-dinner mood

An overburdening sense of the inexpressible

An uncomfortable premonition of fear

An unfailing sweetness and unerring perception

An unpleasant and heavy sensation sat at his heart

An unredeemed dreariness of thought

An unsuspected moral obtuseness

An utter depression of soul

And day peers forth with her blank eyes

And what is all this pother about? [pother = commotion; disturbance]

Animated by noble pride

Anticipation painted the world in rose

Appalled in speechless disgust

Appealing to the urgent temper of youth

Apprehensive solicitude about the future

Ardent words of admiration

Armed all over with subtle antagonisms

Artless and unquestioning devotion

As if smitten by a sudden spasm

As the long train sweeps away into the golden distance

August and imperial names in the kingdom of thought

Awaiting his summons to the eternal

silence

## B

Bandied about from mouth to mouth
Barricade the road to truth
Bartering the higher aspirations of life
Beaming with pleasurable anticipation
Before was the open malignant sea
Beguiled the weary soul of man
Beneath the cold glare of the desolate
night
Bent on the lofty ends of her destiny
Beset by agreeable hallucinations
Beset with smiling hills
Beside himself in an ecstasy of pleasure
Betokening an impulsive character
Beyond the farthest edge of night
Birds were fluting in the tulip-trees
Biting sentences flew about
Black inky night
Blithe with the bliss of the morning
Blown about by every wind of doctrine
Bookish precision and professional

peculiarity
Borne from lip to lip
Borne onward by slow-footed time
Borne with a faculty of willing
compromise
Bowed with a certain frigid and
deferential surprise
Broke in a stupendous roar upon the
shuddering air
Browsing at will on all the uplands of
knowledge and thought
Buffeted by all the winds of passion
Buried hopes rose from their sepulchers
Buried in the quicksands of ignorance
But none the less peremptorily
[peremptorily = ending all debate or
action]
By a curious irony of fate
By a happy turn of thinking
By virtue of his impassioned curiosity

## C

Carried the holiday in his eye
Chafed at the restraints imposed on him
Cheeks furrowed by strong purpose and
feeling
Childlike contour of the body
Cleansed of prejudice and self-interest
Cloaked in prim pretense
Clothed with the witchery of fiction
Clutch at the very heart of the usurping
mediocrity
Cold gaze of curiosity
Collapse into a dreary and hysterical
depression
Comment of rare and delightful flavor

Conjuring up scenes of incredible beauty
and terror
Conscious of unchallenged supremacy
Constant indulgence of wily stratagem
and ambitious craft
Contemptuously indifferent to the
tyranny of public opinion
Covered with vegetation in wild
luxuriance
Crisp sparkle of the sea
Crystallize about a common nucleus
Cultivated with a commensurate zeal
Current play of light gossip
Curtains of opaque rain

## D

Dallying in maudlin regret over the past
[maudlin = tearfully sentimental]
Dark with unutterable sorrows
Darkness oozed out from between the
trees
Dawn had broken

Day stood distinct in the sky
Days of vague and fantastic melancholy
Days that are brief and shadowed
Deep shame and rankling remorse
Deficient in affectionate or tender
impulses

Delicately emerging stars
Delicious throng of sensations
Despite her pretty insolence
Dignity and sweet patience were in her look
Dim opalescence of the moon
Dimly foreshadowed on the horizon
Dimmed by the cold touch of unjust suspicion
Disfigured by passages of solemn and pompous monotony.
Disguised itself as chill critical impartiality
Dismal march of death
Distinguished by hereditary rank or social position
Distract and beguile the soul

Distressing in their fatuous ugliness
Diverted into alien channels
Diverting her eyes, she pondered
Dogs the footsteps
Doled out in miserly measure
Doubt tortured him
Doubts beset her lonely and daring soul
Down the steep of disenchantment
Dreams and visions were surpassed
Dreams that fade and die in the dim west
Drear twilight of realities
Drift along the stream of fancy
Drowned in the deep reticence of the sea
Drowsiness coiled insidiously about him
Dull black eyes under their precipice of brows

E
Earth danced under a heat haze
Easily moved to gaiety and pleasure
Either way her fate was cruel
Embrace with ardor the prospect of serene leisure
Endearing sweetness and manner
Endeavoring to smile away his chagrin
Endlessly shifting moods
Endowed with all those faculties that can make the world a garden of enchantment
Endowed with life and emphasis
Enduring with smiling composure the near presence of people who are distasteful
Enjoyed with astonishing unscrupulousness
Enticed irresistibly by the freedom of an

open horizon
Essay a flight of folly
Evanescent shades of feeling [evanescent = vanishing like vapor]
Events took an unexpected sinister turn
Every curve of her features seemed to express a fine arrogant acrimony and harsh truculence
Everywhere the fragrance of a bountiful earth
Exasperated by what seemed a wilful pretense of ignorance
Exhibits itself in fastidious crotchets
Expectation darkened into anxiety
Experience and instinct warred within her
Exquisite graciousness of manner
Exquisitely stung by the thought

F
Familiar and endearing intimacy
Fatally and indissolubly united
Fathomless depths of suffering
Fear held him in a vice
Feeding his scholarly curiosity
Feeling humiliated by the avowal
Felicitousness in the choice and exquisiteness in the collocation of words

Fettered by poverty and toil
Feverish tide of life
Fine precision of intent
Fitful tumults of noble passion
Fleeting touches of something alien and intrusive
Floating in the clouds of reverie
Fluctuations of prosperity and adversity

122

Flushed with a suffusion that crimsoned her whole countenance
Forebodings possessed her
Foreshadowing summer's end
Forever echo in the heart
Forever sings itself in memory
Formless verbosity and a passionate rhetoric
Fragments of most touching melody
Free from rigid or traditional fetters

Freedom and integrity of soul
Freighted with strange, vague longings
Frosty thraldom of winter [thraldom = servitude; bondage]
Fugitive felicities of thought and sensation
Full of dreams and refinements and intense abstractions
Full of majestic tenderness

## G

Gathering all her scattered impulses into a passionate act of courage
Gaze dimly through a maze of traditions
Generosity pushed to prudence
Gleams of sunlight, bewildered like ourselves, struggled, surprised, through the mist and disappeared
Glowing with haste and happiness
Go straight, as if by magic, to the inner meaning

Goaded on by his sense of strange importance
Graceful length of limb and fall of shoulders
Great shuddering seized on her
Green hills pile themselves upon each other's shoulders
Grim and sullen after the flush of the morning
Guilty of girlish sentimentality

## H

Half choked by a rising paroxysm of rage
Half-suffocated by his triumph
Hardened into convictions and resolves
Haughtiness and arrogance were largely attributed to him
Haunt the recesses of the memory
Haunted with a chill and unearthly foreboding
He accosted me with trepidation
He adroitly shifted his ground
He airily lampooned their most cherished prejudices
He bowed submission
He braced himself to the exquisite burden of life
He condescended to intimate speech with her
He conversed with a colorless fluency
He could detect the hollow ring of fundamental nothingness
He could do absolutely naught
He drank of the spirit of the universe
He drew near to a desperate resolve

He evinced his displeasure by a contemptuous sneer or a grim scowl
He felt an unaccountable loathing
He felt the ironic rebound of her words
He flung diffidence to the winds
He flushed crimson
He found the silence intolerably irksome
He frowned perplexedly
He gave her a baffled stare
He gave himself to a sudden day-dream
He gave his ear to this demon of false glory
He grew wanton with success
He had acted with chivalrous delicacy of honor
He had the eye of an eagle in his trade
He had the gift of deep, dark silences
He held his breath in admiring silence
He laughed away my protestations
He lent no countenance to the insensate prattle
He listened greedily and gazed intent
He made a loathsome object

He made the politest of monosyllabic replies
He murmured a civil rejoinder
He murmured a vague acceptance
He mused a little while in grave thought
He never wears an argument to tatters
He only smiled with fatuous superiority
He paused, stunned and comprehending
He perceived the iron hand within the velvet glove
He raised a silencing hand
He ruled autocratically
He sacrificed the vulgar prizes of life
He sat on thorns
He set his imagination adrift
He shambled away with speed
He sighed deeply, from a kind of mental depletion
He smote her quickening sensibilities
He submitted in brooding silence
He suppressed every sign of surprise
He surrendered himself to gloomy thought
He threaded a labyrinth of obscure streets
He threw a ton's weight of resolve upon his muscles
He threw out phrases of ill-humor
He threw round a measuring eye
He treads the primrose path of dalliance
He used an unguarded adjective
He was a tall, dark, saturnine youth, sparing of speech [saturnine = melancholy; sullen]
He was aware of emotion
He was born to a lively and intelligent patriotism
He was dimly mistrustful of it
He was discreetly silent
He was empty of thought
He was entangled in a paradox
He was giving his youth away by handfuls
He was haunted and begirt by presences
He was measured and urbane
He was most profoundly skeptical
He was nothing if not grandiloquent

He was quaking on the precipice of a bad bilious attack
He was utterly detached from life
He went hot and cold
He would fall into the blackest melancholies
He writhed in the grip of a definite apprehension
He writhed with impotent humiliation
Her blank gaze chilled you
Her bright eyes were triumphant
Her eyes danced with malice
Her eyes dilated with pain and fear
Her eyes were full of wondering interest
Her eyes were limpid and her beauty was softened by an air of indolence and languor [languor = dreamy, lazy mood]
Her face stiffened anew into a gray obstinacy
Her face was lit up by a glow of inspiration and resolve
Her haughty step waxed timorous and vigilant
Her head throbbed dangerously
Her heart appeared to abdicate its duties
Her heart fluttered with a vague terror
Her heart pounded in her throat
Her heart was full of speechless sorrow
Her hurrying thoughts clamored for utterance
Her imagination recoiled
Her interest flagged
Her life had dwarfed her ambitions
Her limbs ran to marble
Her lips hardened
Her lips parted in a keen expectancy
Her mind was a store-house of innocuous anecdote
Her mind was beaten to the ground by the catastrophe
Her mood was unaccountably chilled
Her musings took a sudden and arbitrary twist
Her scarlet lip curled cruelly
Her smile was faintly depreciatory
Her smile was linked with a sigh
Her solicitude thrilled him

Her stare dissolved
Her step seemed to pity the grass it prest
Her strength was scattered in fits of agitation
Her stumbling ignorance which sought the road of wisdom
Her thoughts outstripped her erring feet
Her tone was gathering remonstrance
Her tongue on the subject was sharpness itself
Her tongue stumbled and was silent
Her voice had the coaxing inflections of a child
Her voice trailed off vaguely
Her voice was full of temper, hard-held
Her voice, with a tentative question in it, rested in air
Her wariness seemed put to rout
His accents breathed profound relief
His agitation increased
His brow grew knit and gloomy
His brow was in his hand
His conscience leapt to the light
His constraint was excruciating
His curiosity is quenched
His dignity counseled him to be silent
His ears sang with the vibrating intensity of his secret existence
His eyes had a twinkle of reminiscent pleasantry
His eyes literally blazed with savage fire
His eyes shone with the pure fire of a great purpose
His eyes stared unseeingly
His face caught the full strength of the rising wind
His face dismissed its shadow
His face fell abruptly into stern lines
His face lit with a fire of decision
His face showed a pleased bewilderment
His face torn with conflict
His face was gravely authoritative
His gaze faltered and fell
His gaze searched her face
His gaze seemed full of unconquerable hopefulness
His hand supported his chin

His hands were small and prehensible
[prehensible = capable of being seized]
His heart asserted itself again, thunderously beating
His heart rebuked him
His heart was full of enterprise
His impatient scorn expired
His last illusions crumbled
His lips loosened in a furtively exultant smile
His lips seemed to be permanently parted in a good-humored smile
His mind echoed with words
His mind leaped gladly to meet new issues and fresh tides of thought
His mind was dazed and wandering in a mist of memories
His mood yielded
His mouth quivered with pleasure
His passions vented themselves with sneers
His pulses leaped anew
His reputation had withered
His sensibilities were offended
His shrewd gaze fixed appraisingly upon her
His soul full of fire and eagle-winged
His soul was compressed into a single agony of prayer
His soul was wrung with a sudden wild homesickness
His speech faltered
His swift and caustic satire
His temper was dark and explosive
His thoughts galloped
His thoughts were in clamoring confusion
His tone assumed a certain asperity
[asperity = roughness; harshness]
His torpid ideas awoke again
His troubled spirit shifted its load
His vagrant thoughts were in full career
His voice insensibly grew inquisitorial
His voice was thick with resentment and futile protest
His whole face was lighted with a fierce enthusiasm

His whole frame seemed collapsed and shrinking
His whole tone was flippant and bumptious
His words trailed off brokenly
His youthful zeal was contagious

I

I capitulated by inadvertence
I cut my reflections adrift
I felt a qualm of apprehension
I suffered agonies of shyness
I took the good day from the hands of God as a perfect gift
I was in a somber mood
I was overshadowed by a deep boding
I was piqued [piqued = resentment; indignation]
I yielded to the ingratiating mood of the day
Ill-bred insolence was his only weapon
Ill-dissimulated fits of ambition
Imbued with a vernal freshness [vernal = resembling spring; fresh]
Immense and careless prodigality
Immense objects which dwarf us
Immersed in secret schemes
Immured in a trivial round of duty [immured = confine within]
Impassioned and earnest language
Impatient and authoritative tones
Impervious to the lessons of experience
Implying an immense melancholy
Imprisoned within an enchanted circle
In a deprecating tone of apology
In a flash of revelation
In a gale of teasing merriment
In a misery of annoyance and mortification
In a musing ecstasy of contemplation
In a sky stained with purple, the moon slowly rose
In a spirit of indulgent irony
In a strain of exaggerated gallantry
In a tone of after-dinner perfunctoriness [perfunctoriness = with little interest]
In a tone of musing surprise

Hope was far and dim
How sweet and reasonable the pale shadows of those who smile from some dim corner of our memories
Humiliating paltriness of revenge

In a tumult of self-approval and towering exultation
In a vague and fragmentary way
In a wise, superior, slightly scornful manner
In accents of menace and wrath
In its whole unwieldy compass
In moments of swift and momentous decision
In quest of something to amuse
In requital for various acts of rudeness
In the air was the tang of spring
In the dusky path of a dream
In the face of smarting disillusions
In the flush and heyday of youth and gaiety and loveliness
In the heyday of friendship
In the mild and mellow maturity of age
In the perpetual presence of everlasting verities
In this breathless chase of pleasure
In this chastened mood I left him
Incapable of initiative or boldness
Inconceivable perversion of reasoning
Indolently handsome eyes
Indulge in pleasing discursiveness
Ineffable sensation of irritability
Infantile insensibility to the solemnity of his bereavement
Infantine simplicity and lavish waste
Innumerable starlings clove the air [clove = split]
Insensible to its subtle influence
Inspired by the immortal flame of youth
Intangible and indescribable essence
Intense love of excitement and adventure
Intimations of unpenetrated mysteries
Into her eyes had come a hostile challenge

126

Into the purple sea the orange hues of heaven sunk silently
Into the very vestibule of death
Involuntarily she sighed
Involuntary awkwardness and reserve
Involved in a labyrinth of perplexities
It came to him with a stab of enlightenment
It elicited a remarkably clear and coherent statement
It is a flight beyond the reach of human magnanimity
It is a thing infinitely subtle
It is not every wind that can blow you from your anchorage
It lends no dazzling tints to fancy
It moved me to a strange exhilaration
It parted to a liquid horizon and showed the gray rim of the sea
It proved a bitter disillusion
It seemed intolerably tragic
It seemed to exhale a silent and calm authority
It was a breathless night of suspense
It was a desolating vision
It was a night of little ease to his toiling mind
It was a night of stupefying surprises
It was all infinitely soft and refreshing to the eye
It was an evening of great silences and spaces, wholly tranquil
It was sheer, exuberant, instinctive, unreasoning, careless joy
It was the ecstasy and festival of summer
It was torture of the most exquisite kind

J
Jealousies and animosities which pricked their sluggish blood to tingling
Joy rioted in his large dark eyes

Judging without waiting to ponder over bulky tomes

K
Kind of unscrupulous contempt for gravity

Kiss-provoking lips

L
Laden with the poignant scent of the garden honeysuckle
Language of excessive flattery and adulation
Lapped in soft music of adulation
Lapse into pathos and absurdity
Large, dark, luminous eyes that behold everything about them
Latent vein of whimsical humor
Lead to the strangest aberrations
Leaping from lambent flame into eager and passionate fire [lambent = effortlessly brilliant]
Leave to the imagination the endless vista of possibilities

Life flowed in its accustomed stream
Lights and shadows of reviving memory crossed her face
Lionized by fashionable society
Long intertangled lines of silver streamlets
Lost in a delirious wonder
Lost in irritable reflection
Love hovered in her gaze
Ludicrous attempts of clumsy playfulness and tawdry eloquence
Luke-warm assurance of continued love
Lulled by dreamy musings
Luminous with great thoughts

M
Magnanimous indifference to meticulous niceties

127

Making the ear greedy to remark offense
Marching down to posterity with divine honors
Marked out for some strange and preternatural doom
Mawkishly effeminate sentiment
Memories plucked from wood and field
Memory was busy at his heart
Merged in a sentiment of unutterable sadness and compassion
Microscopic minuteness of eye

Misgivings of grave kinds
Mockery crept into her tone
Molded by the austere hand of adversity
Moments of utter idleness and insipidity
Moods of malicious reaction and vindictive recoil
Morn, in yellow and white, came broadening out of the mountains
Mumble only jargon of dotage
My body is too frail for its moods

## N

Nature seemed to revel in unwonted contrasts [unwonted = unusual]
New ambitions pressed upon his fancy
New dreams began to take wing in his imagination
Night after night the skies were wine-blue and bubbling with stars

Night passes lightly in the open world, with its stars and dews and perfumes
Nights of fathomless blackness
No mark of trick or artifice
Noble and sublime patience
Nursed by brooding thought

## O

Obsessed with the modishness of the hour
Occasional flashes of tenderness and love
Oddly disappointing and fickle
One gracious fact emerges here
One long torture of soul
One of the golden twilights which transfigure the world
Oppressed and disheartened by an all-pervading desolation

Oppressed with a confused sense of cumbrous material [cumbrous = cumbersome]
Outweighing years of sorrow and bitterness
Over and over the paroxysms of grief and longing submerged her
Overhung and overspread with ivy
Overshadowed by a vague depression

## P

Pale and vague desolation
Pallor of reflected glories
Palpitating with rage and wounded sensibility
Panting after distinction
Peace brooded over all
Pelted with an interminable torrent of words
Penetrate beneath the surface to the core
Peopled the night with thoughts
Perpetual gloom and seclusion of life
Pertinent to the thread of the discussion
Pervasive silence which wraps us in a

mantle of content
Piles of golden clouds just peering above the horizon
Platitudinous and pompously sentimental
Plaudits of the unlettered mob
Pleasant and flower-strewn vistas of airy fancy
Pledged with enthusiastic fervor
Plumbing the depth of my own fears
Poignant doubts and misgivings
Power of intellectual metamorphosis
Power to assuage the thirst of the soul
Precipitated into mysterious depths of

nothingness
Preening its wings for a skyward flight
Pressing cares absorbed him
Pride working busily within her
Proclaimed with joyous defiance
Prodigal of discriminating epithets
Prodigious boldness and energy of
intellect

Products of dreaming indolence
Profound and chilling solitude of the
spot
Proof of his imperturbability and
indifference
Provocative of bitter hostility
Pulling the strings of many enterprises
Purge the soul of nonsense

Q
Quickened and enriched by new
contacts with life and truth

Quivering with restrained grief

R
Radiant with the beautiful glamor of
youth
Ransack the vocabulary
Red tape of officialdom
Redolent of the night lamp
Reflecting the solemn and unfathomable
stars
Regarded with an exulting pride
Rehabilitated and restored to dignity
Remorselessly swept into oblivion

Resounding generalities and
conventional rhetoric
Respect forbade downright contradiction
Restless and sore and haughty feelings
were busy within
Retort leaped to his lips
Rigid adherence to conventionalities
Rudely disconcerting in her behavior
Rudely reminded of life's serious issues

S
Sacrificed to a futile sort of treadmill
Sadness prevailed among her moods
Scorched with the lightning of
momentary indignation
Scorning such paltry devices
Scotched but not slain
Scrupulous morality of conduct
Seem to swim in a sort of blurred mist
before the eyes
Seething with suppressed wrath
Seize on greedily
Sensuous enjoyment of the outward
show of life
Serenity beamed from his look
Serenity of paralysis and death
Seriousness lurked in the depths of her
eyes
Served to recruit his own jaded ideas
Set anew in some fresh and appealing
form
Setting all the sane traditions at defiance

Shadowy vistas of sylvan beauty
She affected disdain
She assented in precisely the right terms
She bandies adjectives with the best
She challenged his dissent
She cherished no petty resentments
She curled her fastidious lip
She curled her lip with defiant scorn
She did her best to mask her agitation
She disarmed anger and softened
asperity [asperity = harshness]
She disclaimed fatigue
She fell into a dreamy silence
She fell into abstracted reverie
She felt herself carried off her feet by the
rush of incoherent impressions
She flushed an agitated pink
She forced a faint quivering smile
She frowned incomprehension
She had an air of restrained fury
She had an undercurrent of acidity

She hugged the thought of her own unknown and unapplauded integrity
She lingered a few leisurely seconds
She nodded mutely
She nourished a dream of ambition
She permitted herself a delicate little smile
She poured out on him the full opulence of a proud recognition
She questioned inimically [inimically = unfriendly; hostile]
She recaptured herself with difficulty
She regarded him stonily out of flint-blue eyes
She sat eyeing him with frosty calm
She seemed the embodiment of dauntless resolution
She seemed wrapped in a veil of lassitude
She shook hands grudgingly
She softened her frown to a quivering smile
She spoke with hurried eagerness
She spoke with sweet severity
She stilled and trampled on the inward protest
She stood her ground with the most perfect dignity
She strangled a fierce tide of feeling that welled up within her
She swept away all opposing opinion with the swift rush of her enthusiasm
She thrived on insincerity
She twitted him merrily
She was both weary and placated
She was conscious of a tumultuous rush of sensations
She was demure and dimly appealing
She was exquisitely simple
She was gripped with a sense of suffocation and panic
She was in an anguish of sharp and penetrating remorse
She was oppressed by a dead melancholy
She was stricken to the soul
She wore an air of wistful questioning
Sheer superfluity of happiness

Sickening contrasts and diabolic ironies of life
Silence fell
Singing lustily as if to exorcise the demon of gloom
Skirmishes and retreats of conscience
Slender experience of the facts of life
Slope towards extinction
Slow the movement was and tortuous
Slowly disengaging its significance from the thicket of words
So innocent in her exuberant happiness
Soar into a rosy zone of contemplation
Softened by the solicitude of untiring and anxious love
Solitary and sorely smitten souls
Some dim-remembered and dream-like images
Some exquisite refinement in the architecture of the brain
Some flash of witty irrelevance
Something curiously suggestive and engaging
Something eminently human beaconed from his eyes
Something full of urgent haste
Something indescribably reckless and desperate in such a picture
Something that seizes tyrannously upon the soul
Sore beset by the pressure of temptation
Specious show of impeccability
Spectacular display of wrath
Spur and whip the tired mind into action
Stale and facile platitudes
Stamped with unutterable and solemn woe
Startled into perilous activity
Startling leaps over vast gulfs of time
Stem the tide of opinion
Stern emptying of the soul
Stimulated to an ever deepening subtlety
Stirred into a true access of enthusiasm
Stony insensibility to the small pricks and frictions of daily life
Strange capacities and suggestions both of vehemence and pride

Strange laughings and glitterings of silver streamlets
Stripped to its bare skeleton
Strode forth imperiously [imperious = arrogantly overbearing]
Struck by a sudden curiosity
Struck dumb with strange surprise
Stung by his thoughts, and impatient of rest
Stung by the splendor of the prospect
Subdued passages of unobtrusive majesty
Sublime indifference to contemporary usage and taste
Submission to an implied rebuke
Subtle indications of great mental agitation
Subtle suggestions of remoteness
Such things as the eye of history sees
Such was the petty chronicle
Suddenly a thought shook him

Suddenly overawed by a strange, delicious shyness
Suddenly smitten with unreality
Suddenly snuffed out in the middle of ambitious schemes
Suffered to languish in obscurity
Sugared remonstrances and cajoleries
Suggestions of veiled and vibrant feeling
Summer clouds floating feathery overhead
Sunk in a phraseological quagmire
Sunk into a gloomy reverie
Sunny silence broods over the realm of little cottages
Supreme arbiter of conduct
Susceptibility to fleeting impressions
Sweet smoke of burning twigs hovered in the autumn day
Swift summer into the autumn flowed

T
Taking the larger sweeps in the march of mind
Tears of outraged vanity blurred her vision
Teased with impertinent questions
Tenderness breathed from her
Tense with the anguish of spiritual struggle
Terror filled the more remote chambers of his brain with riot
Tethered to earth
That which flutters the brain for a moment
The accelerated beat of his thoughts
The affluent splendor of the summer day
The afternoon was filled with sound and sunshine
The afternoon was waning
The air and sky belonged to midsummer
The air darkened swiftly
The air is touched with a lazy fragrance, as of hidden flowers
The air was caressed with song
The air was full of fugitive strains of old songs

The air was raw and pointed
The allurements of a coquette
The ambition and rivalship of men
The angry blood burned in his face
The anguish of a spiritual conflict tore his heart
The artificial smile of languor
The awful and implacable approach of doom
The babble of brooks grown audible
The babbledom that dogs the heels of fame
The bait proved incredibly successful
The balm of solitary musing
The beauty straightway vanished
The beckonings of alien appeals
The benign look of a father
The blandishments of pleasure and pomp of power
The blinding mist came down and hid the land
The blue bowl of the sky, all glorious with the blaze of a million worlds
The bound of the pulse of spring
The buzz of idolizing admiration

131

The caressing peace of bright soft
sunshine
The chaotic sound of the sea
The chill of forlorn old age
The chill of night crept in from the street
The chivalric sentiment of honor
The chivalrous homage of respect
The clamorous agitation of rebellious
passions
The clouded, restless, jaded mood
The constant iteration of the sea's wail
The contagion of extravagant luxury
The conversation became desultory
[desultory = haphazardly; random]
The crowning touch of pathos
The current of his ideas flowed full and
strong
The dance whizzed on with cumulative
fury
The dawn is singing at the door
The day sang itself into evening
The day was at once redolent and
vociferous [redolent = emitting
fragrance; aromatic; suggestive;
reminiscent] [vociferous = conspicuously
and offensively loud]
The day was blind with fog
The day was gracious
The days passed in a stately procession
The days when you dared to dream
The debilitating fears of alluring fate
The deep and solemn purple of the
summer night
The deep flush ebbed out of his face
The deep tranquillity of the shaded
solitude
The deepening twilight filled with
shadowy visions
The deepest wants and aspirations of his
soul
The delicatest reproof of imagined
distrust
The demerit of an unworthy alliance
The desire of the moth for the star
The dimness of the sealed eye and soul
The dreamy solicitations of indescribable
afterthoughts

The dying day lies beautiful in the tender
glow of the evening
The early morning of the Indian summer
day was tinged with blue mistiness
The earth looked despoiled
The east alone frowned with clouds
The easy grace of an unpremeditated
agreeable talker
The easy-going indolence of a sedentary
life
The echo of its wrathful roar surged and
boomed among the hills
The empurpled hills standing up, solemn
and sharp, out of the green-gold air
The enchanting days of youth
The eternal questioning of inscrutable
fate
The evening comes with slow steps
The evening star silvery and solitary on
the girdle of the early night
The exaggerations of morbid
hallucinations
The excitement of rival issues
The extraordinary wistful look of
innocence and simplicity
The eye of a scrutinizing observer
The eyes burnt with an amazing fire
The eyes filled with playfulness and
vivacity
The father's vigil of questioning sorrow
The fine flower of culture
The first recoil from her disillusionment
The flawless triumph of art
The flight of the autumnal days
The flower of courtesy
The fluttering of untried wings
The foreground was incredibly shabby
The fragrance of a dear and honored
name
The freshening breeze struck his brow
with a cooling hand
The freshness of some pulse of air from
an invisible sea
The fruit of vast and heroic labors
The general effect was of extraordinary
lavish profusion
The give and take was delicious

The gloom of the afternoon deepened
The gloom of winter dwelt on everything
The gloomy insolence of self-conceit
The glow of the ambitious fire
The golden gloom of the past and the bright-hued hope of the future
The golden riot of the autumn leaves
The golden sunlight of a great summer day
The gray air rang and rippled with lark music
The grimaces and caperings of buffoonery
The grotesque nightmare of a haunting fear
The hand of time sweeps them into oblivion
The haunting melody of some familiar line of verse
The haunting phrase leaped to my brain
The headlong vigor of sheer improvisation
The heights of magnanimity and love
The high-bred pride of an oriental
The hills were clad in rose and amethyst
The hill-tops gleam in morning's spring
The hinted sweetness of the challenge aroused him
The hot humiliation of it overwhelmed her
The hungry curiosity of the mind
The idiosyncratic peculiarities of thought
The idle chatter of the crowd
The immediate tyranny of a present emotion
The inaccessible solitude of the sky
The incarnation of all loveliness
The incoherent loquacity of a nervous patient [loquacity = very talkative]
The indefinable air of good-breeding
The indefinable yearning for days that were dead
The indefinite atmosphere of an opulent nature
The intercepted glances of wondering eyes
The intrusive question faded

The invidious stigma of selfishness [invidious = rousing ill will]
The iron hand of oppression
The irresistible and ceaseless onflow of time
The irrevocable past and the uncertain future
The landscape ran, laughing, downhill to the sea
The leaden sky rests heavily on the earth
The leaves of time drop stealthily
The leaves syllabled her name in cautious whispers
The lights winked
The little incident seemed to throb with significance
The lofty grace of a prince
The loud and urgent pageantry of the day
The low hills on the horizon wore a haze of living blue
The machinations of a relentless mountebank [mountebank = flamboyant charlatan]
The machinations of an unscrupulous enemy
The magical lights of the horizon
The majestic solemnity of the moment yielded to the persuasive warmth of day
The marvelous beauty of her womanhood
The maximum of attainable and communicable truth
The melancholy day weeps in monotonous despair
The melodies of birds and bees
The memory of the night grew fantastic and remote
The meticulous observation of facts
The mind freezes at the thought
The mind was filled with a formless dread
The mocking echoes of long-departed youth
The moment marked an epoch
The moon is waning below the horizon
The more's the pity

133

The morning beckons
The morning droned along peacefully
The most servile acquiescence
The multiplicity of odors competing for your attention
The murmur of soft winds in the tree-tops
The murmur of the surf boomed in melancholy mockery
The murmuring of summer seas
The music and mystery of the sea
The music of her delicious voice
The music of her presence was singing a swift melody in his blood
The music of unforgotten years sounded again in his soul
The mute melancholy landscape
The mystery obsessed him
The naked fact of death
The nameless and inexpressible fascination of midnight music
The narrow glen was full of the brooding power of one universal spirit
The nascent spirit of chivalry
The night was drowned in stars
The old ruddy conviction deserted me
The onrush and vividness of life
The opulent sunset
The orange pomp of the setting sun
The oscillations of human genius
The outpourings of a tenderness reawakened by remorse
The pageantry of sea and sky
The palest abstractions of thought
The palpitating silence lengthened
The panorama of life was unrolled before him
The paraphernalia of power and prosperity
The parting crimson glory of the ripening summer sun
The past slowly drifted out of his thought
The pendulous eyelids of old age
The penetrating odors assailed his memory as something unforgettable
The pent-up intolerance of years of repression

The perfume of the mounting sea saturated the night with wild fragrance
The piquancy of the pageant of life
[piquancy = tart spiciness]
The pith and sinew of mature manhood
The plenitude of her piquant ways
[piquant = engagingly stimulating]
The presage of disaster was in the air
The pressure of accumulated misgivings
The preternatural pomposities of the pulpit
The pristine freshness of spring
The pull of soul on body
The pulse of the rebounding sea
The purging sunlight of clear poetry
The purple vaulted night
The question drummed in head and heart day and night
The question irresistibly emerged
The quick pulse of gain
The radiant serenity of the sky
The radiant stars brooded over the stainless fields, white with freshly fallen snow
The restlessness of offended vanity
The retreating splendor of autumn
The rising storm of words
The river ran darkly, mysteriously by
The river sang with its lips to the pebbles
The roar of the traffic rose to thunder
The romantic ardor of a generous mind
The room had caught a solemn and awful quietude
The rosy-hued sky went widening off into the distance
The rosy twilight of boyhood
The royal arrogance of youth
The sadness in him deepened inexplicably
The scars of rancor and remorse
The scent of roses stole in with every breath of air
The sea heaved silvery, far into the night
The sea slept under a haze of golden winter sun
The sea-sweep enfolds you, satisfying eye and mind

The sea-wind buffeted their faces
The secret and subduing charm of the woods
The see-saw of a wavering courage
The sentimental tourist will be tempted to tarry
The shadows of the night seemed to retreat
The shadows rested quietly under the breezeless sky
The shafts of ridicule
The sheer weight of unbearable loneliness
The shiver of the dusk passed fragrantly down the valley
The silence grew stolid
The silence was uncomfortable and ominous
The silent day perfumed with the hidden flowers
The silver silence of the night
The sinking sun made mellow gold of all the air
The sky grew brighter with the imminent day
The sky grew ensaffroned with the indescribable hue that heralds day
The sky put on the panoply of evening
The sky was a relentless, changeless blue
The sky was dull and brooding
The sky was heavily sprinkled with stars
The sky was turning to the pearly gray of dawn
The smiling incarnation of loveliness
The song of hurrying rivers
The sound of the sea waxed
The spacious leisure of the forest
The spell of a deathless dream was upon them
The star-strewn spaces of the night
The stars looked down in their silent splendor
The stars seemed attentive
The steadfast mind kept its hope
The steady thunder of the sea accented the silence
The still voice of the poet

The stillness of a forced composure
The stillness of the star-hung night
The strangest thought shimmered through her
The stream forgot to smile
The streams laughed to themselves
The strident discord seemed to mock his mood
The stunning crash of the ocean saluted her
The subtle emanation of other influences seemed to arrest and chill him
The sudden rush of the awakened mind
The summit of human attainment
The sun blazed torridly
The sun goes down in flame on the far horizon
The sun lay golden-soft over the huddled hills
The sunlight spread at a gallop along the hillside
The sunset was rushing to its height through every possible phase of violence and splendor
The suspicion of secret malevolence
The swelling tide of memory
The swing of the pendulum through an arch of centuries
The tempered daylight of an olive garden
The tender grace of a day that is fled
The tension of struggling tears which strove for an outlet
The thought leaped
The timely effusion of tearful sentiment
The tone betrayed a curious irritation
The torture of his love and terror crushed him
The trees rustled and whispered to the streams
The tumult in her heart subsided
The tumult in her mind found sudden speech
The tumult of pride and pleasure
The tune of moving feet in the lamplit city
The tyranny of nipping winds and early frosts

The unmasked batteries of her glorious gray eyes
The vacant fields looked blankly irresponsive
The vast and shadowy stream of time
The vast cathedral of the world
The vast unexplored land of dreams
The velvet of the cloudless sky grew darker, and the stars more luminous
The veneer of a spurious civilization
The very pulsation and throbbing of his intellect
The very silence of the place appeared a source of peril
The vision fled him
The vivifying touch of humor
The web of lies is rent in pieces
The wheel of her thought turned in the same desolate groove
The whispering rumble of the ocean
The white seething surf fell exhausted along the shore
The whole exquisite night was his
The whole sea of foliage is shaken and broken up with little momentary shiverings and shadows
The wide horizon forever flames with summer
The wild whirl of nameless regret and passionate sorrow
The wild winds flew round, sobbing in their dismay
The wind charged furiously through it, panting towards the downs
The wind piped drearily
The wind was in high frolic with the rain
The winnowed tastes of the ages
The woods were silent with adoration
The youth of the soul
The zenith turned shell pink
Their ephemeral but enchanting beauty had expired forever [ephemeral = markedly short-lived]
Their eyes met glancingly
Their troth had been plighted
There was a kind of exhilaration in this subtle baiting

There was a mild triumph in her tone
There was a mournful and dim haze around the moon
There was a strange massing and curving of the clouds
There was a thrill in the air
There was a time I might have trod the sunlit heights
There was no glint of hope anywhere
There was no menace in the night's silvern calmness
There was something so kindly in its easy candor
There was spendthrift grandeur
These qualities were raised to the white heat of enthusiasm
They became increasingly turbid and phantasmagorical [phantasmagorical = fantastic imagery]
They escaped the baffled eye
They sit heavy on the soul
They were vastly dissimilar
This exquisite conjunction and balance
This little independent thread of inquiry ran through the texture of his mind and died away
This shadowy and chilling sentiment unaccountably creeps over me
Thought shook through her in poignant pictures
Thoughts came thronging in panic haste
Thrilled by fresh and indescribable odors
Thrilled with a sense of strange adventure
Through a cycle of many ages
Through endless and labyrinthine sentences
Thrilled to the depths of her being
Time had passed unseen
Tinsel glitter of empty titles
Tired with a dull listless fatigue
To all intents and purposes
To speak with entire candor
To stay his tottering constancy
To the scourging he submitted with a good grace
Tossed disdainfully off from young and

ardent lips
Touched every moment with shifting and enchanting beauty
Touched with a bewildering and elusive beauty
Transcendental contempt for money

U
Unapproachable grandeur and simplicity
Unaware of her bitter taunt
Under the vivifying touch of genius
Unearthly in its malignant glee
Unfathomed depths and impossibilities
Unforced and unstudied depth of feeling
Unspoiled by praise or blame
Unspoken messages from some vaster world

V
Vain allurements of folly and fashion
Variously ramified and delicately minute channels of expression
Varnished over with a cold repellent cynicism
Vast sweep of mellow distances
Veiled by some equivocation
Vibrant with the surge of human passions

W
Wantonly and detestably unkind
Waylay Destiny and bid him stand and deliver
Wayward and strangely playful responses
Wearing the white flower of a blameless life
What sorry and pitiful quibbling
When a pleasant countryside tunes the spirit to a serene harmony of mood
When music is allied to words
When the frame and the mind alike seem unstrung and listless
When the profane voices are hushed
When the waves show their teeth in the flying breeze
Whilst the morn kissed the sleep from

Transformed with an overmastering passion
Trouble gathered on his brow
Turning the world topsy-turvey
Twilight creeps upon the darkening mind

Unstable moral equilibrium of boyhood
Until sleep overtakes us at a stride
Untouched by the ruthless spirit of improvement
Upon the mountain-tops of meditation
Urbanely plastic and versatile
Uttering grandiose puerilities [puerilities = childishness, silly]

Vicissitudes of wind and weather [vicissitudes = sudden or unexpected changes]
Vigor and richness of resource
Visible and palpable pains and penalties
Voices that charm the ear and echo with a subtle resonance in the soul
Volcanic upheavings of imprisoned passions

her eyes
Whistled life away in perfect contentment
Wholly alien to his spirit
With a vanquished and weary sigh
Womanly fickleness and caprice
Words and acts easily wrenched from their true significance
Worn to shreds by anxiety
Wrapped in a sudden intensity of reflection
Wrapped in an inaccessible mood
Wrapped in scudding rain
Wrapt in his odorous and many-colored robe
Wrapt in inward contemplation
Wrought of an emotion infectious and

137

splendidly dangerous
Wrought out of intense and tragic

experience

Y
Yielding to a wave of pity
Your mind enthroned in the seventh

circle of content

# SECTION 8
# STRIKING SIMILES

A

A blind rage like a fire swept over him

A book that rends and tears like a broken saw

A breath of melancholy made itself felt like a chill and sudden gust from some unknown sea

A cloud in the west like a pall creeps upward

A cloud like a flag from the sky

A cluster of stars hangs like fruit in the tree

A confused mass of impressions, like an old rubbish-heap

A cry as of a sea-bird in the wind

A dead leaf might as reasonably demand to return to the tree

A drowsy murmur floats into the air like thistledown

A face as imperturbable as fate

A face as pale as wax

A face tempered like steel

A fatigued, faded, lusterless air, as of a caged creature

A few pens parched by long disuse

A figure like a carving on a spire

A fluttering as of blind bewildered moths

A giant galleon overhead, looked like some misty monster of the deep

A glacial pang of pain like the stab of a dagger of ice frozen from a poisoned well

A glance that flitted like a bird

A great moon like a red lamp in the sycamore

A grim face like a carved mask

A hand icily cold and clammy as death

A heart from which noble sentiments sprang like sparks from an anvil

A jeweler that glittered like his shop

A lady that lean'd on his arm like a queen in a fable of old fairy days

A life, a Presence, like the air

A life as common and brown and bare as the box of earth in the window there

A light wind outside the lattice swayed a branch of roses to and fro,

shaking out their perfume as from a swung censer

A lightning-phrase, as if shot from the quiver of infallible wisdom

A list of our unread books torments some of us like a list of murders

A little breeze ran through the corn like a swift serpent

A little weed-clogged ship, gray as a ghost

A long slit of daylight like a pointing finger

A memory like a well-ordered cupboard

A mighty wind, like a leviathan, plowed the brine

A mind very like a bookcase

A mystery, soft, soothing and gentle, like the whisper of a child murmuring its happiness in its sleep

A name which sounds even now like the call of a trumpet

A note of despairing appeal which fell like a cold hand upon one's living soul

A purpose as the steady flame

A question deep almost as the mystery of life

A quibbling mouth that snapped at verbal errors like a lizard catching flies

A radiant look came over her face, like a sudden burst of sunshine on a cloudy day

A reputation that swelled like a sponge

A ruby like a drop of blood

A shadow of melancholy touched her lithe fancies, as a cloud dims the waving of golden grain

A silver moon, like a new-stamped coin, rode triumphant in the sky
A slow thought that crept like a cold worm through all his brain
A smile flashed over her face, like sunshine over a flower
A soft and purple mist like a vaporous amethyst
A soft haze, like a fairy dream, is floating over wood and stream
A soul as white as heaven
A sound like the throb of a bell
A stooping girl as pale as a pearl
A sudden sense of fear ran through her nerves like the chill of an icy wind
A sweet voice caroling like a gold-caged nightingale
A thin shrill voice like the cry of an expiring mouse
A thing of as frail enchantment as the gleam of stars upon snow
A vague thought, as elusive as the smell of a primrose
A vanishing loveliness as tender as the flush of the rose leaf and as ethereal as the light of a solitary star
A voice as low as the sea
A voice soft and sweet as a tune that one knows
A white bird floats there, like a drifting leaf
Against a sky as clear as sapphire
Age, like winter weather
Agile as a leopard
Agitated like a storm-tossed ship
Air like wine
All around them like a forest swept the deep and empurpled masses of her tangled hair
All like an icicle it seemed, so tapering and cold
All my life broke up, like some great river's ice at touch of spring
All silent as the sheeted dead
All sounds were lost in the whistle of air humming by like the flight of a million arrows

All that's beautiful drifts away like the waters
All the world lay stretched before him like the open palm of his hand
All unconscious as a flower
Alone, like a storm-tossed wreck, on this night of the glad New Year
An anxiety hung like a dark impenetrable cloud
An ardent face out-looking like a star
An ecstasy which suddenly overwhelms your mind like an unexpected and exquisite thought
An envious wind crept by like an unwelcome thought
An ideal as sublime and comprehensive as the horizon
An immortal spirit dwelt in that frail body, like a bird in an outworn cage
An impudent trick as hackneyed as conjuring rabbits out of a hat
An indefinable resemblance to a goat
An isle of Paradise, fair as a gem
An old nodding negress whose sable head shined in the sun like a polished cocoanut
An omnibus across the bridge crawls like a yellow butterfly
An undefined sadness seemed to have fallen about her like a cloud
An unknown world, wild as primeval chaos
An unpleasing strain, like the vibration of a rope drawn out too fast
And a pinnace like a flutter'd bird came flying from afar
And a tear like silver, glistened in the corner of her eye
And all our thoughts ran into tears like sunshine into rain
And at first the road comes moving toward me, like a bride waving palms
And Dusk, with breast as of a dove, brooded
And eyes as bright as the day
And fell as cold as a lump of clay
And her cheek was like a rose

140

And here were forests ancient as the hills
And many a fountain, rivulet, and pond,
as clear as elemental diamond, or serene
morning air
And melting like the stars in June
And night, as welcome as a friend
And silence like a poultice comes to heal
the blows of sound
And spangled o'er with twinkling points,
like stars
And the smile she softly uses fills the
silence like a speech
As a child in play scatters the heaps of
sand that he has piled on the seashore
As a cloud that gathers her robe like
drifted snow
As a flower after a drought drinks in the
steady plunging rain
As a leaf that beats on a mountain
As a lion grieves at the loss of her whelps
As a man plowing all day longs for
supper and welcomes sunset
As a sea disturbed by opposing winds
As amusing as a litter of likely young
pigs
As arbitrary as a cyclone and as killing as
a pestilence
As austere as a Roman matron
As beautiful as the purple flush of dawn
As blind as a mole
As brief as sunset clouds in heaven
As bright as sunlight on a stream
As busy as a bee
As cattle driven by a gadfly
As chimney sweepers come to dust
As clear as a whistle
As clear as the parts of a tree in the
morning sun
As close as oak and ivy stand
As delicate and as fair as a lily
As delightful to the mind as cool well-
water to thirsty lip
As diamond cuts diamond
As direct and unvarying as the course of
a homing bird
As distinct as night and morning
As dry as desert dust

As dumb as a fish
As easily as the sun shines
As easy as a turn of the hand
As elastic as a steel spring
As extinct as the dodo
As faint as the memory of a sound
As familiar to him as his alphabet
As fatal as the fang of the most
venomous snake
As fleeting and elusive as our dreams
As foam from a ship's swiftness
As fresh and invigorating as a sea-breeze
As full of eager vigor as a mountain
stream
As full of spirit as a gray squirrel
As gay and busy as a brook
As gently as the flower gives forth its
perfume
As gently as withered leaves float from a
tree
As graceful as a bough
As grave as a judge
As great as the first day of creation
As high as heaven
As I dropped like a bolt from the blue
As I dwelt like a sparrow among the
spires
As if a door were suddenly left ajar into
some world unseen before
As impossible as to count the stars in
illimitable space
As in the footsteps of a god
As inaccessible to his feet as the clefts
and gorges of the clouds
As inexorable as the flight of time
As innocent as a new laid egg
As iridescent as a soap bubble
As locusts gather to a stream before a fire
As mellow and deep as a psalm
As men strip for a race, so must an
author strip for the race with time
As merry as bees in clover
As nimble as water
As one who has climbed above the
earth's eternal snowline and sees only
white peaks and pinnacles
As pale as any ghost

As patient as the trees
As quick as the movement of some wild animal
As quiet as a nun breathless with adoration
As radiant as the rose
As readily and naturally as ducklings take to water
As reticent as a well-bred stockbroker
As ruthlessly as the hoof of a horse tramples on a rose
As shallow streams run dimpling all the way
As simple as the intercourse of a child with its mother
As sleep falls upon the eyes of a child tired with a long summer day of eager pleasure and delight
As some vast river of unfailing source
As stars that shoot along the sky
As still as a stone
As stupid as a sheep
As sudden as a dislocated joint slipping back into place
As summer winds that creep from flower to flower
As supple as a step-ladder
As swaggering and sentimental as a penny novellete [novellete = short novel]
As swift as thought

B
Babbling like a child
Balmy in manner as a bland southern morning
Be like the granite of thy rock-ribbed land
Beauteous she looks as a water-lily
Beautiful as the dawn, dominant as the sun
Beauty maddens the soul like wine
Beheld great Babel, wrathful, beautiful, burn like a blood-red cloud upon the plain
Beneath a sky as fair as summer flowers
Bent like a wand of willow
Black as a foam-swept rock

As the accumulation of snowflakes makes the avalanche
As the bubble is extinguished in the ocean
As the dew upon the roses warms and melts the morning light
As the fair cedar, fallen before the breeze, lies self-embalmed amidst the moldering trees
As the light straw flies in dark'ning whirlwinds
As the lightning cleaves the night
As the loud blast that tears the skies
As the slow shadows of the pointed grass mark the eternal periods
As those move easiest who have learn'd to dance
As though a rose should shut, and be a bud again
As though Pharaoh should set the Israelites to make a pin instead of a pyramid
As unapproachable as a star
As weird as the elfin lights
As well try to photograph the other side of the moon
At extreme tension, like a drawn bow
Away he rushed like a cyclone
Awkward as a cart-horse

Black his hair as the wintry night
Blithe as a bird [blithe = carefree and lighthearted]
Bounded by the narrow fences of life
Bowed like a mountain
Breaking his oath and resolution like a twist of rotten silk
Breathed like a sea at rest
Bright as a diamond in the sun
Bright as a fallen fragment of the sky
Bright as the coming forth of the morning, in the cloud of an early shower
Bright as the sunbeams
Bright as the tear of an angel, glittered a lonely star

Brilliant and gay as a Greek
Brisk as a wasp in the sunshine
Brittle and bent like a bow
Bronze-green beetles tumbled over
stones, and lay helpless on their backs
with the air of an elderly clergyman
knocked down by an omnibus
Brown as the sweet smelling loam
Brute terrors like the scurrying of rats in
a deserted attic
Buried in his library like a mouse in a
cheese
Burns like a living coal in the soul
But across it, like a mob's menace, fell
the thunder
But thou art fled, like some frail
exhalation
Butterflies like gems

C
Calm as the night
Calm like a flowing river
Calm like a mountain brooding o'er the
sea
Calmly dropping care like a mantle from
her shoulders
Cast thy voice abroad like thunder
Charm upon charm in her was packed,
like rose-leaves in a costly vase
Chaste as the icicle
Cheeks as soft as July peaches
Chill breath of winter
Choked by the thorns and brambles of
early adversity
Cities scattered over the world like ant-
hills
Cities that rise and sink like bubbles
Clear and definite like the glance of a
child or the voice of a girl
Clear as a forest pool
Clear as crystal
Clenched little hands like rumpled roses,
dimpled and dear
Cloud-like that island hung afar
Clouds like the petals of a rose

Cloudy mirror of opinion
Cold and hard as steel
Cold as the white rose waking at
daybreak
Cold, glittering monotony like frosting
around a cake
Collapsed like a concertina
Colored like a fairy tale
Companionless as the last cloud of an
expiring storm whose thunder is its knell
Consecration that like a golden thread
runs through the warp and woof of one's
life [warp = lengthwise threads] [woof =
crosswise threads]
Constant as gliding waters
Contending like ants for little molehill
realms
Continuous as the stars that shine
Cowslips, like chance-found gold
Creeds like robes are laid aside
Creeping like a snail, unwillingly to
school
Cruel as death
Curious as a lynx
Cuts into the matter as with a pen of fire

D
Dainty as flowers
Dance like a wave of the sea
Dark and deep as night
Dark as pitch
Dark trees bending together as though
whispering secrets
Dazzling white as snow in sunshine
Deafening and implacable as some
elemental force

Dear as remembered kisses after death
Dear as the light that visits these sad eyes
Dearer than night to the thief
Debasing fancies gather like foul birds
Deep as the fathomless sea
Deep dark well of sorrow
Delicate as nymphs
Delicate as the flush on a rose or the
sculptured line on a Grecian urn

Denominational lines like stone walls
Dependency had dropped from her like a cast-off cloak
Despondency clung to him like a garment that is wet
Destructive as the lightning flash
Die like flies
Dip and surge lightly to and fro, like the red harbor-buoy
Disappearing into distance like a hazy sea
Dissatisfaction had settled on his mind

E
Each like a corpse within its grave
Each moment was an iridescent bubble fresh-blown from the lips of fancy
Eager-hearted as a boy
Eager with the headlong zest of a hunter for the game
Ears that seemed as deaf as dead man's ears
Easy as a poet's dream
Emotions flashed across her face like the sweep of sun-rent clouds over a quiet landscape
Eternal as the skies
Evanescent as bubbles [evanescent = vanishing like vapor]
Every flake that fell from heaven was like an angel's kiss
Every lineament was clear as in the sculptor's thought [lineament =

F
Faces pale with bliss, like evening stars
Fade away like a cloud in the horizon
Faint and distant as the light of a sun that has long set
Faintly, like a falling dew
Fair and fleet as a fawn
Fair as a star when only one is shining in the sky
Fallen like dead leaves on the highway
Falling away like a speck in space
Fanciful and extravagant as a caliph's dream

like a shadow
Dissolve like some unsubstantial vision faded
Do make a music like to rustling satin
Dogging them like their own shadow
Dost thou not hear the murmuring nightingale like water bubbling from a silver jar?
Drop like a feather, softly to the ground
Drowned like rats
Dull as champagne

characteristic feature]
Everyone on the watch, like a falcon on its nest
Every phrase is like the flash of a scimitar
Exploded like a penny squib
Eyes as deeply dark as are the desert skies
Eyes as luminous and bright and brown as waters of a woodland river
Eyes half veiled by slumberous tears, like bluest water seen through mists of rain
Eyes like a very dark topaz
Eyes like deep wells of compassionate gloom
Eyes like limpid pools in shadow
Eyes like mountain water that o'erflowing on a rock

Fawning like dumb neglected lap-dogs
Felt her breath upon his cheek like a perfumed air
Fields of young grain and verdured pastures like crushed velvet
Fierce as a bear in defeat
Fierce as the flames
Fills life up like a cup with bubbling and sparkling liquor
Fit closely together as the close-set stones of a building
Fix'd like a beacon-tower above the

waves of a tempest
Flame like a flag unfurled
Flap loose and slack like a drooping sail
Flashed with the brilliancy of a well-cut jewel
Fled like sweet dreams
Fleet as an arrow
Flitted like a sylph on wings
Flowers as soft as thoughts of budding love
Fluent as a rill, that wanders silver-footed down a hill
Fluid as thought

G
Gazed like a star into the morning light
Glaring like noontide
Gleam like a diamond on a dancing girl
Glistening like threads of gold
Glitter like a swarm of fire-flies tangled in a silver braid
Glittering like an aigrette of stars [aigrette = ornamental tuft of upright plumes]
Gone astray as a sheep that is lost

H
Hair as harsh as tropical grass and gray as ashes
Hangs like a blue thread loosen'd from the sky
Hard, sharp, and glittering as a sword
Harnessed men, like beasts of burden, drew it to the river-side
Haunts you like the memory of some former happiness
He began to laugh with that sibilant laugh which resembles the hiss of a serpent [sibilant = producing a hissing sound]
He bent upon the lightning page like some rapt poet o'er his rhyme
He bolted down the stairs like a hare
He clatters like a windmill
He danced like a man in a swarm of hornets
He fell as falls some forest lion, fighting

Fluttered like gilded butterflies in giddy mazes
Fragile as a spider's web
Free as the air, from zone to zone I flew
Free as the winds that caress
Fresh and unworn as the sea that breaks languidly beside them
Fresh as a jewel found but yesterday
Fresh as the first beam glittering on a sail
Frightened like a child in the dark
Full-throated as the sea
Furious as eagles

Gone like a glow on the cloud at the close of day
Gone like tenants that quit without warning
Gorgeous as the hues of heaven
Grazing through a circulating library as contentedly as cattle in a fresh meadow
Great scarlet poppies lay in drifts and heaps, like bodies fallen there in vain assault

well
He fell down on my threshold like a wounded stag
He had acted exactly like an automaton
He lay as straight as a mummy
He lay like a warrior taking his rest
He lived as modestly as a hermit
He looked fagged and sallow, like the day [fagged = worked to exhaustion]
He looked with the bland, expressionless stare of an overgrown baby
He played with grave questions as a cat plays with a mouse
He radiated vigor and abundance like a happy child
He sat down quaking like a jelly
He saw disaster like a ghostly figure following her
He snatched furiously at breath like a tiger snatching at meat

He spoke with a uniformity of emphasis that made his words stand out like the raised type for the blind
He swayed in the sudden grip of anger
He sweeps the field of battle like a monsoon
He that wavereth is like a wave of the sea, driven with the wind and tossed
He turned on me like a thunder-cloud
He turned white as chalk
He wandered restlessly through the house, like a prowling animal
He was as splendidly serious as a reformer
He was as steady as a clock
He was as wax in those clever hands
He was bold as the hawk
He was so weak now, like a shrunk cedar white with the hoar-frost
Hearts unfold like flowers before thee
Heavy was my heart as stone
Heeled like an avalanche to leeward
Her arms like slumber o'er my shoulders crept
Her banners like a thousand sunsets glow
Her beauty broke on him like some rare flower
Her beauty fervent as a fiery moon
Her breath is like a cloud
Her cheeks are like the blushing cloud
Her cheeks were wan and her eyes like coals
Her dusky cheek would burn like a poppy
Her expression changed with the rapidity of a kaleidoscope
Her eyes as bright as a blazing star
Her eyes as stars of twilight fair
Her eyes, glimmering star-like in her pale face
Her eyes were as a dove that sickeneth
Her face changed with each turn of their talk, like a wheat-field under a summer breeze
Her face collapsed as if it were a pricked balloon

Her face was as solemn as a mask
Her face was dull as lead
Her face was like a light
Her face was passionless, like those by sculptor graved for niches in a temple
Her hair dropped on her pallid cheeks, like sea-weed on a clam
Her hair hung down like summer twilight
Her hair shone like a nimbus
Her hair was like a coronet
Her hands are white as the virgin rose that she wore on her wedding day
Her hands like moonlight brush the keys
Her head dropped into her hands like a storm-broken flower
Her heart has grown icy as a fountain in the fall
Her holy love that like a vestal flame had burned
Her impulse came and went like fireflies in the dusk
Her lashes like fans upon her cheek
Her laugh is like a rainbow-tinted spray
Her lips are like two budded roses
Her lips like a lovely song that ripples as it flows
Her lips like twilight water
Her little lips are tremulous as brook-water is [tremulous = timid or fearful]
Her long black hair danced round her like a snake
Her mouth as sweet as a ripe fig
Her neck is like a stately tower
Her pale robe clinging to the grass seemed like a snake
Her pulses flutter'd like a dove
Her skin was as the bark of birches
Her sweetness halting like a tardy May
Her two white hands like swans on a frozen lake
Her voice cut like a knife
Her voice like mournful bells crying on the wind
Her voice was like the voice the stars had when they sang together
Her voice was rich and vibrant, like the

middle notes of a 'cello

Her words sounding like wavelets on a summer shore

Herding his thoughts as a collie dog herds sheep

Here and there a solitary volume greeted him like a friend in a crowd of strange faces

Here in statue-like repose, an old wrinkled mountain rose

Hers was the loveliness of some tall white lily cut in marble, splendid but chill

His bashfulness melted like a spring frost

His brow bent like a cliff o'er his thoughts

His cheeks were furrowed and writhen like rain-washed crags [writhen = twisted]

His eyes blazed like deep forests

His eyes glowed like blue coals

His eyes were hollows of madness, his hair like moldy hay

His face burnt like a brand

His face was glad as dawn to me

His face was often lit up by a smile like pale wintry sunshine

His fingers were knotted like a cord

His formal kiss fell chill as a flake of snow on the cheek

His fortune melted away like snow in a thaw

His glorious moments were strung like pearls upon a string

His indifference fell from him like a garment

His invectives and vituperations bite and flay like steel whips [invective = abusive language] [vituperation = abusive language]

His mind murmurs like a harp among the trees

His mind was like a lonely wild

His mind was like a summer sky

His nerves thrilled like throbbing violins

His retort was like a knife-cut across the sinews

His revenge descends perfect, sudden, like a curse from heaven

His spirits sank like a stone

His talk is like an incessant play of fireworks

His voice is as the thin faint song when the wind wearily sighs in the grass

His voice rose like a stream of rich distilled perfumes

His voice was like the clap of thunder which interrupts the warbling birds among the leaves

His whole soul wavered and shook like a wind-swept leaf

His words gave a curious satisfaction, as when a coin, tested, rings true gold

Hopeful as the break of day

How like a saint she sleeps

How like a winter hath my absence been

How like the sky she bends over her child

Howling in the wilderness like beasts

Huge as a hippopotamus

Humming-birds like lake of purple fire

Hushed as the grave

Hushed like a breathless lyre

I

I had grown pure as the dawn and the dew

I have heard the Hiddon People like the hum of swarming bees

I have seen the ravens flying, like banners of old wars

I saw a face bloom like a flower

I saw a river of men marching like a tide

I saw his senses swim dizzy as clouds

I wander'd lonely as a cloud

I was as sensitive as a barometer

I was no more than a straw on the torrent of his will

I will face thy wrath though it bite as a sword

Ideas which spread with the speed of

light
Idle hopes, like empty shadows
Impassive as a statue
Impatient as the wind
Impregnable as Gibraltar
Impressive as a warrant of arrest for high treason
Incredible little white teeth, like snow shut in a rose
Infrequent carriages sped like mechanical toys guided by manikins
In honor spotless as unfallen snow
In that head of his a flame burnt that was like an altar-fire
In yonder cottage shines a light, far-gleaming like a gem
Instantly she revived like flowers in water
Intangible as a dream
It came and faded like a wreath of mist at eve
It cuts like knives, this air so chill

It drops away like water from a smooth statue
It pealed through her brain like a muffled bell
It poured upon her like a trembling flood
It racked his ears like an explosion of steam-whistles
It ran as clear as a trout-brook
It seems as motionless and still as the zenith in the skies
It set his memories humming like a hive of bees
It staggered the eye, like the sight of water running up hill
It stung like a frozen lash
It was as futile as to oppose an earthquake with argument
It was as if a door had been opened into a furnace, so the eyes blazed
It would collapse as if by enchantment
Its temples and its palaces did seem like fabrics of enchantment piled to Heaven

## J
Jealousy, fierce as the fires

## K
Kindle like an angel's wings the western skies in flame
Kindly mornings when autumn and

winter seemed to go hand in hand like a happy aged couple
Kingdoms melt away like snow

## L
Laboring like a giant
Languid streams that cross softly, slowly, with a sound like smothered weeping
Laughter like a beautiful bubble from the rosebud of baby-hood
Laughter like the sudden outburst of the glad bird in the tree-top
Lazy merchantmen that crawled like flies over the blue enamel of the sea
Leapt like a hunted stag
Let his frolic fancy play, like a happy child
Let in confusion like a whirling flood
Let thy mouth murmur like the doves
Life had been arrested, as the horologist,

with interjected finger, arrests the beating of the clock [horologist = one who repairs watches]
Life stretched before him alluring and various as the open road
Life sweet as perfume and pure as prayer
Light as a snowflake
Lights gleamed there like stars in a still sky
Like a ball of ice it glittered in a frozen sea of sky
Like a blade sent home to its scabbard
Like a blast from a horn
Like a blast from the suddenly opened door of a furnace

Like a blossom blown before a breeze, a white moon drifts before a shimmering sky
Like a bright window in a distant view
Like a caged lion shaking the bars of his prison
Like a calm flock of silver-fleeced sheep
Like a cloud of fire
Like a cold wind his words went through their flesh
Like a crowd of frightened porpoises a shoal of sharks pursue
Like a damp-handed auctioneer
Like a deaf and dumb man wondering what it was all about
Like a dew-drop, ill-fitted to sustain unkindly shocks
Like a dipping swallow the stout ship dashed through the storm
Like a distant star glimmering steadily in the darkness
Like a dream she vanished
Like a festooned girdle encircling the waist of a bride
Like a flower her red lips parted
Like a game in which the important part is to keep from laughing
Like a glow-worm golden
Like a golden-shielded army
Like a great express train, roaring, flashing, dashing head-long
Like a great fragment of the dawn it lay
Like a great ring of pure and endless light
Like a great tune to which the planets roll
Like a high and radiant ocean
Like a high-born maiden
Like a jewel every cottage casement showed
Like a joyless eye that finds no object worth its constancy
Like a knight worn out by conflict
Like a knot of daisies lay the hamlets on the hill
Like a lily in bloom
Like a living meteor

Like a locomotive-engine with unsound lungs
Like a long arrow through the dark the train is darting
Like a mirage, vague, dimly seen at first
Like a miser who spoils his coat with scanting a little cloth [scanting = short]
Like a mist the music drifted from the silvery strings
Like a moral lighthouse in the midst of a dark and troubled sea
Like a murmur of the wind came a gentle sound of stillness
Like a noisy argument in a drawing-room
Like a pageant of the Golden Year, in rich memorial pomp the hours go by
Like a pale flower by some sad maiden cherished
Like a poet hidden
Like a river of molten amethyst
Like a rocket discharging a shower of golden stars
Like a rose embower'd in its own green leaves
Like a sea of upturned faces
Like a shadow never to be overtaken
Like a shadow on a fair sunlit landscape
Like a sheeted ghost
Like a ship tossed to and fro on the waves of life's sea
Like a slim bronze statue of Despair
Like a snow-flake lost in the ocean
Like a soul that wavers in the Valley of the Shadow
Like a stalled horse that breaks loose and goes at a gallop through the plain
Like a star, his love's pure face looked down
Like a star that dwelt apart
Like a star, unhasting, unresting
Like a stone thrown at random
Like a summer cloud, youth indeed has crept away
Like a summer-dried fountain
Like a swift eagle in the morning glare breasting the whirlwind with impetuous

flight
Like a thing at rest
Like a thing read in a book or
remembered out of the faraway past
Like a tide of triumph through their
veins, the red, rejoicing blood began to
race
Like a triumphing fire the news was
borne
Like a troop of boys let loose from school,
the adventurers went by
Like a vaporous amethyst
Like a vision of the morning air
Like a voice from the unknown regions
Like a wandering star I fell through the
deeps of desire
Like a watch-worn and weary sentinel
Like a wave of the sea driven with the
wind and tossed
Like a whirlwind they went past
Like a withered leaf the moon is blown
across the bay
Like a world of sunshine
Like a yellow silken scarf the thick fog
hangs
Like an alien ghost I stole away
Like an eagle clutching his prey, his arm
swooped down
Like an eagle dallying with the wind
Like an engine of dread war, he set his
shoulder to the mountain-side
Like an enraged tiger
Like an enthusiast leading about with
him an indifferent tourist
Like an icy wave, a swift and tragic
impression swept through him
Like an unbidden guest
Like an unbodied joy whose race is just
begun
Like an unseen star of birth
Like an unwelcome thought
Like apparitions seen and gone
Like attempting to number the waves on
the snore of a limitless sea
Like bells that waste the moments with
their loudness
Like blasts of trumpets blown in wars

Like bright Apollo
Like bright lamps, the fabled apples glow
Like building castles in the air
Like bursting waves from the ocean
Like cliffs which have been rent asunder
Like clouds of gnats with perfect
lineaments [lineaments = distinctive
shape]
Like cobwebs woven round the limbs of
an infant giant
Like crystals of snow
Like dead lovers who died true
Like Death, who rides upon a thought,
and makes his way through temple,
tower, and palace
Like dew upon a sleeping flower
Like dining with a ghost
Like drawing nectar in a sieve
Like earth's decaying leaves
Like echoes from a hidden lyre
Like echoes from an antenatal dream
Like fixed eyes, whence the dear light of
sense and thought has fled
Like footsteps upon wool
Like fragrance from dead flowers
Like ghosts, from an enchanter fleeing
Like ghosts the sentries come and go
Like golden boats on a sunny sea
Like great black birds, the demons haunt
the woods
Like green waves on the sea
Like having to taste a hundred exquisite
dishes in a single meal
Like Heaven's free breath, which he who
grasps can hold not
Like helpless birds in the warm nest
Like iridescent bubbles floating on a foul
stream
Like kindred drops mingled into one
Like laying a burden on the back of a
moth
Like lead his feet were
Like leaves in wintry weather
Like leviathans afloat
Like lighting a candle to the sun
Like making a mountain out of a mole-
hill

Like mariners pulling the life-boat
Like mice that steal in and out as if they feared the light
Like mountain over mountain huddled
Like mountain streams we meet and part
Like music on the water
Like notes which die when born, but still haunt the echoes of the hill
Like oceans of liquid silver
Like one pale star against the dusk, a single diamond on her brow gleamed with imprisoned fire
Like one who halts with tired wings
Like one who talks of what he loves in dream
Like organ music came the deep reply
Like pageantry of mist on an autumnal stream
Like phantoms gathered by the sick imagination
Like planets in the sky
Like pouring oil on troubled waters
Like roses that in deserts bloom and die
Like rowing upstream against a strong downward current
Like scents from a twilight garden
Like separated souls
Like serpents struggling in a vulture's grasp
Like sheep from out the fold of the sky, stars leapt
Like ships that have gone down at sea
Like shy elves hiding from the traveler's eye
Like skeletons, the sycamores uplift their wasted hands
Like some grave night thought threading a dream
Like some new-gathered snowy hyacinth, so white and cold and delicate it was
Like some poor nigh-related guest, that may not rudely be dismist
Like some suppressed and hideous thought which flits athwart our musings, but can find no rest within a pure and gentle mind

Like some unshriven churchyard thing, the friar crawled
Like something fashioned in a dream
Like sounds of wind and flood
Like splendor-winged moths about a taper
Like stepping out on summer evenings from the glaring ball-room upon the cool and still piazza
Like straws in a gust of wind
Like summer's beam and summer's stream
Like sunlight, in and out the leaves, the robins went
Like sweet thoughts in a dream
Like the awful shadow of some unseen power
Like the bellowing of bulls
Like the boar encircled by hunters and hounds
Like the bubbles on a river sparkling, bursting, borne away
Like the cold breath of the grave
Like the creaking of doors held stealthily ajar
Like the cry of an itinerant vendor in a quiet and picturesque town
Like the dance of some gay sunbeam
Like the dawn of the morn
Like the detestable and spidery araucaria [araucaria = evergreen trees of South America and Australia]
Like the dew on the mountain
Like the dim scent in violets
Like the drifting foam of a restless sea when the waves show their teeth in the flying breeze
Like the embodiment of a perfect rose, complete in form and fragrance
Like the faint cry of unassisted woe
Like the faint exquisite music of a dream
Like the fair flower dishevel'd in the wind
Like the fair sun, when in his fresh array he cheers the morn, and all the earth revealeth
Like the falling thud of the blade of a

murderous ax
Like the fierce fiend of a distempered dream
Like the fitting of an old glove to a hand
Like the foam on the river
Like the great thunder sounding
Like the jangling of all the strings of some musical instrument
Like the jewels that gleam in baby eyes
Like the kiss of maiden love the breeze is sweet and bland
Like the long wandering love, the weary heart may faint for rest
Like the moon in water seen by night
Like the music in the patter of small feet
Like the prodigal whom wealth softens into imbecility
Like the quivering image of a landscape in a flowing stream
Like the rainbow, thou didst fade
Like the rustling of grain moved by the west-wind
Like the sap that turns to nectar, in the velvet of the peach
Like the sea whose waves are set in motion by the winds
Like the sea-worm, that perforates the shell of the mussel, which straightway closes the wound with a pearl
Like the setting of a tropical sun
Like the shadow of a great hill that reaches far out over the plain
Like the shadows of the stars in the upheaved sea
Like the shudder of a doomed soul
Like the silver gleam when the poplar trees rustle their pale leaves listlessly
Like the soft light of an autumnal day
Like the Spring-time, fresh and green
Like the stern-lights of a ship at sea, illuminating only the path which has been passed over
Like the sudden impulse of a madman
Like the swell of Summer's ocean
Like the tattered effigy in a cornfield
Like the vase in which roses have once been distill'd

Like the visits of angels, short and far between
Like the whole sky when to the east the morning doth return
Like thistles of the wilderness, fit neither for food nor fuel
Like those great rivers, whose course everyone beholds, but their springs have been seen by but few
Like thoughts whose very sweetness yielded proof that they were born for immortality
Like to diamonds her white teeth shone between the parted lips
Like torrents from a mountain source, we rushed into each other's arms
Like troops of ghosts on the dry wind past
Like two doves with silvery wings, let our souls fly
Like two flaming stars were his eyes
Like vaporous shapes half seen
Like village curs that bark when their fellows do
Like wasted hours of youth
Like winds that bear sweet music, when they breathe through some dim latticed chamber
Like wine-stain to a flask the old distrust still clings
Like winged stars the fire-flies flash and glance
Like young lovers whom youth and love make dear
Lingering like an unloved guest
Lithe as a panther
Little white hands like pearls
Lofty as a queen
Loneliness struck him like a blow
Looked back with faithful eyes like a great mastiff to his master's face
Looking as sulky as the weather itself
Looking like a snarling beast baulked of its prey [baulked = checked, thwarted]
Loose clouds like earth's decaying leaves are shed
Lost like the lightning in the sullen clod

Love as clean as starlight
Love brilliant as the morning
Love had like the canker-worm consumed her early prime
Love is a changing lord as the light on a turning sword
Love like a child around the world doth run

Love like a miser in the dark his joys would hide
Love shakes like a windy reed your heart
Love smiled like an unclouded sun
Love that sings and has wings as a bird
Lovely as starry water
Lovely the land unknown and like a river flowing

## M

March on my soul nor like the laggard stay
Me on whose heart as a worm she trod
Meaningless as the syllables of an unknown tongue
Men moved hither and thither like insects in their crevices
Mentality as hard as bronze
Mentally round-shouldered and decrepit
Merge imperceptibly into one another like the hues of the prism
Meteors that dart like screaming birds
Milk-white pavements, clear and richly pale, like alabaster
More variegated than the skin of a serpent
Motion like the spirit of that wind whose soft step deepens slumber
Motionless as a plumb line
Mountains like frozen wrinkles on a sea
Moving in the same dull round, like blind horses in a mill
Mute as an iceberg
My age is as a lusty Winter
My body broken as a turning wheel
My breath to Heaven like vapor goes
My head was like a great bronze bell

with one thought for the clapper
My heart is as some famine-murdered land
My heart is like a full sponge and must weep a little
My heart like a bird doth hover
My heart will be as wind fainting in hot grass
My life floweth away like a river
My life was white as driven snow
My love for thee is like the sovereign moon that rules the sea
My love's like the steadfast sun
My lungs began to crow like chanticleer [chanticleer = rooster]
My mind swayed idly like a water-lily in a lake
My muscles are as steel
My skin is as sallow as gold
My soul was as a lampless sea
My spirit seemed to beat the void, like the bird from out the ark
My thoughts came yapping and growling round me like a pack of curs
My thoughts ran leaping through the green ways of my mind like fawns at play

## N

Night falls like fire
No longer shall slander's venomed spite crawl like a snake across his perfect name
Now every nerve in my body seemed like a strained harp-string ready to snap at a touch
Now like a wild nymph she veils her

shadowy form
Now like a wild rose in the fields of heaven slipt forth the slender figure of the Dawn
Now memory and emotion surged in my soul like a tempest
Now thou seemest like a bankrupt beau, stripped of his gaudy hues

153

## O

Obscured with wrath as is the sun with cloud
Odorous as all Arabia
Often enough life tosses like a fretful stream among rocky boulders
Oh, lift me as a wave, a leaf, a cloud
Old as the evening star
Old happy hours that have long folded their wings
Once again, like madness, the black shapes of doubt swing through his brain
One bleared star, faint glimmering like a bee
One bright drop is like the gem that decks a monarch's crown
One by one flitting like a mournful bird

One deep roar as of a cloven world
One winged cloud above like a spread dragon overhangs the west
Oppressed by the indefiniteness which hung in her mind, like a thick summer haze
Or shedding radiance like the smiles of God
Our enemies were broken like a dam of river reeds
Our hearts bowed down like violets after rain
Our sail like a dew-lit blossom shone
Overhead the intense blue of the noonday sky burst like a jewel in the sun

## P

Pale and grave as a sculptured nun
Pale as a drifting blossom
Passed like a phantom into the shadows
Passive and tractable as a child
Peaceful as a village cricket-green on Sunday
Peevish and impatient, like some ill-trained man who is sick
Perished utterly, like a blown-out flame
Philosophy evolved itself, like a vast spider's loom
Pillowed upon its alabaster arms like to a child o'erwearied with sweet toil
Polished as the bosom of a star
Poured his heart out like the rending sea in passionate wave on wave

Pouting like the snowy buds o' roses in July
Presently she hovered like a fluttering leaf or flake of snow
Pride and self-disgust served her like first-aid surgeons on the battlefield
Proud as the proudest of church dignitaries
Pure as a wild-flower
Pure as the azure above them
Pure as the naked heavens
Pure as the snowy leaves that fold over the flower's heart
Purple, crimson, and scarlet, like the curtains of God's tabernacle
Put on gravity like a robe

## Q

Quaking and quivering like a short-haired puppy after a ducking
Questions and answers sounding like a continuous popping of corks
Quiet as a nun's face

Quietly as a cloud he stole
Quietude which seemed to him beautiful as clear depths of water
Quivering like an eager race-horse to start

## R

Rage, rage ye tears, that never more should creep like hounds about God's footstool

Ran like a young fawn
Rattle in the ear like a flourish of trumpets

Rays springing from the east like golden arrows
Red as the print of a kiss might be
Redolent with the homely scent of old-fashioned herbs and flowers
Reflected each in the other like stars in a lake
Refreshed like dusty grass after a shower
Refreshing as descending rains to sunburnt climes
Remote as the hidden star
Restless as a blue-bottle fly on a warm summer's day
Revealed his doings like those of bees in a glass hive
Rich as the dawn
Ride like the wind through the night

Rivers that like silver threads ran through the green and gold of pasture lands
Roared like mountain torrents
Rolling it under the tongue as a sweet morsel
Round my chair the children run like little things of dancing gold
Ruddy as sunrise
Ruddy his face as the morning light
Ruffling out his cravat with a crackle of starch, like a turkey when it spreads its feathers
Running to and fro like frightened sheep
Rushing and hurrying about like a June-bug

## S

Sanctuaries where the passions may, like wild falcons, cover their faces with their wings
Sayings that stir the blood like the sound of a trumpet
Scattered love as stars do light
Sea-gulls flying like flakes of the sea
Sentences level and straight like a hurled lance
Shadowy faces, known in dreams, pass as petals upon a stream
Shake like an aspen leaf
Shaken off like a nightmare
Shapeless as a sack of wool
Shattered like so much glass
She brightened like a child whose broken toy is glued together
She could summon tears as one summons servants
She danced like a flower in the wind
She disclaimed the weariness that dragged upon her spirits like leaden weights
She exuded a faint and intoxicating perfume of womanliness, like a crushed herb
She felt like an unrepentant criminal
She fled like a spirit from the room

She flounders like a huge conger-eel in an ocean of dingy morality
She gave him a surprised look, like a child catching an older person in a foolish statement
She gave off antipathies as a liquid gives off vapor
She has great eyes like the doe
She heard him like one in a dream
She let the soft waves of her deep hair fall like flowers from Paradise
She looked like a tall golden candle
She looked like the picture of a young rapt saint, lost in heavenly musing
She moved like mirth incarnate
She nestles like a dove
She played with a hundred possibilities fitfully and discursively as a musician runs his fingers over a key-board
She played with grave cabinets as a cat plays with a mouse
She saw this planet like a star hung in the glistening depths of even
She seemed as happy as a wave that dances on the sea
She shall be sportive as the fawn
She stood silent a moment, dropping before him like a broken branch

She that passed had lips like pinks
She walked like a galley-slave
She walks in beauty like the night
She was as brilliant, and as hard too, as electric light
She was silent, standing before him like a little statuesque figure
Shining like the dewy star of dawn
Shivering pine-trees, like phantoms
Showy as damask-rose and shy as musk
Shrill as the loon's call
Shrivel like paper thrust into a flame
Shy as the squirrel
Sights seen as a traveling swallow might see them on the wing
Silence deep as death
Silence now is brooding like a gentle spirit o'er the still and pulseless world
Silence that seemed heavy and dark; like a passing cloud
Sinks clamorous like mill-waters at wild play
Sits like the maniac on his fancied throne
Skies as clear as babies' eyes
Sleek and thick and yellow as gold
Slender and thin as a slender wire
Slowly as a tortoise
Slowly as the finger of a clock, her shadow came
Slowly moved off and disappeared like shapes breathed on a mirror and melting away
Slowly, unnoted, like the creeping rust that spreads insidious, had estrangement come
Small as a grain of mustard seed
Smooth as a pond
Smooth as the pillar flashing in the sun
Snug as a bug in a rug
Soaring as swift as smoke from a volcano springs
So elusive that the memory of it afterwards was wont to come and go like a flash of light
So my spirit beat itself like a caged bird against its prison bars in vain
Soft as a zephyr

Soft as sleep the snow fell
Soft as Spring
Soft as the down of the turtle dove
Soft as the landscape of a dream
Soft as the south-wind
Soft in their color as gray pearls
Soft vibrations of verbal melody, like the sound of a golden bell rung far down under the humming waters
Some gleams of feeling pure and warm as sunshine on a sky of storm
Some like veiled ghosts hurrying past as though driven to their land of shadows by shuddering fear
Some minds are like an open fire--how direct and instant our communication with them
Something divine seemed to cling around her like some subtle vapor
Something resistant and inert, like the obstinate rolling over of a heavy sleeper after he has been called to get up
Something sharp and brilliant, like the glitter of a sword or a forked flash of lightning
Sorrowful eyes like those of wearied kine spent from the plowing [kine = cows]
Spread like wildfire
Squirrel-in-the-cage kind of movement
Stamping like a plowman to shuffle off the snow
Stared about like calves in a pen
Steadfast as the soul of truth
Steals lingering like a river smooth
Still as death
Stood like a wave-beaten rock
Straight as a ray of light
Straight as an arrow
Streamed like a meteor through the troubled air
Streamed o'er his memory like a forest flame
Streaming tears, like pearl drops from a flint
Striking with the force of an engine of destruction
Strong as a bison

Style comes, if at all, like the bloom upon fruit, or the glow of health upon the cheek
Subtle as jealousy
Sudden a thought came like a full-blown rose, flushing his brow
Sudden sprays of rain, like volleys of sharp arrows, rattled gustily against the windows
Suddenly, like death, the truth flashed on them
Sunbeams flashing on the face of things like sudden smilings of divine delight
Sunday mornings which seem to put on,

T

Talking and thinking became to him like the open page of a monthly magazine
Tall lance-like reeds wave sadly o'er his head
That like a wounded snake drags its slow length along
The anemone that weeps at day-break, like a silly girl before her lover
The army blazed and glowed in the golden sunlight like a mosaic of a hundred thousand jewels
The army like a witch's caldron seethed
The beating of her heart was like a drum
The beauty of her quiet life was like a rose in blowing
The billows burst like cannon down the coast
The birds swam the flood of air like tiny ships
The boat cuts its swift way through little waves like molten gold and opal
The boom of the surf grew ever less sonorous, like the thunder of a retreating storm
The breast-plate of righteousness
The breathless hours like phantoms stole away
The breeze is as a pleasant tune
The calm white brow as calm as earliest morn
The camp fire reddens like angry skies

like a Sabbath garment, an atmosphere of divine quietude
Supple and sweet as a rose in bloom
Sway like blown moths against the rosewhite flame
Sweet as a summer night without a breath
Sweet as music she spoke
Sweet as the rain at noon
Sweet as the smile of a fairy
Swift as a swallow heading south
Swift as lightning
Swift as the panther in triumph
Swifter than the twinkling of an eye

The chambers of the house were haunted by an incessant echoing, like some dripping cavern
The church swarmed like a hive
The city is all in a turmoil; it boils like a pot of lentils
The clouds that move like spirits o'er the welkin clear [welkin = sky]
The clustered apples burnt like flame
The colored bulbs swung noon-like from tree and shrub
The crimson close of day
The curl'd moon was like a little feather
The curling wreaths like turbans seem
The dark hours are swept away like crumbling ashes
The dark mass of her hair shook round her like a sea
The dawn is rising from the sea, like a white lady from her bed
The dawn had whitened in the mist like a dead face
The dawn with silver-sandaled feet crept like a frightened girl.
The day stunned me like light upon some wizard way
The day was sweeter than honey and the honey-comb
The day have trampled me like armed men
The dead past flew away over the fens

like a flight of wild swans

The deep like one black maelstrom
round her whirls

The deepening east like a scarlet poppy
burnt

The desolate rocky hills rolled like a solid
wave along the horizon

The dome of heaven is like one drop of
dew

The dreams of poets come like music
heard at evening from the depth of some
enchanted forest

The eagerness faded from his eyes,
leaving them cold as a winter sky after
sunset

The earth was like a frying-pan, or some
such hissing matter

The eternal sea, which like a childless
mother, still must croon her ancient
sorrows to the cold white moon

The evening sky was as green as jade

The excitement had spread through the
whole house, like a piquant and
agreeable odor

The excitement of the thought buoyed
his high-strung temperament like a tonic

The feathery meadows like a lilac sea

The firm body like a slope of snow

The first whiff of reality dissipated them
like smoke

The floor, newly waxed, gleamed in the
candle-light like beaten moonbeams

The fragrant clouds of hair, they flowed
round him like a snare

The gathering glory of life shone like the
dawn

The gesture was all strength and will,
like the stretching of a sea-bird's wings

The girl's voice rang like a bird-call
through his rustling fancies

The glimmer of tall flowers standing like
pensive moon-worshipers in an ecstasy
of prayerless bloom

The guides sniffed, like chamois, the air
[chamois = extremely agile goat
antelope]

The heavens are like a scroll unfurled

The hills across the valley were purple as
thunder-clouds

The hoofs of the horses rang like the
dumb cadence of an old saga

The hours crawled by like years

The hum of the camp sounds like the sea

The hurrying crowds of men gather like
clouds

The ideas succeeded each other like a
dynasty of kings

The impalpable presence of the new
century rose like a vast empty house
through which
no human feet had walked

The inexorable facts closed in on him
like prison-warders hand-cuffing a
convict

The lake glimmered as still as a mirror

The land of gold seemed to hold him like
a spell

The land was like a dream

The level boughs, like bars of iron across
the setting sun

The light of London flaring like a dreary
dawn

The lights blazed up like day

The lilies were drooping, white, and
wan, like the head and skin of a dying
man

The mellowing hand of time

The melody rose tenderly and lingeringly
like a haunting perfume of pressed
flowers

The Milky Way lay like diamond-dust
upon the robe of some great king

The monk's face whitened like sea-foam

The moon drowsed between the trees
like a great yellow moth

The moon on the tower slept soft as snow

The moonbeams rest like a pale spotless
shroud

The moonlight lay like snow

The moonlight, like a fairy mist, upon
the mesa spreads

The mortal coldness of the soul, like
death itself comes down

The mountain shadows mingling, lay like

pools above the earth
The mountains loomed up dimly, like phantoms through the mist
The music almost died away, then it burst like a pent-up flood
The name that cuts into my soul like a knife
The nervous little train winding its way like a jointed reptile
The new ferns were spread upon the earth like some lacy coverlet
The night like a battle-broken host is driven before
The night yawned like a foul wind
The ocean swelled like an undulating mirror of the bowl of heaven
The old books look somewhat pathetically from the shelves, like aged dogs wondering why no one takes them for a walk
The old infamy will pop into daylight like a toad out of fissure in the rock
The penalty falls like a thunderbolt from heaven
The phrase was like a spear-thrust
The pine trees waved as waves a woman's hair
The place was like some enchanted town of palaces
The plains to northward change their color like the shimmering necks of doves
The poppy burned like a crimson ember
The prime of man has waxed like cedars
The public press would chatter and make odd ambiguous sounds like a shipload of monkeys in a storm
The purple heather rolls like dumb thunder
The rainbows flashed like fire
The river shouted as ever its cry of joy over the vitality of life, like a spirited boy before the face of inscrutable nature
The roofs with their gables like hoods
The roses lie upon the grass like little shreds of crimson silk
The satire of the word cut like a knife
The scullion with face shining like his

pans
The sea reeled round like a wine-vat splashing
The sea-song of the trampling waves is as muffled bells
The sea spread out like a wrinkled marble floor
The sea, that gleamed still, like a myriad-petaled rose
The sea was as untroubled as the turquoise vault which it reflected
The setting of the sun is like a word of peace
The sharp hail rattles against the panes and melts on my cheeks like tears
The ships, like sheeted phantoms coming and going
The silence seemed to crush to earth like a great looking-glass and shiver into a million pieces
The silvery morning like a tranquil vision fills the world
The sky burned like a heated opal
The sky gleamed with the hardness and brilliancy of blue enamel
The sky was as a shield that caught the stain of blood and battle from the dying sun
The sky was clear and blue, and the air as soft as milk
The sky was like a peach
The sky where stars like lilies white and fair shine through the mists
The solid air around me there heaved like a roaring ocean
The solid mountains gleamed like the unsteady sea
The soul is like a well of water springing up into everlasting life
The sound is like a noon-day gale
The sound is like a silver-fountain that springeth in a golden basin
The sound of a thousand tears, like softly pattering wings
The sound of your running feet that like the sea-hoofs beat
The spear-tongued lightning slipped like

159

a snake
The Spring breaks like a bird
The stacks of corn in brown array, like
tattered wigwams on the plain
The stars come down and trembling
glow like blossoms on the waves below
The stars lay on the lapis-lazuli sky like
white flower-petals on still deep water
[lapis-lazuli = opaque to translucent
blue, violet-blue, or greenish-blue
gemstone]
The stars pale and silent as a seer
The strange cold sense of aloofness that
had numbed her senses suddenly gave
way like snow melting in the spring
The sudden thought of your face is like a
wound when it comes unsought
The sun, like a great dragon, writhes in
gold
The sun on the sea-wave lies white as the
moon
The surf was like the advancing lines of
an unknown enemy flinging itself upon
the shore
The terrible past lay afar, like a dream
left behind in the night
The tide was in the salt-weed, and like a
knife it tore
The time, gliding like a dream
The torrent from the hills leaped down
their rocky stairways like wild steeds
The tree whose plumed boughs are soft
as wings of birds
The uproar and contention pierced him
like arrows
The veiled future bowed before me like a
vision of promise
The velvet grass that is like padding to
earth's meager ribs
The villa dips its foot in the lake, smiling
at its reflection like a bather lingering on
the brink
The voice of Fate, crying like some old
Bellman through the world
The voice that rang in the night like a
bugle call
The warm kindling blood burned her

cheeks like the breath of a hot wind
The waves were rolling in, long and lazy,
like sea-worn travelers
The whole truth, naked, cold, and fatal
as a patriot's blade
The wind all round their ears hissed like
a flight of white-winged geese
The wind comes and it draws its length
along like the genii from the earthen pot
The wine flows like blood
The woman seemed like a thing of stone
The words kept ringing in my ears like
the tolling of a bell
The words of the wise fall like the tolling
of sweet, grave bells upon the soul
The world had vanished like a
phantasmagoria
The world is bitter as a tear
The world is in a simmer, like a sea
The world wavers within its circle like a
dream
The years stretched before her like some
vast blank page out to receive the record
of her toil
The years vanished like a May snowdrift
The yellow apples glowed like fire
Their glances met like crossed swords
Their joy like sunshine deep and broad
falls on my heart
Their minds rested upon the thought, as
chasing butterflies might rest together on
a flower
Their music frightful as the serpent's hiss
Their touch affrights me as a serpent's
sting
Then fall unheeded like the faded flower
Then felt I like some watcher of the skies
Then it swelled out to rich and glorious
harmonies like a full orchestra playing
under the sea
Then the lover sighing like furnace
Theories sprouted in his mind like
mushrooms
There is an air about you like the air that
folds a star
There, like a bird, it sits and sings
There seemed to brood in the air a quiet

benevolence of a Father watching His myriad children at play

There she soars like a seraph

There she stood straight as a lily on its stem

There slowly rose to sight, a country like a dragon fast asleep

There streamed into the air the sweet smell of crushed grass, as though many fields had been pressed between giant's fingers and so had been left

These eyes like stars have led me

These final words snapped like a whip-lash

These thoughts pierced me like thorns

They are as cruel as creeping tigers

They are as white foam on the swept sands

They are as white swans in the dusk, thy white hands

They are painted sharp as death

They broke into pieces and fell on the ground, like a silvery, shimmering shower of hail

They dropped like panthers

They fly like spray

They had hands like claws

They had slipped away like visions

They have as many principles as a fish has bones

They have faces like flowers

They hurried down like plovers that have heard the call [plovers = wading birds]

They look like rose-buds filled with snow

They seem like swarming flies, the crowd of little men

They seemed like floating flowers

They shine as sweet as simple doves

They stand like solitary mountain forms on some hard, perfectly transparent day

They vanished like the shapes that float upon a summer's dream

Thick as wind-blown leaves innumerable

Thickly the flakes drive past, each like a childish ghost

Thine eyes like two twin stars shining

This life is like a bubble blown up in the air

This love that dwells like moonlight in your face

This thought is as death

This tower rose in the sunset like a prayer

Those ancestral themes past which so many generations have slept like sea-going winds over pastures

Those death-like eyes, unconscious of the sun

Those eyelids folded like a white rose-leaf

Those eyes like bridal beacons shine

Thou art to me but as a wave of the wild sea

Thou as heaven art fair and young

Thou hadst a voice whose sound was like the sea

Thou must wither like a rose

Thou shalt be as free as mountain winds

Thou wouldst weep tears bitter as blood

Though bright as silver the meridian beams shine

Though thou be black as night

Thoughts vague as the fitful breeze

Three-cornered notes fly about like butterflies

Through the forest, like a fairy dream through some dark mind, the ferns in branching beauty stream

Through the moonlit trees, like ghosts of sounds haunting the moonlight, stole the faint tinkle of a guitar

Through the riot of his senses, like a silver blaze, ran the legend

Thy beauty like a beast it bites

Thy brown benignant eyes have sudden gleams of gladness and surprise, like woodland brooks that cross a sunlit spot

Thy carven columns must have grown by magic, like a dream in stone

Thy favors are but like the wind that kisses everything it meets

Thy heart is light as a leaf of a tree

Thy name burns like a gray and flickering candle flame

Thy name will be as honey on men's lips
Till death like sleep might steal on me
Till he melted like a cloud in the silent
summer heaven
Time drops in decay, like a candle burnt
out
Time like a pulse shakes fierce
To drag life on, which like a heavy chain
lengthens behind with many a link of
pain
To forsake as the trees drop their leaves
in autumn

Toys with smooth trifles like a child at
play
Transitory as clouds without substance
Transparent like a shining sun
Tree and shrub altered their values and
became transmuted to silver sentinels
Trees that spread their forked boughs
like a stag's antlers
Trembling like an aspen-leaf
Truths which forever shine as fixed stars
Turning easily and securely as on a
perfect axle

## U

Unbends like a loosened bow
Unbreakable as iron
Unconscious as an oak-tree of its growth
Under the willow-tree glimmered her
face like a foam-flake drifting over the
sea
Unheralded, like some tornado loosed
out of the brooding hills, it came to pass
Unknown, like a seed in fallow ground,
was the germ of a plan
Unmoving as a tombstone

Untameable as flies
Unutterable things pressing on my soul
like a pent-up storm craving for outlet
Upcast like foam of the effacing tide
Uplifting the soul as on dovelike wings
Uplifting their stony peaks around us
like the walls and turrets of a gigantic
fortress
Urgent as the seas
Uttering wild cries like a creature in
pain

## V

Vague as a dream
Vague thoughts that stream shapelessly
through her mind like long sad vapors
through the twilight sky
Vanish into thin air, like ghosts at the
cockcrow

Vanished like snow when comes a thaw
Vanished like vapor before the sun
Vibrations set quivering like harp strings
struck by the hand of a master
Vociferous praise following like a noisy
wave

## W

Walking somewhat unsteadily like a
blind man feeling his way
Waves glittered and danced on all sides
like millions of diamonds
We left her and retraced our steps like
faithless hounds
Weak and frail like the vapor of a vale
Wearing their wounds like stars
Weary wind, who wanderest like the
world's rejected guest
When a draft might puff them out like a
guttering candle [guttering = To melt

through the side of the hollow in a
candle formed by a burning wick; to
burn low and unsteadily; flicker]
When arm in arm they both came swiftly
running, like a pair of turtle-doves that
could not live asunder day or night
When cards, invitations, and three-
corn'd notes fly about like white
butterflies
When she died, her breath whistled like
the wind in a keyhole
When the fever pierced me like a knife

Where a lamp of deathless beauty shines like a beacon
Where heroes die as leaves fall
Where the intricate wheels of trade are grinding on, like a mill
Where the source of the waters is fine as a thread
Whilst the lagging hours of the day went by like windless clouds o'er a tender sky
Whistled sharply in the air like a handful of vipers
White as a ghost from darkness
White as chalk
White as dove or lily, or spirit of the light
White as the driven snow
White as the moon's white flame
White as the sea-bird's wing
White clouds like daisies
White hands she moves like swimming swans
White hands through her hair, like white doves going into the shadow of a wood
White like flame
White sails of sloops like specters
Whose bodies are as strong as alabaster
Whose hair was as gold raiment on a king
Whose laugh moves like a bat through silent haunted woods
Whose little eyes glow like the sparks of fire
Whose music like a robe of living light reclothed each new-born age
Windy speech which hits all around the

mark like a drunken carpenter
Winged like an arrow to its mark
With a sting like a scorpion
With all the complacency of a homeless cat
With an angry broken roar, like billows on an unseen shore, their fury burst
With hate darkling as the swift winter hail
With music sweet as love
With sounds like breakers
With strength like steel
With the whisper of leaves in one's ear
With words like honey melting from the comb
Wits as sharp as gimlets [gimlet = small hand tool for boring holes]
Women with tongues like polar needles
Words as fresh as spring verdure [verdure = lush greenness of flourishing vegetation]
Words as soft as rain
Words like the gossamer film of the summer
Words sweet as honey from his lips distill'd
Words were flashing like brilliant birds through the boughs overhead
Wordsworth, thy music like a river rolls
Worthless like the conjurer's gold
Wrangle over details like a grasping pawnbroker
Wrinkled and scored like a dried apple
Writhing with an intensity that burnt like a steady flame

Y
Yielding like melted snow
Yonder flimsy crescent, bent like an archer's bow above the snowy summit
You are as gloomy to-night as an undertaker out of employment
You are as hard as stone
You gave me such chill embraces as the snow-covered heights receive from clouds
Your blood is red like wine

Your charms lay like metals in a mine
Your eyes are like fantastic moons that shiver in some stagnant lake
Your eyes as blue as violets
Your eyes they were green and gray like an April day
Your frail fancies are swallowed up, like chance flowers flung upon the river's current
Your hair was golden as tints of sunrise

Your heart is as dry as a reed
Your locks are like the raven
Your love shall fall about me like sweet
rain
Your step's like the rain to summer vexed
farmer
Your thoughts are buzzing like a swarm
of bees
Your tongue is like a scarlet snake
Your voice had a quaver in it just like the
linnet [linnet = small finch]
Youth like a summer morn

# SECTION 9
# CONVERSATIONAL PHRASES

## A

A most extraordinary idea!
A thousand hopes for your success
Accept my best wishes
All that is conjecture
Allow me to congratulate you
An unfortunate comparison, don't you think?
And even if it were so?
And how am I to thank you?
And in the end, what are you going to make of it?
And yet the explanation does not wholly satisfy me

Apparently I was wrong
Are we wandering from the point?
Are you a trifle--bored?
Are you fully reconciled?
Are you not complicating the question?
Are you prepared to go to that length?
Are you still obdurate? [obdurate = Hardened in wrongdoing; stubbornly impenitent]
As it happens, your conjecture is right
Assuredly I do
At first blush it may seem fantastic

## B

Banish such thoughts
But are you not taking a slightly one-sided point of view?
But consider for a moment
But I look at the practical side
But I wander from my point
But now I'll confide something to you
But perhaps I'm hardly fair when I say that
But seriously speaking, what is the use of it?
But surely that is inconsistent

But that's a tremendous hazard
But the thing is simply impossible
But there's one thing you haven't said
But, wait, you haven't heard the end
But what do you yourself think about it?
But who could foresee what was going to happen?
But you are open to persuasion?
But you do not know for certain
But you must tell me more
By a curious chance, I know it very well
By no means desirable, I think

## C

Can I persuade you?
Can you imagine anything so horrible?
Certain circumstances make it undesirable
Certainly not, if it displeases you

Certainly, with the greatest pleasure
Come, where's your sense of humor?
Consult me when you want me--at any time

## D

Decidedly so
Dine with me to-morrow night?--if you are free?
Do I presume too much?
Do I seem very ungenerous?

Do not misunderstand me
Do not the circumstances justify it?
Don't be so dismal, please
Don't delude yourself
Don't let me encroach on your good

nature
Don't think I am unappreciative of your kindness
Do you attach any particular meaning to that?
Do you know, I envy you that
Do you know what his chief interests are now?

E
Either way is perplexing
Eminently proper, I think

F
Fanciful, I should say
For the simplest of reasons
Forgive me if I seem disobliging
Fortunate, to say the least

G
Give me your sympathy and counsel
Glorious to contemplate

H
Happily there are exceptions to every rule
Has it really come to that?
Have I incurred your displeasure?
Have you any rooted objection to it?
Have you anything definite in your mind?
Have you reflected what the consequences might be to yourself?
He does me too much honor
He feels it acutely
He has a queer conception of the proprieties
He is a poor dissembler [dissemble = conceal behind a false appearance]
He is anything but obtuse
He is so ludicrously wrong
He is the most guileless of men
He was so extremely susceptible
He writes uncommonly clever letters
Heaven forbid that I should wound your sensibility

Do you mind my making a suggestion?
Do you press me to tell?
Do you really regard him as a serious antagonist?
Do you think there is anything ominous in it?
Does it please you so tremendously?
Does it seem incredible?

Everyone looks at it differently
Excuse my bluntness

Frankly, I don't see why it should
Frugal to a degree
Fulsome praise, I call it

Good! that is at least something
Gratifying, I am sure

His sense of humor is unquenchable
How amiable you are to say so
How can I tell you how much I have enjoyed it all?
How can I thank you?
How can you be so unjust?
How delightful to meet you
How does the idea appeal to you?
How droll you are!
How extraordinary!
How intensely interesting!
How perfectly delightful!
How utterly abominable
How very agreeable this is!
How very interesting
How very surprising
How well you do it!
However, I should like to hear your views
Human nature interests me very much indeed

166

I

I admire your foresight
I admit it most gratefully
I agree--at least, I suppose I do
I agree that something ought to be done
I always welcome criticism so long as it is sincere
I am absolutely bewildered
I am afraid I am not familiar enough with the subject
I am afraid I cannot suggest an alternative
I am afraid I've allowed you to tire yourself
I am afraid I must confess my ignorance
I am afraid you will call me a sentimentalist
I am always glad to do anything to please you
I am anxious to discharge the very onerous debt I owe you
I am appealing to your sense of humor
I am at your service
I am bound to secrecy
I am compelled to, unluckily
I am curious to learn what his motive was
I am deeply flattered and grateful
I am delighted to hear you say so
I am dumb with admiration
I am entirely at your disposal
I am extremely glad you approve of it
I am far from believing the maxim
I am fortunate in being able to do you a service
I am glad to be able to think that
I am glad to have had this talk with you
I am glad to say that I have entirely lost that faculty
I am glad you can see it in that way
I am glad you feel so deeply about it
I am giving you well-deserved praise
I am going to make a confession
I am grateful for your good opinion
I am honestly indignant
I am, I confess, a little discouraged
I am in a chastened mood

I am inclined to agree with you
I am incredulous
I am indebted to you for the suggestion
I am listening--I was about to propose
I am lost in admiration
I am luckily disengaged to-day
I am more grieved than I can tell you
I am naturally overjoyed
I am not a person of prejudices
I am not an alarmist
I am not as unreasonable as you suppose
I am not at all in the secret of his ambitions
I am not capable of unraveling it
I am not going into sordid details
I am not going to let you evade the question
I am not going to pay you any idle compliments
I am not impervious to the obligations involved
I am not in sympathy with it
I am not in the least surprised
I am not inquisitive
I am not prepared to say
I am not sure that I can manage it
I am not vindictive
I am overjoyed to hear you say so
I am perfectly aware of what I am saying
I am persuaded by your candor
I am quite convinced of that
I am quite discomfited
I am quite interested to see what you will do
I am quite ready to be convinced
I am rather of the opinion that I was mistaken
I am ready to make great allowances
I am really afraid I don't know
I am really gregarious
I am sensible of the flattery
I am seriously annoyed with myself about it
I am so glad you think that
I am so sorry--so very sorry
I am sorry to disillusionize you

I am sorry to interrupt this interesting discussion
I am sorry to say it is impossible
I am speaking plainly
I am still a little of an idealist
I am suppressing many of the details
I am sure it sounds very strange to you
I am sure you could pay me no higher compliment
I am sure you will hear me out
I am surprised, I confess
I am sustained by the prospect of a good dinner
I am vastly obliged to you
I am vastly your debtor for the information
I am very far from being a fanatic
I am very glad of this opportunity
I am very grateful--very much flattered
I am wholly in agreement with you
I am willing to accept all the consequences
I am wonderfully well
I am wondering if I may dare ask you a very personal question?
I am your creditor unawares
I anticipate your argument
I appreciate your motives
I assure you it is most painful to me
I assure you my knowledge of it is limited
I bear no malice about that
I beg your indulgence
I beg your pardon, but you take it too seriously
I brazenly confess it
I can easily understand your astonishment
I can explain the apparent contradiction
I can find no satisfaction in it
I can hardly agree with you there
I can never be sufficiently grateful
I can only tell you the bare facts
I can scarcely accept the offer
I can scarcely boast that honor
I can scarcely imagine anything more disagreeable

I can sympathize with you
I cannot altogether acquit myself of interested motives
I cannot explain it even to myself
I cannot find much real satisfaction in it
I cannot forbear to press my advantage
I cannot imagine what you mean
I cannot precisely determine
I can't pretend to make a jest of what I'm going to say
I cannot say definitely at the moment
I cannot say that in fact it is always so
I cannot see how you draw that conclusion
I cannot thank you enough for all your consideration
I compliment you on your good sense
I confess, I find it difficult
I could ask for nothing better
I could never forgive myself for that
I dare say your intuition is quite right
I decline to commit myself beforehand
I detest exaggeration
I didn't mean that--exactly
I do not comprehend your meaning
I don't deny that it is interesting
I don't doubt it for a moment
I do not doubt the sincerity of your arguments
I do not exactly understand you
I do not feel sure that I entirely share your views
I don't feel that it is my business
I do not find it an unpleasant subject
I don't insist on your believing me
I don't justify my presumption
I don't know quite why you should say that
I don't know that I can do that
I don't know when I have heard anything so lamentable
I don't know why you should be displeased
I don't make myself clear, I see
I don't pretend to explain
I don't see anything particularly wonderful in it

I don't underrate his kindness
I don't want to disguise that from you
I don't want to exaggerate
I don't want to seem critical
I doubt the truth of that saying
I endorse it, every word
I entirely approve of your plan
I fancy it's just that
I fear I cannot help you
I fear that's too technical for me
I feel a certain apprehension
I feel an unwonted sense of gaiety
[unwonted = unusual]
I feel it my duty to be frank with you
I feel myself scarcely competent to judge
I feel very grateful to you for your kind
offer
I find it absorbing
I find it rather monotonous
I find this agreeable mental exhilaration
I frankly confess that
I generally trust my first impressions
I give my word gladly
I give you my most sacred word of honor
I had better begin at the beginning
I had no intention of being offensive
I hadn't thought of it in that light
I hardly think that could be so
I have a hundred reasons for thinking so
I have a peculiar affection for it
I have an immense faith in him
I have been constrained by
circumstances
I have been decidedly impressed
I have been longing to see more of you
I have been puzzling over a dilemma
I have every reason to think so
I have given you the best proof of it
I have gone back to my first impressions
I have known striking instances of the
kind
I have never heard it put so well
I have no delusions on that score
I have not succeeded in convincing
myself of that
I have not the influence you think
I have not the least doubt of it

I haven't the remotest idea
I have often a difficulty in deciding
I have often marveled at your courage
I have quite changed my opinion about
that
I have something of great importance to
say to you
I have sometimes vaguely felt it
I have the strongest possible prejudice
against it
I heartily congratulate you
I hope it will not seem unreasonable to
you
I hope we may meet again
I hope you will forgive an intruder
I hope you will not think me irreverent
I hope you will pardon my seeming
carelessness
I indulge the modest hope
I know it is very presumptuous
I know my request will appear singular
I like it immensely
I like your frankness
I make no reflection whatever
I mean it literally
I might question all that
I mistrust these wild impulses
I most certainly agree with you
I most humbly ask pardon
I must add my congratulations on your
taste
I must apologize for intruding upon you
I must ask you one more question, if I
may
I must confess I have never thought of
that
I must refrain from any comment
I must respectfully decline to tell you
I must take this opportunity to tell you
I need not remind you that you have a
grave responsibility
I never heard anything so absurd
I offer my humblest apologies
I owe the idea wholly to you
I partly agree with you
I personally owe you a great debt of
thankfulness

I place myself entirely at your service
I place the most implicit reliance on your good sense
I prefer to reserve my judgment
I purposely evaded the question
I quite appreciate the very clever way you put it
I quite see what the advantages are
I really am curious to know how you guessed that
I realize how painful it must be to you
I recollect it clearly
I rely on your good sense
I remember the occasion perfectly
I resent that kind of thing
I respect you for that
I respect your critical faculty
I say it in all modesty
I see disapproval in your face
I see it from a different angle
I see you are an enthusiast
I see your point of view
I seem to have heard that sentiment before
I shall at once proceed to forget it
I shall await your pleasure
I shall be glad if you will join me
I shall be interested to watch it develop
I shall be most proud and pleased
I shall certainly take you at your word
I shall feel highly honored
I shall make a point of thinking so
I shall never forget your kindness
I shall respect your confidence
I should appreciate your confidence greatly
I should be very ungrateful were I not satisfied with it
I should feel unhappy if I did otherwise
I should like your opinion of it
I should not dream of asking you to do so
I should think it very unlikely
I simply cannot endure it
I spoke only in jest
I stand corrected
I suppose I ought to feel flattered
I surmised as much

I sympathize deeply with you
I take that for granted
I think extremely well of it
I think he has very noble ideals
I think I can answer that for you
I think I know what you are going to say
I think it has its charm
I think it is superb!
I think it quite admirable
I think its tone is remarkably temperate
I think that is rather a brilliant idea
I think what you say is reasonable
I think you are quibbling
I think you are rather severe in your opinions
I think you have great appreciation of values
I think you have summed it up perfectly
I think your candor is charming
I thoroughly agree with you
I thought it most amusing
I thought you were seriously indisposed
I trust you will not consider it an impertinence
I understand exactly how you feel about it
I understand your delicacy of feeling
I venture to propose another plan
I very rarely allow myself that pleasure
I want to have a frank understanding with you
I was at a loss to understand the reason for it
I was hoping that I could persuade you
I was on the point of asking you
I was speaking generally
I watched you with admiration
I will answer you frankly
I will listen to no protestations
I will take it only under compulsion
I will tell you what puzzles me
I will think of it, since you wish it
I will, with great pleasure
I wish I could explain my point more fully
I wish I knew what you meant by that
I wish to be perfectly fair

I wish to put things as plainly as possible
I wonder how much truth there is in it?
I wonder if you have the smallest
recollection of me?
I would agree if I understood
I wouldn't put it just that way
If ever I can repay it, command me
If I mistake not you were there once?
If I speak strongly, it is because I feel
strongly
If I were disposed to offer counsel
If I were sure you would not
misunderstand my meaning
If you don't mind my saying so
If you insist upon it
If you will pardon me the frankness
In a manner that sometimes terrifies me
In one respect you are quite right
In that case let me rob you of a few
minutes
In what case, for example?
Incredible as it sounds, I had for a
moment forgotten
Indeed, but it is quite possible
Indeed! How?
Indeed, you are wholly wrong
Indifferently so, I am afraid
Irony was ten thousand leagues from my
intention
Is it sane--is it reasonable?
Isn't it amazing?
Isn't it extraordinarily funny?
Isn't it preposterous?
Isn't that a trifle unreasonable?
Isn't that rather a hasty conclusion?
Is that a fair question?
It always seemed to me impossible
It amuses you, doesn't it?
It blunts the sensibilities
It could never conceivably be anything
but popular
It depends on how you look at it
It depends upon circumstances
It doesn't sound plausible to me
It has a lovely situation as I remember it
It has amused me hugely
It has been a relief to talk to you

It has been an immense privilege to see
you
It has never occurred to me
It is a curious fact
It is a great pleasure to meet you
It is a huge undertaking
It is a most unfortunate affair
It is a perfectly plain proposition
It is a rather melancholy thought
It is a truth universally acknowledged
It is all very inexcusable
It is all very well for you to be
philosophical
It is altogether probable
It is an admirable way of putting it
It is an error of taste
It is an extreme case, but the principle is
sound
It is an ingenious theory
It is an uncommonly fine description
It is extremely interesting, I can assure
you
It is for you to decide
It is historically true
It is I who should ask forgiveness
It is incredible!
It is indeed generous of you to suggest it
It is inexplicable
It is interesting, as a theory
It is literally impossible
It is merely a mood
It is most unfortunate
It is my deliberately formed opinion
It is my opinion you are too
conscientious
It is nevertheless true
It is not a matter of the slightest
consequence
It is not always fair to judge by
appearances
It is not so unreasonable as you think
It is often very misleading
It is one of the grave problems of the day
It is only a fancy of mine
It is perfectly defensible
It is perfectly trite
It is permissible to gratify such an

impulse
It is possible, but I rather doubt it
It is quite an easy matter
It is quite conceivable
It is quite too absurd
It is rather startling
It is really impressive
It is really most callous of you to laugh
It is sheer madness
It is sickening and so insufferably arrogant
It is simply a coincidence
It is the most incomprehensible thing in the world
It is to you that I am indebted for all this
It is true, I am grieved to say
It is true none the less
It is very amusing
It is very far from being a fiction
It is very good of you to do this for my pleasure
It is very ingenious
It is very splendid of you
It is wanton capriciousness
It is your privilege to think so
It's a difficult and delicate matter to discuss
It's a matter of immediate urgency
It's absolute folly
It's absurd--it's impossible
It's all nonsense
It's as logical as it can be under the circumstances
It's been a strange experience for you
It's deliciously honest
It's going to be rather troublesome
It's inconceivable that it should ever be necessary
It's mere pride of opinion
It's my chief form of recreation
It's not a matter of vast importance
It's past my comprehension
It's quite wonderful how logical and simple you make it
It's really very perplexing
It's so charming of you to say that
It's so kind of you to come

It's such a bore having to talk about it
It's the natural sequence
It's too melancholy
It's very wonderful
It makes it all quite interesting
It may sound strange to you
It must be a trifle dull at times
It must be fascinating
It must be very gratifying to you
It must have been rather embarrassing
It seems an age since we've last seen you
It seems entirely wonderful to me
It seems incredible
It seems like a distracting dream
It seems preposterous
It seems the height of absurdity
It seems to me that you have a perfect right to do so
It seems unspeakably funny to me
It seems very ridiculous
It shall be as you wish
It should not be objectionable
It sounds plausible
It sounds profoundly interesting
It sounds rather appalling
It sounds very alluring
It strikes me as rather pathetic
It was an unpardonable liberty
It was inevitable that you should say that
It was most stupid of me to have forgotten it
It was not unkindly meant
It was peculiarly unfortunate
It was really an extraordinary experience
It was so incredible
It was the most amazing thing I ever heard
It was very good of you to come out and join us
It will create a considerable sensation
It will divert your thoughts from a mournful subject
It will give me pleasure to do it
It will not alter my determination
It would be ill-advised
It would interest me very much
It would seem to be a wise decision

It would take too long to formulate my thought

## J
Join us, please, when you have time moment
Just trust to the inspiration of the

Justify it if you can

## L
Let me persuade you
Let me say how deeply indebted I feel for your kindness
Let me speak frankly

Let us grant that for the sake of the argument
Let us take a concrete instance

## M
Many thanks--how kind and good you are!
May I ask to whom you allude?
May I be privileged to hear it?
May I speak freely?
May I venture to ask what inference you would draw from that?
Might I suggest an alternative?
Most dangerous!

My attitude would be one of disapproval
My confidence in you is absolute
My idea of it is quite the reverse
My information is rather scanty
My meaning is quite the contrary
My point of view is different, but I shall not insist upon it
My views are altered in many respects

## N
No, I am speaking seriously
No, I don't understand it
Not at all
Not to my knowledge

Nothing could be more delightful
Now is it very plain to you?
Now you are flippant

## O
Obviously the matter is settled
Of course, but that again isn't the point
Of course I am delighted
Of course I don't want to press you against your will
Of course you will do what you think best
Oh, certainly, if you wish it
Oh, do not form an erroneous impression
Oh, I appreciate that in you!
Oh, that's mere quibbling
Oh, that's splendid of you!
Oh, that was a manner of speaking

Oh, yes, I quite admit that
Oh, yes, you may take that for granted
Oh, you are very bitter
Oh, you may be as scornful as you like
On the contrary, I agree with you thoroughly
On the face of it, it sounds reasonable
One assumption you make I should like to contest
One has no choice to endure it
One must be indulgent under the circumstances
One thing I beg of you

## P
Pardon me, but I don't think so

Pardon me, I meant something different

Perhaps I am indiscreet
Perhaps not in the strictest sense
Perhaps you do not feel at liberty to do so
Perhaps you think me ungrateful
Personally I confess to an objection
Please continue to be frank
Please do not think I am asking out of
mere curiosity
Please forgive my thoughtlessness

Please make yourself at home
Pray don't apologize
Pray forgive me for intruding on you so
unceremoniously
Pray go on!
Precisely, that is just what I meant
Put in that way it certainly sounds very
well

## Q
Question me, if you wish
Quibbling, I call it

Quite so
Quite the wisest thing you can do

## R
Rather loquacious, I think [loquacious =
very talkative]
Reading between the lines
Really? I should have thought otherwise
Really--you must go?

Reassure me, if you can
Reflect upon the possible consequences
Relatively speaking
Reluctantly I admit it
Reverting to another matter

## S
Shall we have a compact?
She has an extraordinary gift of
conversation
She is easily prejudiced
She seems uncommonly appreciative
She will be immensely surprised
Show me that the two cases are
analogous
So far so good
So I inferred
So much the better for me
So you observe the transformation?

Something amuses you
Sometimes the absurdity of it occurs to
me
Speaking with all due respect
Still, you might make an exception
Strangely it's true
Such conduct seems to me unjustifiable
Surely there can be no question about
that
Surely we can speak frankly
Surely you sound too harsh a note
Surely you would not countenance that

## T
Tell me in what way you want me to
help you
Thank you for telling me that
Thank you for your good intentions
That, at least, you will agree to
That depends on one's point of view
That doesn't sound very logical
That is a counsel of perfection
That is a fair question, perhaps
That is a question I have often proposed
to myself

That is a stroke of good fortune
That is a superb piece of work
That is a very practical explanation
That is admirably clear
That is certainly ideal
That is eminently proper
That is hardly consistent
That is inconceivable
That is just like you, if you will forgive
me for saying so
That is most fortunate

That is most kind of you
That is most unexpected and distressing
That is not fair--to me
That is not to be lightly spoken of
That is precisely what I mean
That is quite true, theoretically
That is rather a difficult question to answer
That is rather a strange request to make
That is rather awkward
That is really good of you
That is the prevailing idea
That is tragic
That is true and I think you are right
That is very amiable in you
That is very curious
That is very felicitous
That is very gracious
That is what I call intelligent criticism
That is what I meant to tell you
That is a humiliating thought
That is a most interesting idea
That is such a hideous idea
That is the most incredible part of it
That might involve you in life-long self-reproach
That must be exceedingly tiresome
That ought to make you a little lenient
That reassures me
That shows the infirmity of his judgment
That theory isn't tenable
That was exceedingly generous
That was intended ironically
That was very thoughtful of you
That was very well reasoned
That will blast your chances, I am afraid
That will suit me excellently
That would be somewhat serious
That would be very discreditable
The agreement seems to be ideal
The idea is monstrous
The inference is obvious

U
Undeniably true
Unfortunately I must decline the proposal

The notion is rather new to me
The pleasure is certainly not all on your side
The reason is not so far to seek
The same problem has perplexed me
The sentiment is worthy of you
The simplest thing in the world
The situation is uncommonly delicate
The story seems to me incredible
The subject is extremely interesting
The tone of it was certainly hostile
The very obvious moral is this
The whole thing is an idle fancy
Then I have your permission?
Then you're really not disinclined?
Then you merely want to ask my advice?
There are endless difficulties
There are reasons which make such a course impossible
There is a good deal of sense in that
There is a grain of truth in that, I admit
There is food for reflection in that
There is my hand on it
There is no resisting you
There is nothing I should like so much
There is one inevitable condition
There is something almost terrifying about it
There must be extenuating circumstances
They amuse me immensely
This is a most unexpected pleasure
This is charmingly new to me
This is indeed good fortune
This is really appalling
This is really not a laughing matter
Those are my own private feelings
Those things are not forgotten at once
To me it's simply outrageous
To speak frankly, I do not like it
True, I forgot!

Unlikely to be so
Unquestionably superior
Unwholesome influence, I would say

## V

Very good, I'll do so
Very well, I will consent
Vivacity is her greatest charm

Virtually accomplished, I believe
Vouch for its truth

## W

We are all more or less susceptible
We are drifting away from our point
We are impervious to certain rules
We are merely wasting energy in this duel
We can safely take it for granted
We couldn't have a better topic
We had better agree to differ
We have had some conclusions in common
We must judge it leniently
We must not expose ourselves to misinterpretation
We owe you a debt of gratitude
We shall be glad to see you, if you care to come
We will devoutly hope not
Well, as a matter of fact, I have forgotten
Well done! I congratulate you
Well, I'm not going to argue that
Well, I call it scandalous
Well, I confess they don't appeal to me
Well, more's the pity
Well, perhaps it is none of my affair
Well, that is certainly ideal!
Well, this is good fortune
Well, yes--in a way
Well, you are a dreamer!
What a beautiful idea
What a charming place you have here
What a curious coincidence!
What a pretty compliment!

What a tempting prospect!
What an extraordinary idea!
What are your misgivings?
What can you possibly mean?
What conceivable reason is there for it?
What do you imagine my course should be?
What do you propose?
What is the next step in your argument?
What is there so strange about that?
What, may I ask, is your immediate object?
What unseemly levity on his part
What very kind things you say to me
What would you expect me to do?
What you have just said is even truer than you realize
What you propose is utterly impossible
Who is your sagacious adviser?
[sagacious = sound judgment, wise]
Why ask such embarrassing questions?
Why did you desert us so entirely?
Why do you take it so seriously?
Will you allow me to ask you a question?
Will you be more explicit?
Will you have the kindness to explain?
Will you pardon my curiosity?
Will you permit me a brief explanation?
Would you apply that to everyone?
Would you mind telling me your opinion?

## Y

Yes and no
Yes, but that is just what I fail to comprehend
Yes, I dare say
Yes, if you will be so good
Yes, it was extraordinarily fine
Yes, that is my earnest wish

Yes, that's undeniable
Yes? You were saying?
You agree with me, I know
You are a profound philosopher
You are a severe critic
You are delightfully frank
You are greatly to be envied

You are heartily welcome
You are incomprehensible
You are incorrigible
You are kind and comforting
You are most kind
You are not consistent
You are not serious, I hope
You are not seriously displeased with me?
You are quite delightful
You are rather puzzling to-day
You are right to remind me of that
You are unduly distressing yourself
You are very complimentary
You are very gracious
You're so tremendously kind about it
You're succeeding admirably
You're taking it all much too seriously
You're talking nonsense!
You're very good, I'm sure
You ask me--but I shouldn't wonder if you knew better than I do
You astonish me greatly
You behaved with great forbearance
You can hardly be serious
You cannot regret it more than I do
You could not pay me a higher compliment
You did it excellently
You did not clearly understand what I meant
You don't seem very enthusiastic
You excite my curiosity
You flatter my judgment
You have a genius for saying the right thing
You have asked me a riddle
You have asked the impossible
You have been wrongly informed
You have done me a great service
You have had a pleasant time, I hope
You have my deepest sympathy
You have my unbounded confidence
You have received a false impression
You have such an interesting way of putting things

You interest me deeply
You judge yourself too severely
You know I'm in an agony of curiosity
You know I'm not given to sentimentality
You know the familiar axiom
You leave no alternative
You look incredulous
You may be sure of my confidence
You may rely on me absolutely
You might make an exception
You must have misunderstood me
You must not fail to command me
You overwhelm me with your kindness
You really insist upon it?
You rebuke me very fairly
You say that as though you were surprised
You see how widely we differ
You see, it's all very vague
You see things rose-colored
You seem to be in a happy mood
You seem to take a very mild interest in what I propose
You shock me more than I can say
You speak in enigmas
You speak with authority
You surely understand my position
You take a great deal for granted
You take a pessimistic view of things
You take me quite by surprise
You will admit I have some provocation
You will become morbid if you are not careful
You will have ample opportunity
You will, of course, remember the incident
You will please not be flippant
You will understand my anxiety
Your argument is facile and superficial
Your consideration is entirely misplaced
Your judgments are very sound
Your logic is as clever as possible
Your opinion will be invaluable to me
Your request is granted before it is made
Your statement is somewhat startling

# SECTION 10
# PUBLIC SPEAKING PHRASES

A

A fact of vast moment
A few words will suffice to answer
A further objection is
A great many people have said
A little indulgence may be due to those
A majority of us believe
A man in my situation has
A more plausible objection is found
A proof of this is
A servile mind can never know
A short time since
A specific answer can be given
A thought occurred to me
Able men have reasoned out
Above all things, let us not forget
Absolutely true it is
Abundant reason is there
Accordingly by reason of this
circumstance
Add this instance to
After a careful study of all the evidence
After full deliberation
After reminding the hearer
After this it remains only to say
Again, can we doubt
Again, I ask the gentleman
Again, in this view
Again, it is quite clear that
Again, it is urged
Again, let us compare
Again, very numerous are the cases
Again, we have abundant instances
Against all this concurring testimony
All confess this to be true
All I ask is
All of us know
All that I will say now
All the facts which support this
All the signs of the time indicate
All these things you know
All this being considered

All this is historical fact
All this is very well
All this suggests
All this we take for granted
Allow me for a moment to turn to
Allow me to tell a story
Altho I say it to myself
Amazing as it may seem
Am I mistaken in this
Among many examples
Among the distinguished guests who
honor
Among the problems that confront us
An answer to this is now ready
An argument has often been put forward
An example or two will illustrate
An indescribably touching incident
An opinion has now become established
And again, it is said
And again, it is to be presumed
And coming nearer to our own day
And did a man try to persuade me
And do you really think
And everybody here knows
And for myself, as I said
And further, all that I have said
And hence the well-known doctrine
And here again, when I speak
And here allow me to call your attention
And here I am led to observe
And here I come to the closing evidence
And here I have an opportunity
And here I reproach
And here I wish you to observe
And here let me define my position
And here let me give my explanation
And here let us recall to mind
And how is it possible to imagine
And I am bound to say
And I beg of you
And I call on you

And I might say this
And I refuse assent
And I rejoice to know
And I say, it were better for you
And I should in like manner repudiate
And I speak with reverence
And I submit to you
And I trust that you will consider
And I will make a practical suggestion
And I will tell you why
And I would, moreover submit
And if a man could anywhere be found
And if any of you should question
And if I know anything of my
countrymen
And if I may presume to speak
And if I take another instance
And if this be true
And if you come to a decision
And if you think it your duty
And in conclusion
And in like manner
And in order to see this
And in thus speaking, I am not denying
And is not this lamentable
And is there not a presumption
And it happens
And it is certainly true
And it is doubtful if
And it is not difficult to see
And it is not plain
And it is one of the evidences
And it is precisely in this
And it is strikingly suggested to us
And it is undeniable, I say
And it is well that this should be so
And last of all
And lest anyone should marvel
And let it be observed
And lo! and behold
And more than this
And next I would ask
And now allow me to call attention
And now behold a mystery
And now consider
And now having discussed
And now I beg that I may be permitted

And now I go back to the statement
And now I have completed my review
And now I have said enough to explain
And now I must touch upon one point
And now if I may take for granted
And now it would be very pleasant for
me
And now observe how
And now, sir, what I had first to say
And now supposing this point to be
settled
And now that I have mentioned
And now the chief points of it
And now the question is asked me
And now, to close, let me give you
And now, to what purpose do I mention
And, of course, you are aware
And of this I am perfectly certain
And quite as difficult is it to create
And right here lies the cause
And, sir, a word
And so, again, as regard
And so I am reminded of a story
And so I leave these words with you
And so I may point out
And so I might recount to you
And so, in the other cases, I have named
And so in the present case
And so on
And so through all phases
And so, upon every hand
And sometimes it will be difficult
And that gave another distorted view
And the reason is very obvious
And the same holds good
And then again
And then hastily to conclude
And then I may be reminded
And then there is another thought
And then when it is said
And there are reasons why
And there is also this view
And therefore am I truly glad
And therefore it is not unfrequently
quoted
And therefore it is not without regret
And this brings me to the last thing

179

And this is really the sense
And this leads me to say a word
And thus consistently
And thus it is conceivable
And thus it seems to me
And thus we are led on then to further
question
And to all this must be added
And to return to the topic
And to this conclusion you must come
And unquestionably
And we are brought to the same
conclusion
And what do you suppose will be
And when I have shown to you
And when I recall that event
And when we pass beyond the bounds of
And where, let me ask
And why should I insist
And will you still insist
And with these thoughts come others
And yet I can not but reflect
And yet I feel justified in believing
And yet I think we all feel
And yet let me say to you
And yet one more quotation
And yet this notion is, I conceive
And yet though this be true
And yet we ought, if we are wise
And you may also remember this
Another circumstance that adds to the
difficulty
Another consideration which I shall
adduce [adduce = cite as an example]
Another instance of signal success
Another of these presumptions
Another point is made as clear as crystal
Another reason of a kindred nature
Another reflection which occurs to me

B
Be assured, then
Be confident, therefore
Be it so
Be not deceived
Be sure that in spite of
Be these things as they may

Another sign of our times
Another signal advantage
Another striking instance
Answers doubtless may be given
Are there not many of us
Are we content to believe
Are we forever to deprive ourselves
Are we not startled into astonishment
Are we satisfied to assume
As a general rule I hold
As a last illustration
As a matter of fact
As a proof of this
As an illustration of this truth
As briefly as I may
As far as my limits allow
As far as this is true
As far as this objection relates
As far as we know
As for the rest
As I have now replied to
As I look around on this assembly
As I rise to respond to the sentiment
As I understand this matter
As memory scans the past
As society is now constituted
As some one has well said
As the foregoing instances have shown
As to the particular instance before us
As well might we compare
As we shall see in a few moments
Assuredly it is this
At the outset of this inquiry
At the risk of digression
At the same time, I candidly state
At the utmost we can say
At this juncture
At this solemn moment
Away then with the notion

Be your interests what they may be
Bear with me for a few moments
Bearing on this point
Before attempting to answer this
question
Before going further

180

Before I close I will particularly remark
Before I come to the special matter
Before I proceed to compare
Being fully of the opinion
Being persuaded then
Believing, as I do
Beyond all question we
Bidden by your invitation to a discussion
Broadly speaking
But, above all things, let us
But after all, I think no one can say
But again, when we carefully consider
But am I wrong in saying
But apart from the fact
But besides these special facts
But can this question
But depend upon it
But despite all this
But do not let us depend
But do you imagine
But doubts here arise
But even admitting these possibilities
But everyone who deserves
But first of all, remark, I beg you
But, further, I shall now demonstrate
But, gentlemen, I must be done
But grave problems confront us
But here I am discussing
But here let me say
But how can we pass over
But how shall I describe my emotions
But however that may be
But I am bound to say
But I am certain from my own
experience
But I am very sorry to say
But I am willing enough to admit
But I can at least say
But I can not conceive
But I can promise
But I cherish the hope
But I confess that I should be glad
But I digress
But I do not propose all these things
But I do say this
But I have been insisting simply
But I have heard it argued

But I have no fear of the future
But I leave this train of thought
But I may be permitted to speak
But I may say in conclusion
But I need hardly assert
But I pass that over
But I propose to speak to you
But I repeat
But I resist the temptation
But I return to the question
But I shall go still further
But I simply ask
But I submit the whole subject
But I trust that you will all admit
But I venture to assure you
But I will allude
But I will not further impress any idea
But I would earnestly impress upon you
But if I may even flatter myself
But if I seek for illustrations
But if you want more evidence
But if you wish to know
But in making this assertion
But in my opinion there is no need
But in the course of time
But is it quite possible to hold
But is this any reason why
But it does not follow from this
But it happens very fortunately
But it has been suggested to me
But it is a fact
But it is impossible for one
But it is necessary to explain
But it is no use protesting
But it is not fair to assert
But it is not my intention
But it is not necessary to suppose
But it is not possible to believe
But it is not really so
But it is otherwise with
But it is sometimes said
But it may be doubted whether
But it may happen that I forgot
But it will be a misfortune
But it will naturally be asked
But it will perhaps be argued
But it would be vain to attempt

181

But let me ask you to glance
But let me before closing refer
But let none of you think
But let us also keep ever in mind
But let us look a little further
But lo! all of a sudden
But mark this
But more than all things else
But my allotted time is running away
But my answer to this objection
But, my friends, pause for a moment
But never was a grosser wrong
But not for one moment
But notwithstanding all this
But now look at the effect
But now take notice of
But on the other hand
But on what ground are we
But passing these by
But perhaps I ought to speak distinctly
But perhaps you are not yet weary
But putting these questions aside
But quite contrary to this, you will find
But recollect, I pray you, how
But, sir, it is manifest
But some other things are to be noted
But some will ask me
But sooner or later
But still, I repeat
But suppose the fact
But surely, you can not say
But that I may not divert you from
But that is not all
But that must be always the impression
But the fact is
But the final value
But the greatest proof of all
But the most formidable problem

But the necessity of the case
But the question may arise
But, then, let us ask ourselves
But there is another duty imposed
But there is much more than this
But this I do not hesitate to say
But this I fearlessly affirm
But this I know
But this is a circuitous argument
But this is no place for controversy
But this is not all
But this is what I mean
But this much I affirm as true
But this warns me
But this we may put aside
But to go still further
But to say the truth
But we are met with the assertion
But we are to recollect
But we ask, perhaps
But we may depend upon it
But we think it is not wise
But we want something more for
explanation
But what a blunder would be yours
But what is the fact
But what we must needs guard against
But when it is declared
But when we look a little deeper
But while it may be admitted
But who has not seen
But why do I numerate these details
But with these exceptions
But yet nothing can be more splendid
But you should know
By no means
By the way, I have not mentioned
By this time it will be suspected

C
Can it be supposed
Can the long records of humanity teach
us
Can there be a better illustration
Can we pretend
Can you lightly contemplate
Can you yield yourselves

Cautious and practical thinkers ask
Certain it is
Certainly I am not blind to the faults
Certainly, one can conceive
Clearly enough
Coming back to the main subject
Coming down to modern times

Coming to present circumstances
Common sense indicates
Consequently, I am not discussing this

matter
Consider, I beg you, what
Contemplating these marvelous changes

## D

Delude not yourselves with the belief
Depend upon it
Did it ever occur to you
Difficult then as the question may be
Do I need to describe
Do me the honor of believing
Do not imagine
Do not let us conceal from ourselves
Do not suppose for a moment
Do not talk to me of
Do not think me guilty of
Do we not know
Do what you will

Do you ask how that can be
Do you believe this can be truthfully said
Do you not know I am speaking of
Do you remember a concrete instance
Do you think, then
Does any man say
Does it ever occur to you
Does it not seem something like idiocy to
Does it not shock you to think
Does not the event show
Does not the nature of every man revolt
Doubtless the end is sought

## E

Every now and then you will find
Every one has asked himself

Every one therefore ought to look to
Every reader of history can recall

## F

Far from it
Few indeed there are
Few subjects are more fruitful
Few things impress the imagination more
Finally, it is my most fervent prayer
First in my thoughts are
First of all I ask
For, be assured of this
For behold
For I must tell you
For if any one thinks that there is
For, in truth, if you please to recollect
For instance, I can fancy
For is it not true
For it is not right to
For let it be observed first
For mark you
For my own part, I believe

For myself, certainly I think
For observe what the real fact is
For one I deny
For, perhaps, after all
For, perhaps, some one may say
For so it generally happens
For the sake of my argument
For this is what I say
For this reason, indeed, it is
For we all know
Fortunately for us
Fortunately I am not obliged
From one point of view we are
From the circumstances already
explained
From the standpoint of
From this statement you will perceive

## G

Generally speaking
God be praised

Grant this true
Granting all this

**H**

Had I time for all that might be said
Had my limits allowed it
Happily for us
Hardly less marvelous
Hardly will anyone venture to say
Have I exaggerated
Have you ever noticed
Having taken a view of
Having thus described what appears to me
He is the best prophet who
He seems at times to confuse
He was an eminent instance of
He who is insensible to
Hence arises a grave mischief
Hence, as I have said
Hence it follows
Here again the testimony corroborates
Here arises the eternal question
Here comes the practical matter
Here for a moment I seem
Here, however, it may be objected
Here I am considering
Here I end my illustrations
Here I must pause for a moment
Here I only insist upon
Here I ought to stop
Here is another strange thing
Here is good hope for us
Here is no question
Here let me meet one other question
Here, then, I am brought to the consideration

Here then I take up the subject
Here then is the key
Here, then, it is natural at last
Here then, we are brought to the question
Here, then, we are involved
Here undoubtedly it is
Here we can not but pause to contemplate
Here we come into direct antagonism with
Here we come to the very crux of
Here we have it on high authority
History is replete with predictions
Hitherto I have spoken only of
Holding this view, I am concerned
How can we help believing
How do you account for
How does it happen
How human language staggers when
How infinitely difficult it is
How infinitely superior must it appear
How is this to be explained
How many a time
How momentous, then
How much better, I say, if
How much more rational it would be
How shall I attempt to enumerate
How shall I describe to you
However, I am viewing the matter
However, I will not in any way admit
However, it is to me a very refreshing thing

**I**

I abide by my statement
I add a few suggestions
I adduce these facts [adduce = cite as an example]
I admire the main drift of
I admit, of course, at once
I admit the extreme complexity
I again ask
I allude to
I always delight to think
I always will assert the right to

I am a great admirer
I am a little at a loss to know
I am about to supplement
I am agitated by conflicting emotions
I am alarmed, indeed, when I see
I am also bound to say
I am also satisfied
I am apprehensive
I am asked to-night to propose
I am assured and fully believe
I am at a loss for adequate terms

I am bold to say
I am but saying
I am by no means certain
I am certain that you will give me credit
I am certainly in earnest sympathy
I am confronted by the hope
I am conscious of the fact
I am convinced by what I have seen
I am deeply imbued with the conviction
I am deeply insensible of the compliment
I am determined
I am even bold enough to hazard
I am exceeding my necessary limits
I am exceedingly glad of this opportunity
I am extremely obliged to you
I am familiar with
I am far from asserting
I am filled with admiration
I am firmly convinced
I am free to admit
I am fully convinced
I am giving voice to what you all feel
I am glad of this public opportunity
I am glad to answer to the toast
I am glad to express the belief
I am glad to notice
I am going to spare you and myself
I am grateful to you for this honor
I am greatly alarmed
I am greatly indebted to you
I am happy to be with you
I am here by the favor of your invitation
I am here the advocate of
I am here to introduce
I am in favor of
I am in sympathy with
I am inclined sometimes to believe
I am inclined to suspect
I am indebted for the honor
I am, indeed, most solicitous
I am informed
I am led on by these reflections
I am led to believe
I am mainly concerned
I am most deeply sensible of the welcome
I am most grateful for the opportunity
I am myself greatly indebted

I am nevertheless too sensible
I am not a stranger to
I am not at liberty to discuss
I am not at present concerned
I am not about to defend
I am not advocating
I am not altogether clear
I am not aware of a single instance
I am not blind to the faults of
I am not bold enough to
I am not catching at sharp arguments
I am not concerned to argue
I am not defending myself
I am not dreaming of denying
I am not going into vexed questions
I am not going to reproach
I am not here to defend
I am not insensible
I am not of those who pretend
I am not prepared to dispute the word
I am not presumptuous to assert
I am not proposing to set forth
I am not ripe to pass sentence
I am not so unreasonable as to tell you
I am not surprised
I am not taking into account
I am not unaware
I am not undertaking to deliver
I am now going to attempt
I am obliged to add
I am obliged to go still further
I am often reminded
I am old enough to remember
I am one of those who believe
I am only too sensible of the fact
I am perfectly willing to admit
I am persuaded
I am prepared to back that opinion by
I am privileged to speak to
I am quite conscious that
I am rather disposed to think
I am ready to do battle
I am reassured by the presence here
I am reluctantly but forcibly reminded
I am resolved not to permit
I am sensible, sir
I am simply endeavoring to show

I am so surrounded on every hand
I am sometimes inclined to think
I am somewhat relieved to know
I am sorry to say
I am suggesting the reason why
I am sure, at any rate
I am sure every impartial man will agree
I am sure I feel no hostility
I am sure that I echo the sentiment
I am sure this generous audience will
pardon me
I am sure you all hope
I am sure you feel the truth
I am sure you will acquit me
I am sure you will be kind enough
I am sure you will do me the justice
I am sure you will not be surprised
I am surely not here to assert
I am tempted further to offer to you
I am thankful for the privilege
I am thoroughly convinced
I am to speak to you this evening
I am to urge the interest of
I am told occasionally
I am told on authority
I am too well aware of the difficulties
I am totally at a loss to conceive
I am trespassing too long on your time
I am unable to understand
I am unconscious of intentional error
I am under a very great obligation
I am under the deepest feeling of
gratitude
I am under the impression
I am unwillingly bound to add
I am uttering no paradox when I say
I am very far from thinking.
I am very glad to have the honor
I am very happy to be here
I am very much in the condition of
I am very sure that if you ponder
I am very sure you will believe
I am well aware
I am willing to know
I anticipate with pleasing expectation
I appeal in the first place
I appeal to any man to say

I appeal to the better judgment
I appreciate the significance
I argue this cause
I ask again
I ask no greater blessing
I ask permission to speak to you
I ask the attention
I ask the audience
I ask the audience to return with me
I ask this of you
I ask you calmly and dispassionately
I ask you gentlemen, do you think
I ask you if it is possible
I ask you, if you please, to rise and give
the toast
I ask you in all candor
I ask you now to follow me
I ask you to consider
I ask you to join me in drinking a toast
I ask you to pledge with me
I ask your attention
I ask your indulgence
I assert, sir, that it is
I assure myself
I assure you, of my own personal
knowledge
I attribute it to
I avail myself of the opportunity
I beg again to thank you for the honor
I beg all to remember
I beg and implore of you
I beg emphatically to say
I beg leave to make some observations
I beg of you to remember
I beg to tender my most fervent wishes
I beg you not to mistake my meaning
I beg you to accept my grateful
expression
I begin by observing
I begin with expressing a sentiment
I believe from my own personal
experience
I believe I can speak for all
I believe I shall make it clear to you
I believe I voice the sentiment
I believe it to be the simple truth
I believe most profoundly

I believe that I am within the mark
I believe that in this instance
I bid you a most cordial and hearty welcome
I bow with you in reverent commemoration
I call on you to answer
I call to mind how
I can by no calculation justify
I call hardly conceive
I can make allowance for
I can most truthfully assure you
I call never sufficiently express my gratitude
I can not allow myself to believe
I can not avoid confessing
I can not be content with
I can not believe, I will not believe
I can not better illustrate this argument
I can not better sum up
I can not boast of
I can not bound my vision
I can not but reflect
I can not but see what mischief
I can not charge myself with
I can not close without giving expression
I can not conceive a greater honor
I can not feel any doubt myself
I can not forbear from offering
I can not give you a better illustration
I can not help expressing a wish
I can not help speaking urgently
I can not here go into details
I can not hesitate to say
I can not hope adequately to respond
I can not justly be responsible because
I can not let this opportunity pass
I can not persuade myself
I can not prevail on myself
I can not refrain from saying for myself
I can not resist the train of thought
I can not say how glad I am
I can not say with confidence
I can not stop to give in detail
I can not sufficiently thank you
I can not take back my word
I can not take it for granted

I can not thank you enough
I can not well avoid saying
I can only congratulate you
I can only hope for indulgence
I can readily understand
I can scarcely concede anything more important
I can scarcely find fitting words
I can strongly recommend
I can understand, moreover
I can with propriety speak here
I certainly have not so good an opinion
I challenge any man
I cheerfully own
I cheerfully submit myself
I claim a share also for
I class them altogether under the head
I close with the words
I close with this sentiment
I come at length to
I come next to the question of
I come to the other assumption
I conceive this to be
I confess I feel not the least alarmed
I confess I have had my doubts
I confess I have little sympathy
I confess it affects me very deeply to
I confess it is very difficult to
I confess that I do not entirely approve
I confess that it is a comfort to me
I confess that my notions are widely different
I confess to a little embarrassment
I confess to you that I have no fear
I confine myself to saying
I congratulate you upon the auspicious character
I consider I have said enough in proof
I consider it amply explains
I contend
I content myself with pursuing
I could do no less than
I could easily mention
I could enlarge upon it
I could never understand
I could wish that this belief
I dare say you know

I dare venture the remark
I declare to you
I deem it both necessary and just
I deem it proper here to remind
I deem myself honored
I deny, once and for all
I deny the inference
I desire to be brief
I desire to bear my testimony
I desire to call attention
I desire to know
I desire to lay emphatic stress
I dissent from the opinion
I distrust all general theories of
I do again and again urge upon you
I do, indeed, recollect
I do not absolutely assert
I do not advocate
I do not argue
I do not ask you to
I do not at this moment remember
I do not believe it possible
I do not belong to those who
I do not choose to consume
I do not complain of
I do not consider it necessary
I do not contend
I do not countenance for a moment
I do not deem it incumbent upon me
I do not depreciate for a moment
I do not desire to call in question
I do not desire to put too much emphasis
I do not despair of surmounting
I do not disguise the fact
I do not enter into the question
I do not fail to admire
I do not fear a contradiction
I do not feel at liberty
I do not forget the practical necessity
I do not hesitate to say
I do not imagine
I do not in the least degree
I do not indeed deny
I do not indulge in the delusion
I do not know how anyone can believe
I do not know whether you are aware of
it

I do not know why
I do not know with what correctness
I do not mean anything so absurd
I do not mean now to go further than
I do not mean to impute
I do not merely urge
I do not mistrust
I do not myself pretend to be
I do not need to remind you
I do not, of course, deny
I do not pretend to argue
I do not propose to take up your time
I do not question for a moment
I do not recount all
I do not say anything about the future
I do not say this with any affectation
I do not see how it is possible
I do not see much difference between
I do not seek to palliate
I do not speak exclusively
I do not stop to discuss
I do not, therefore, wonder
I do not think it necessary to warn you
I do not think it possible
I do not think it unfair reasoning
I do not think myself obliged to dwell
I do not think that I need further discuss
I do not think this at all an exaggeration
I do not think we can go far wrong
I do not think you will often hear
I do not understand how it can apply
I do not vouch for
I do not want to discourage you
I do not wish to be considered egotistic
I do not wish to be misrepresented
I do not wonder
I doubt very much whether
I dwell with pleasure on the
considerations
I earnestly maintain
I embrace with peculiar satisfaction
I end as I began
I entertain great apprehension for
I entertain no such chimerical hopes
[chimerical = highly improbable]
I entertain the hope and opinion
I entirely dissent from the view

I especially hail with approval
I even add this
I even venture to deny
I fancy I hear you say
I fear I may seem trifling
I fear lest I may
I fearlessly appeal
I fearlessly challenge
I feel a great necessity to
I feel bound to add my expression
I feel constrained to declare
I feel entirely satisfied
I feel I have a right to say
I feel it a proud privilege
I feel keenly myself impelled by every duty
I feel only a great emotion of gratitude
I feel respect and admiration
I feel some explanation is due
I feel sure
I feel tempted to introduce here
I feel that I have a special right to
I feel that it is not true
I feel the greatest satisfaction
I feel the task is far beyond my power
I fervently trust
I find it difficult to utter in words
I find it more easy
I find my reference to this
I find myself called upon to say something
I find myself in the position of
I find no better example than
I find no fault with
I find numberless cases
I flatter myself
I, for my part, would rather
I, for one, greatly doubt
I forbear to inquire
I foresaw the consequence
I fully recognize
I gave notice just now
I give you, in conclusion, this sentence
I go further
I grant all this
I grant with my warmest admiration
I gratefully accept

I greatly deplore
I had a kind of hope
I had almost said
I had in common with others
I had occasion to criticize
I happen to differ
I hardly dare to dwell longer
I hardly know anything more strange
I hasten to concede
I have a dark suspicion
I have a great admiration for
I have a pleasing and personal duty
I have a profound pity for those
I have a right to consider
I have a strong belief
I have a very high respect for
I have abstained from
I have acquired some useful experience
I have all along implied
I have all but finished
I have already alluded to
I have already shown the ground of my hope
I have already stated, and now repeat
I have always been under the impression
I have always listened with the greatest satisfaction
I have always maintained
I have another objection
I have another observation to add
I have anticipated the objection
I have assumed throughout
I have attempted thus hastily
I have barely touched some of the points
I have been allowcd the privilege
I have been asked several times
I have been extremely anxious
I have been given to understand
I have been glad to observe
I have been heretofore treating
I have been insisting then on this
I have been interested in hearing
I have been pointing out how
I have been profoundly moved
I have been requested to say a word
I have been told by an eminent authority
I have been too long accustomed to hear

I have been touched by the large generosity
I have been trying to show
I have before me the statistics
I have but one more word to add
I have demonstrated to you
I have depicted
I have endeavored to emphasize
I have enlarged on this subject
I have felt it almost a duty to
I have found great cause for wonder
I have frequently been surprised at
I have gazed with admiration
I have generally observed
I have gone so far as to suggest
I have good reason for
I have had steadily in mind
I have had the honor
I have had to take a long sweep
I have heard it objected
I have heard with relief and pleasure
I have hitherto been adducing instances
[adduce = cite as an example]
I have hitherto been engaged in showing
I have in a measure anticipated
I have in my possession
I have incidentally dwelt on
I have introduced it to suggest
I have labored to maintain
I have laid much stress upon
I have lately observed many strong indications
I have listened with the utmost interest
I have little hope that I can add anything
I have lived to see
I have long ago insisted
I have long been of the conviction
I have never heard it suggested
I have never whispered a syllable
I have no acquaintance with
I have no doubt whatever
I have no excuse for intruding
I have no fear of myself
I have no fears for the success
I have no hesitation in asserting
I have no intention to moralize
I have no particular inclination

I have no prejudice on the subject
I have no pretention to be regarded
I have no reason to think
I have no scruple in saying
I have no such gloomy forebodings
I have no sympathy with the men
I have no thought of venturing to say
I have no wish at all to preach
I have not accustomed myself
I have not allowed myself
I have not been able to deny
I have not particularly referred to
I have not said anything yet
I have not the means of forming a judgment
I have not the right to reproach
I have not time to present
I have nothing more to say
I have noticed of late years
I have now explained to you
I have now made bold to touch upon
I have now rather more than kept my word
I have now said all that occurs to me
I have often been impressed with
I have often been struck with the resemblance
I have often lingered in fancy
I have one step farther to go
I have only partially examined
I have partly anticipated
I have pleasant memories of
I have pointed out
I have pride and pleasure in quoting
I have racked this brain of mine
I have read with great regret
I have said and I repeat
I have said over and over again
I have said what I solemnly believe
I have scant patience
I have seen for myself
I have seen it stated in a recent journal
I have seen some signs of encouragement
I have shown
I have some sort of fear
I have sometimes asked myself
I have sometimes fancied

I have sometimes wondered whether
I have still two comments to make
I have taken pains to know
I have the confident hope
I have the greatest possible confidence
I have the honor to propose
I have then to investigate
I have thought it incumbent on me
I have thought it right on this day
I have thought it well to suggest
I have throughout highly appreciated
I have thus been led by my feelings
I have thus stated the reason
I have to confess with a feeling of melancholy
I have to force my imagination
I have touched very cursorily
I have tried to convey to you
I have undertaken to speak
I have very much less feeling of
I have watched with some attention
I have witnessed the extraordinary
I have yet a more cogent reason
I have yet to learn
I hazard nothing in saying
I hear it sometimes said
I hear you say to yourselves
I heartily feel the singular claims
I hesitate to take an instance
I hold it to be clearly expedient
I hold myself obliged to
I hold the maxim no less applicable
I hold this to be a truth
I hold to the principle
I hope by this time we are all convinced
I hope for our own sakes
I hope I have expressed myself explicitly
I hope I may be allowed to intimate
I hope I shall not be told
I hope it is no disparagement
I hope most sincerely and truly
I hope none who hear me
I hope not to occupy more than a few minutes
I hope that I shall not be so unfortunate
I hope the day may be far distant
I hope the time may come again

I hope to be excused if
I hope to be forgiven if
I hope we may forget
I hope you will not accuse me
I imagine that no one will be disposed
I insist upon it
I intend to propose
I know from experience how
I know full well
I know I am treading on thin ice
I know it has been questioned
I know it is said
I know it will be said
I know many reasons why
I know not how else to express
I know not in what direction to look
I know not of my own knowledge
I know not where else to find
I know perfectly well
I know that it is impossible for me to
I know that this is the feeling
I know that what I may say is true
I know there are some who think
I know there is a theory among us
I know too well
I know very well the difference between
I know well it is not for me
I know well the sentiments
I know you are all impatient to hear
I know you will do all in your power
I know you will interpret what I say
I labor under a degree of prejudice
I lately heard it affirmed
I lay it down as a principle
I leave history to judge
I leave it to you
I leave the arduous task
I leave to others to speak
I long to speak a word or two
I look hopefully to
I look in vain
I look with encouragement
I look with inexpressible dread
I look with mingled hope and terror
I make my appeal to
I make no extravagant claim
I make this abrupt acknowledgment

191

I marvel that
I may add, speaking for my own part
I may be allowed to make one remark
I may be permitted to add
I may confess to you
I may safely appeal
I may say to you calmly
I may seem to have been diffuse
I may take as an instance
I may venture upon a review
I mean by this
I mean, moreover
I mean something more than that
I mention it to you to justify
I mention these facts because
I mention this, not by way of complaint
I might bring you another such case
I might deny that
I might enter into such detail
I might go further
I might go on indefinitely
I might go on to illustrate
I might of course point first
I might reasonably question the justice
I might try to explain
I might venture to claim
I might well have desired
I might well think
I must ask an abrupt question
I must be careful about what I say
I must be contented with
I must be excused if I say
I must bow in reverence
I must call your attention for a moment
I must conclude abruptly
I must confess that I became rather
alarmed
I must consider this as
I must crave your indulgence
I must express to you again
I must fairly tell you
I must find some fault with
I must for want of time omit
I must here admit
I must lament
I must leave any detailed development
I must mention with praise

I must not allow myself to indulge
I must not for an instant be supposed
I must not overlook
I must now beg to ask
I must pause a moment to
I must proceed
I must qualify the statement
I must remind my hearers of
I must reply to some observations
I must return to the subject
I must say that I am one of those
I must speak plainly
I must suppose, however
I must take occasion to say
I must thank you once more
I must try to describe to you
I myself have boundless faith
I need not assure this brilliant company
I need not dwell
I need not enter into
I need not follow out the application
I need not, I am certain, assure you
I need not say how much I thank you
I need not show how inconsistent
I need not specially recommend to you
I need not wander far in search
I need only to observe
I need say nothing in praise
I need scarcely observe
I need to guard myself right here
I neither affirm nor deny
I next come to the implicit assumption
I note with particular pleasure
I notice it as affording an instance
I noticed incidentally the fact
I now address you on a question
I now come, sir, to the second head
I now have the pleasure of presenting to
you
I now pass to the question of
I now proceed to inquire
I now reiterate
I object strongly to the use
I observe, then, in the first place
I only ask a favorable construction of
I only marvel
I only wish you to recognize

I open the all-important question
I ought to give an illustration
I own I can not help feeling
I particularly allude to
I pass on from that
I pass then to our second division
I pause for a moment to say
I pause to confess once more
I pay tribute to
I personally know that it is so
I pray God I may never
I predict that you will
I prefer a practical view
I presume I shall have to admit
I presume that I shall not be disbelieved
I proceed to another important phase
I profess
I propose briefly to glance at
I propose, therefore to consider
I protest I never had any doubt
I purposely have avoided
I question whether
I quite endorse what has been said
I rather look forward to a time
I readily grant
I really can not think it necessary to
I really do not know
I really thought that you would excuse me
I recall another historical fact
I recognize the high compliment conveyed
I recollect hearing a sagacious remark [sagacious = sound judgment]
I refer especially
I refuse to believe
I regard as an erroneous view
I regard it as a tribute
I regard it as a very great honor
I regret that I am not able to remember
I regret that it is not possible for me
I regret the time limits me
I regret this the less
I rejoice in an occasion like this
I rejoice that events have occurred
I rejoice to think I remark here
I remember a reference made

I remember an intimation
I remember full well
I remember the enjoyment with which
I remember to have heard
I repeat, I am not speaking
I repeat my statement in another form
I respectfully counsel
I respectfully submit
I rest my opinion on
I rise in behalf
I rise to express my disapprobation [approbation = warm approval; praise]
I rise to thank you
I rise with some trepidation
I return, in conclusion, to
I return you my most grateful thanks
I said a little way back
I said it would be well
I said that I thought
I salute with profound reverence
I sanction with all my heart
I saw an ingenious argument the other day
I say frankly
I say in moderation
I say it is extremely important
I say it most confidently
I say no more of these things
I say not one syllable against
I say, then, my first point is
I say this is no disparagement of
I say this the more gladly
I say without fear of contradiction
I see around me
I see as clearly as any man possibly can
I see little hope of
I see no exception
I see no possibility of
I see no reason for doubting
I seem to hear you say
I seize upon this opportunity
I seriously desire
I set out with saying
I shall add a few words
I shall address myself to a single point
I shall ask you to look very closely
I shall be told

I shall best attain my object
I shall bestow a little attention upon
I shall certainly admit
I shall consider myself privileged
I shall desist from
I shall endeavor to be guided
I shall give it in the words of
I shall here briefly recite the
I shall here use the word to denote
I shall hope to interest you
I shall invite you to follow me
I shall just give the summary of
I shall never believe
I shall never cease to be grateful
I shall not acknowledge
I shall not attempt a detailed narrative
I shall not end without appealing
I shall not enlarge upon
I shall not force into the discussion
I shall not go so far as to say
I shall not hesitate to say something
I shall not tax your patience
I shall not undertake to prophesy
I shall not weary your patience
I shall now give you some instances
I shall now proceed to show
I shall often have to advert to
I shall pass by all this
I shall presently show
I shall proceed without further preface
I shall recur to certain questions
I shall say all this without entering into
I shall show that I am not
I shall speak first about
I shall speak with becoming frankness
I shall take a broader view of the subject
I shall take it for granted here
I shall therefore endeavor
I shall touch upon one or two questions
I shall waste no time in refuting
I shall with your sanction
I should be false to my own manhood
I should be surprised if
I should be the last man to deny
I should fail in my duty if
I should find it hard to discover
I should have forfeited my own self-

respect
I should like at least to mention
I should like to emphasize
I should like to go a step farther
I should like to refer to two events
I should like to see that view answered
I should like to-day to examine briefly
I should much prefer
I should not be satisfied with myself
I should think it too absurd
I shrink from the contemplation
I shudder at the doctrine
I simply lay my finger on a fact
I simply pause here to ask
I sincerely regret the absence
I sincerely wish it were in my power
I solemnly declare
I sometimes hear a wish expressed
I sorrowfully call to mind
I speak forth my sentiment
I speak from no little personal
observation
I speak of this to show
I speak the fact when I tell you
I speak the secret feeling of this company
I speak what I know when I say
I speak wholly without authority
I speak with feeling upon this point
I speak with some degree of
encouragement
I speak with the utmost sincerity
I speak within the hearing of
I stand in awed amazement before
I stand in the midst of men
I still view with respect
I submit it to every candid mind
I submit that in such a case
I submit that it is high time
I submit this proposition
I summon you to do your share
I suppose it is right to answer
I suppose it to be entirely true
I suppose most men will recollect
I suppose that everyone who listens to
me
I suppose there is no one here
I suppose we are all of one opinion

194

I suspect that is why we so often
I sympathize most heartily
I take a broader and bolder position
I take it for granted
I take leave to say
I take one picture as an illustration
I take pleasure in saying
I take the liberty of observing
I take this instance at random
I take two views of
I tell him in reply
I tell you, gentlemen
I tender my thanks to you
I thank you for having allowed me
I thank you for the appreciative tone
I thank you for the honor
I thank you for your most generous greeting
I thank you for your thoughtful courtesy
I thank you from the bottom of my heart
I thank you very gratefully
I thank you very sincerely for the honor
I think I am correct in saying
I think I am not the first to utter
I think I can claim a purpose
I think I can sincerely declare
I think I have a right to look upon
I think I have rightly spoken
I think I might safely say
I think I need not say more
I think it is not too much to say
I think it is quite right
I think it may be necessary to consider
I think it might be said with safety
I think it my duty to
I think it observable
I think it probable
I think it will astonish you
I think it will be granted
I think no Wise man can be indifferent
I think, on the contrary
I think something may be said in favor of
I think that all will agree
I think that I can explain
I think that I can venture to say
I think that, in these last years
I think that none of us will deny

I think there is no better evidence
I think there is no call on me to listen
I think we are justified
I think we can hardly hope
I think we may all easily see
I think we may ask in reply
I think we may safely conclude
I think we may say, therefore
I think we may well be proud of
I think we may well congratulate each other
I think we must draw a distinction
I think we need neither doubt nor fear
I think we ought to recur a moment to
I think we shall all recognize
I think we should do well to call to mind
I think we take too narrow a view
I think when we look back upon
I think you may well rejoice in
I think you will all agree
I think you will pardon my saying
I think you will see
I thus explicitly reply
I tremble at the task
I tremble to think
I trust I may be indulged
I trust it is not presumptuous
I trust that as the years roll on
I trust that I shall have the indulgence
I trust that this will not be regarded as
I turn, gentlemen, to the case
I use the word advisedly
I use the word in the sense
I use very plain language
I utter this word with the deepest affection
I value very much the honor
I venture to ask permission
I venture to say
I verily believe
I very confidently submit
I view that prospect with the greatest misgiving
I want to bespeak your attention
I want to know the character
I want to make some simple applications
I want to say just a few words

195

I want to say one word more
I want to say to you seriously
I want to think with you
I warn and exhort you
I was astonished to learn
I was constantly watchful to
I was exceedingly interested
I was honored with the acquaintance
I was lost in admiration
I was not slow to accept and believe
I was not without some anxiety
I was overwhelmed
I was sincerely astonished
I was very much interested
I was very much thrilled
I well recollect the time
I well remember an occasion
I will accept the general proposition
I will add the memorable words
I will ask the indulgence
I will ask you to accompany me
I will ask you to bear witness
I will dwell a little longer
I will endeavor in a brief way
I will endeavor to illustrate
I will endeavor to show you
I will enlarge no further
I will even express a hope at the outset
I will even go further and say
I will first call your attention to
I will give one more illustration
I will illustrate this point by
I will merely mention
I will neither affirm nor deny
I will not allude
I will not argue this
I will not attempt to note
I will not be content until
I will not condescend to
I will not enumerate at present
I will not pause to maintain
I will not positively say
I will not pretend to inquire into
I will not quarrel with
I will not relinquish the confidence
I will not repeat the arguments here
I will not try to gauge

I will now consider with you
I will now leave this question
I will now take an instance
I will only speak to one point
I will only sum up my evidence
I will only take an occasion to express
I will only venture to remind you
I will point out to your attention
I will say at once
I will speak but a word or two more
I will speak plainly
I will state with perfect distinctness
I will suppose the objection to be
I will take one more instance
I will take the precaution to add
I will tell you what I think of
I will try to make the thing intelligible
I will venture a single remark
I will venture to add
I will venture to express the hope
I will yield the whole question
I willingly admit
I wish also to declare positively
I wish at the outset
I wish emphatically to reaffirm
I wish I had the time and the power
I wish it first observed
I wish rather to call your attention
I wish, sir, that justice might be done
I wish to ask if you honestly and
candidly believe
I wish to be allowed to enforce in detail
I wish to begin my statement
I wish to confine what I have to say
I wish to do full justice to
I wish to draw your attention
I wish to express my profound
gratification
I wish to give these arguments their full
weight
I wish to know whether
I wish to offer a few words relative to
I wish to remind you in how large a
degree
I wish to say a word or two
I wish to state all this as a matter of fact
I wish you success and happiness

I wish you to observe
I would also gratefully acknowledge
I would as soon believe
I would desire to speak simply and directly
I would enter a protest
I would further point out to you
I would have you understand
I would infinitely rather
I would like to say one word just here
I would not be understood as belittling
I would not dwell upon that matter if
I would not push the suggestion so far
I would now gladly lay before you
I would rather a thousand times
I would recommend to your consideration
I would suggest first of all
I would that my voice could reach the ear
I would urge and entreat you
I would urge upon you
I would venture to point out
I yielded to the earnest solicitations
If any man be so persuaded
If anyone could conceive
If anyone is so dim of vision
If any other answer be made
If at first view this should seem
If, however, you determine to
If I am asked for the proof
If I am wrong
If I can carry you with me
If I can succeed in describing
If I could find words
If I have done no more than view the facts
If I have in any way deserved
If I may be allowed a little criticism
If I may be allowed modestly to suggest
If I may be allowed to refer
If I may reverently say so
If I may say so without presumption
If I may so speak
If I may take for granted
If I may venture to say anything
If I mistake not the sentiment

If I recollect aright
If I understand the matter at all
If I venture a few remarks
If I were asked
If I were to act upon my conviction
If I were to recapitulate
If I wished to prove my contention
If, in consequence we find it necessary
If in the glow of conscious pride
If in the years of the future
If it be difficult to appreciate
If it be so
If it be true
If it is contended
If it means anything, it means this
If more were needed to illustrate.
If my opinions are true
If on the contrary, we all foresee
If, on the other hand, I say
If one seeks to measure
If only we go deep enough
If still you have further doubt
If the bare facts were studied
If the experience of the world is worth anything
If, then, I am asked
If, then, I should here rest my cause
If there be any among us
If there be one lesson more than another
If this be so
If this seems doubtful to anyone
If, unhappily, the day should ever come
If we accept at all the argument
If we are not blind to
If we are rightly informed
If we are to reason on the fact
If we cast our glance back
If we embark upon a career
If we had the whole case before us
If we isolate ourselves
If we may trust to experience
If we pursue a different course
If we pursue our inquiries through
If we sincerely desire
If we survey
If we would not be beguiled
If what has been said is true

If you remain silent
If you seek the real meaning of
If you think for a moment
If you want to look
If you were asked to point out
If you will allow me to prophesy
If you will forgive me the expression
If you wish for a more interesting example
If you wish to get at the bottom of facts
If you would see the most conclusive proof
If your view is right
In a significant paragraph
In a wider sense
In a word, gentlemen
In a word, I conceive
In actual life, I suspect
In addition to these arguments
In addressing myself to the question
In addressing you I feel
In agreement with this obvious conclusion
In all ages of the world
In all or any of these views
In all times and places
In an unguarded moment
In answering the inquiry
In any view of the case
In closing my speech, I ask each of you
In conclusion, let me say
In conclusion, may I repeat
In consequence it becomes a necessity
In contemplating the causes
In days to come
In examining this part of the subject
In fine, it is no extravagance to say
In former ages and generations
In further illustration
In further proof of my assertion
In illustration of what I have said
In like manner are to be explained
In like manner I would advise
In listening to the kind words
In looking about me
In many instances
In meeting this difficulty, I will not urge

In most cases I hold
In my estimation
In my humble opinion
In my view
In offering to you these counsels
In one other respect
In one point I wish no one to mistake me
In one sense this is undoubtedly true
In order to appreciate the force of
In order to complete the proof
In order to do justice to the question
In order to prove plainly and intelligibly
In order to realize adequately
In other words
In our estimate of the past
In point of fact
In precisely the same way
In pursuance of these views
In pursuing the great objects
In regard to
In rising to return my sincere thanks
In saying all of this, I do not forget
In saying this, I am not disposed to deny
In short, I say
In solving this difficulty
In something of a parallel way
In spite of the fact
In such cases, strictly speaking
In support of this assertion
In that matchless epitome
In that mood of high hope
In the anomalies of fortune
In the course of these remarks
In the existing circumstances
In the first place, therefore, I consider
In the first place we see
In the first place, we should be all agreed
In the fullest sense
In the fullness of time
In the last suggestion
In the meantime I will commend to you
In the next place, be assured
In the presence of this vast assembly
In the present situation
In the progress of events
In the remarks I have made
In the same manner I rely

In the second place it is quite clear
In the suggestion I have made
In the very brief space at our disposal
In these extraordinary circumstances
In these sentiments I agree
In this brief survey
In this connection, I may be permitted to refer
In this connection I remind myself
In this necessarily brief and imperfect review
In this rapid and slight enumeration
In this respect
In this sense only
In this there is no contradiction
In very many instances
In very truth
In view of these reflections
In what has now been said
In what I have now further to say
In widening our view
Indeed, can anyone tell me
Indeed, I am not convinced
Indeed, I can not do better
Indeed, I have heard it whispered
Indeed, I may fairly say
Indeed, it will generally be found
Indeed we know
Instances abound
Is it logically consistent
Is it not legitimate to recognize
Is it not marvelous
Is it not obvious
Is it not quite possible
Is it not, then, preposterous
Is it not universally recognized
Is it not wise to argue
Is it possible, can it be believed
Is it, then, any wonder
Is not that the common sentiment
Is there any evidence here
Is there any language of reproach
Is there any possibility of mistaking
Is there any reason in the world
It affords me gratification
It also pleases me very much
It amounts to this

It appears from what has been said
It appears to me, on the contrary
It can rightly be said
It certainly follows, then
It comes to this
It could not be otherwise
It does not necessarily follow
It exhibits a state of mind
It follows as a matter of course
It follows inevitably
It gives us an exalted conception
It grieves me to relate
It hardly fits the character
It has at all times been a just reproach
It has been a very great pleasure for me
It has been generally assumed
It has been justly objected
It has been my privilege
It has been suggested fancifully
It has been well said
It has ever been my ambition
It has struck me very forcibly
It is a circumstance of happy augury [augury = sign of something coming; omen]
It is a common error
It is a curious trait
It is a fact well known
It is a falsehood to say
It is a familiar charge against
It is a good augury of success [augury = sign of something coming; omen]
It is a great pleasure to me
It is a living truth
It is a matter of absorbing interest
It is a matter of amusement
It is a matter of fact
It is a matter of just pride
It is a melancholy story
It is a memory I cherish
It is a mischievous notion
It is a mistake to suppose
It is a most extraordinary thing
It is a most pertinent question
It is a noble thing
It is a peculiar pleasure to me
It is a perversion of terms

199

It is a pleasing peculiarity
It is a popular idea
It is a rare privilege
It is a recognized principle
It is a remarkable and striking fact
It is a strange fact
It is a sure sign
It is a theme too familiar
It is a thing commonly said
It is a touching reflection
It is a true saying
It is a very significant fact
It is a vision which still inspires us
It is a wholesome symptom
It is, all things considered, a fact
It is all very fine to think
It is all very well to say
It is almost proverbial
It is also possible
It is also probably true
It is always pleasant to respond
It is amazing how little
It is an easy matter
It is an egregious mistake [egregious =
conspicuously and outrageously
reprehensible]
It is an established rule
It is an incredible thing
It is an interesting fact
It is an unforgivable offense
It is an unquestionable truth
It is appropriate that we should celebrate
It is asserted
It is assumed as an axiom
It is at once inconsistent
It is but fair to say
It is but too true
It is by no means my design
It is certainly especially pleasant
It is certainly remarkable
It is common in these days to lament
It is commonly assumed
It is comparatively easy
It is curious sophistry
It is curious to observe
It is desirable for us
It is difficult for me to respond fitly

It is difficult to avoid saying
It is difficult to describe
It is difficult to overstate
It is difficult to put a limit
It is difficult to surmise
It is doubtful whether
It is easy enough to add
It is easy to instance cases
It is easy to understand
It is eminently proper
It is every man's duty to think
It is evident that the answer to this
It is evidently supposed by many people
It is exceedingly gratifying to hear
It is exceedingly unfortunate
It is fair that you should hear
It is fair to suppose
It is far from me to desire
It is fatal to suppose
It is fitting
It is for me to relate
It is for others to illustrate
It is for this reason
It is for us to ask
It is greatly assumed
It is gratifying to have the honor
It is hardly for me
It is hardly necessary to pass judgment
It is idle to think of
It is immaterial whether
It is impossible to avoid saying
It is in every way appropriate
It is in the highest degree worthy
It is in this characteristic
It is in vain
It is in your power to give
It is indeed a strange doctrine
It is indeed not a little remarkable
It is indeed true
It is indeed very clear
It is indispensable to have
It is interesting and suggestive
It is interesting to know
It is just so far true
It is likewise necessary
It is made evident
It is manifest

It is manifestly absurd to say
It is merely common sense to say
It is more than probable
It is my agreeable duty
It is my belief
It is my earnest wish
It is my grateful duty to address you
It is my hope
It is my present purpose
It is natural to ask the question
It is necessary to refer
It is necessary to take some notice
It is needful to a complete understanding
It is needless before this audience to
repeat
It is no doubt true
It is no exaggeration to say
It is no part of my business
It is no significant thing
It is no small indication
It is no wonder
It is not a practical question
It is not altogether satisfactory
It is not an unknown occurrence
It is not by any means
It is not difficult to comprehend
It is not difficult to discern
It is not easy for me to find words
It is not enough to say
It is not entirely clear to me
It is not evident
It is not for me on this occasion
It is not given to many men
It is not likely that any of you
It is not logical to say
It is not my intention to enter into
It is not my purpose to discuss
It is not necessarily true
It is not necessary for me even to sketch
It is not necessary for our purpose
It is not often in these modern days
It is not ours to pronounce
It is not out of place to remind you
It is not possible to recount
It is not quite clear
It is not to me so very surprising
It is not too much to say

It is not unknown to you
It is not within the scope of this address
It is now high time for me
It is now perfectly plain
It is observable enough
It is obvious
It is of course difficult
It is of great importance to show
It is of no moment
It is of very little importance
It is often remarked
It is on these grounds
It is one of the burning questions of the
day
It is one of the most natural visions
It is one of the most significant things
It is one of the queerest freaks of fate
It is only a few short years since
It is only just to say
It is our duty to examine
It is ours to bear witness
It is owing to this truth
It is peculiarly befitting at this time
It is perfectly apparent
It is pitiable to reflect
It is pleasant to meet this brilliant
company
It is rather a pleasant coincidence
It is rather an arduous task
It is rather startling
It is related
It is ridiculous to say
It is said, and I think said truly
It is said to be impossible
It is satisfactory to notice
It is scarcely necessary to insist
It is scarcely questioned
It is self-evident
It is sometimes hard to determine
It is still an open question
It is still more surprising
It is substantially true
It is surely necessary for me
It is the clear duty of
It is the doctrine of
It is the fashion to extol
It is the universal testimony

It is therefore evident
It is therefore necessary
It is this which lies at the foundation
It is to be expected
It is to be remembered
It is to me a very sincere satisfaction
It is told traditionally
It is too plain to be argued
It is true
It is unnecessary for me to remind you
It is upon this line of reasoning
It is very common to confuse
It is very doubtful whether
It is very interesting and pleasant
It is well known
It is with great pleasure
It is with pity unspeakable
It is within the memory of men now
living
It is worth while to notice
It may appear absurd
It may at first sight seem strange
It may be added
It may be conjectured
It may be imagined
It may be plausibly objected
It may be rightly said
It may be useful to trace
It may be worth your while to keep in
view
It may indeed be unavoidable
It may not be altogether certain
It may not be uninteresting to any of you
It may or may not be true
It may, perhaps, seem wonderful
It may seem a little strange
It may still more probably be said
It must be a cause of delight
It must be borne in mind
It must be the verdict of history
It must create astonishment
It must doubtless be admitted
It must ever be recollected
It must never be forgotten
It must not be supposed
It must seem to every thoughtful man
It needs scarcely be said

It now becomes my pride and privilege
It only remains now to speak
It ought to animate us
It proves a great deal
It remains only to speak briefly
It remains that I inform you of
It remains that I should say a few words
It reminds me of an anecdote
It reminds one of the compliment
It requires no effort of imagination
It scarcely seems to be in keeping
It seems almost desperate to think of
It seems almost incredible
It seems now to be generally admitted
It seems strange to be told
It seems then that on the whole
It seems to me a striking circumstance
It seems to me idle to ask
It seems to me singularly appropriate
It seems to me the primary foundation
It seems to me unphilosophical
It should always be borne in mind
It should be remembered
It so happens
It sometimes seems to me
It still remains to be observed
It strikes me with wonder
It suggests at the outset
It summons our imagination
It surely is not too much to expect
It therefore astonishes me
It used to be a reproach
It was a brilliant answer
It was a fine and delicate rebuke
It was a fit and beautiful circumstance
It was a propitious circumstance
[propitious = auspicious, favorable]
It was certainly a gracious act
It was in the full understanding
It was my good fortune
It was not to be expected
It was said by one who ought to know
It was, therefore, inevitable
It was under these circumstances
It will appeal to
It will appear from what has been said
It will be asked me how

It will be easy to say too much
It will be easy to trace the influence
It will be evident to you
It will be idle to imply
It will be interesting to trace
It will be just as reasonable to say
It will be rather to our advantage
It will be recollected
It will be seen at a glance
It will be well and wise
It will carry out my meaning more fully
It will, I suppose, be denied
It will not be expected from me
It will not be safe
It will not do for a man to say
It will not, I trust, be concluded
It will not surely be objected
It will not take many words to sum up
It will thus be seen
It would be a misfortune

It would be a proud distinction
It would be a very remarkable fact
It would be absurd to pretend
It would be an inexcusable omission
It would be idle for me
It would be imprudent in me
It would be invidious for me [invidious = rousing ill will, animosity]
It would be natural on such an occasion
It would be no less impracticable
It would be out of place here
It would be preposterous to say
It would be presumptuous in me
It would be the height of absurdity
It would be unfair to praise
It would be unjust to deny
It would be well for us to reflect
It would indeed be unworthy
It would seem perhaps most fitting

## J

Just the reverse is true

## L

Language is inadequate to voice my appreciation
Lastly, I do not understand
Lastly, it can not be denied
Less than this could not be said
Lest I should be accused of quibbling
Let all of us labor in this work
Let anyone imagine to himself
Let anyone who doubts
Let everyone consider
Let it be clearly understood, I repeat it
Let it be remembered
Let it not be objected
Let it not be supposed that I impute [impute = relate to a particular cause or source]
Let me add another thing
Let me add my final word
Let me add one other hint
Let me also say a word in regard
Let me answer these questions
Let me ask you to imagine

Let me ask your leave to propose
Let me be allowed to devote a few words
Let me call attention to another fact
Let me commend to you
Let me direct your attention now to
Let me entreat you to examine
Let me give one more instance
Let me give one parting word
Let me give you an illustration
Let me here make one remark
Let me here say
Let me hope that I have said enough
Let me illustrate again
Let me make myself distinctly understood
Let me make use of an illustration
Let me not be thought offensive
Let me now conclude with
Let me once more urge upon you
Let me protest against the manner
Let me quite temperately defend
Let me rather make the supposition

Let me say a practical word
Let me simply declare
Let me tell you an interesting reminiscence
Let me thank you once more
Let me urge you earnestly
Let no man congratulate himself
Let our conception be enlarged
Let our object be
Let that question be answered by
Let the facts be granted
Let these instances suffice
Let this be the record made
Let this inspire us with abhorrence of
Let us approach the subject from another side
Let us attempt a survey
Let us be perfectly just
Let us be quite practical
Let us bear perpetually in mind
Let us begin at the beginning
Let us begin by examining
Let us briefly review
Let us brush aside once for all
Let us cherish
Let us confirm our opinion
Let us consider for a moment
Let us devote ourselves
Let us discard all prejudice
Let us do all we can
Let us draw an illustration
Let us endeavor to understand
Let us enumerate
Let us figure to ourselves
Let us for the moment put aside
Let us get a clear understanding
Let us heed the voice
Let us hope and believe
Let us hope that future generations
Let us imitate
Let us inquire also

M
Mainly, I believe
Making allowances for differences of opinion
Many of us have had the good fortune

Let us labor and pray
Let us likewise remember
Let us look briefly at a few particulars
Let us look nearer home
Let us not be fearful
Let us not be misled
Let us not be misunderstood
Let us not flatter ourselves
Let us not for a moment forget
Let us not limit our view
Let us now apply the views presented
Let us now consider the characteristics
Let us now see the results
Let us now turn our consideration
Let us observe this analogy
Let us pass on to another fact
Let us pause a moment
Let us push the inquiry yet further
Let us rather listen to
Let us reflect how vain
Let us remember this
Let us remind ourselves
Let us resolve
Let us scrutinize the facts
Let us suppose, for argument's sake
Let us suppose the case to be
Let us take, for instance
Let us, then, be assured
Let us, then, be worthy of
Let us, therefore, say once for all
Let us try to form a mental picture
Let us turn to the contemplation of
Let your imagination realize
Like all citizens of high ideals
Likely enough
Little wonder therefore
Long have I been convinced
Look at it in another way
Look at some of these questions
Look at the situation

Many of you, perhaps, recollect
May I ask you to believe
May I not speak here
May I try to show that every effort

May I venture to suggest
May it not also be advanced
May the day come quickly
Meantime it is encouraging to think
Meanwhile let us freely recognize
Men are in the habit of saying
Men are telling us nowadays
Men everywhere testify
More and more it is felt
More than once have I had to express
More than this need not be said
Moreover, I have insisted
Moreover, I would counsel you
Moreover, when we pass judgment
Much has been said and written about
My appreciation has been quickened

My belief, therefore, is
My duty is to endeavor to show
My experience tells me
My first duty is to express to you
My friends, do you really believe
My friends, I propose
My heart tells me
My idea, therefore, is
My last criticism upon
My mind is not moved by
My mind most perfectly acquiesces
My next objection is
My own private opinion is
My present business is
My regret is intensified by the thought

## N

Nay, I boldly say
Nay, it will be a relief to my mind
Nay, there is a general feeling
Need I say that I mean
Neither should you deceive
Never before have I so strongly felt
Never can I cease to feel
Never did there devolve
Never for a moment believe
Never have I felt so forcibly
Never was a weaker defense attempted
Never was there a greater mistake
Never was there an instance
Nevertheless we can admit
Next, from what has been said it is plain
Next, I consider
Next, it will be denied
No argument can overwhelm a fact
No defense is to be found
No distinct test can be named
No doubt, in the first instance
No doubt there are many questions
No doubt to most of us
No finer sentence has come down to us
No greater service could be rendered
No longer do we believe
No man regrets more than I do
No one can feel this more strongly
No one can, I think, pretend

No one can see the end
No one here, I am sure
No one, I suppose, would say
No one, I think, can fail to observe
No one, I think, will dispute the
statement
No one need to exaggerate
No one will accuse me
No true man ever believes
None can have failed to observe
Nor am I disparaging or discouraging
Nor can I forget either
Nor can it justly be said
Nor can we afford to waste time
Nor can we forget how long
Nor can we now ask
Nor do I believe
Nor do I doubt
Nor do I pretend
Nor do I think there can be found
Nor does it matter much
Nor has there been wanting
Nor indeed am I supposing
Nor is it a fair objection
Nor is it probable
Nor is this all
Nor let me forget to add here
Nor must I be understood as saying
Nor must it be forgotten

Nor need we fear to speak
Nor should any attempt be made
Nor will history fail to record
Nor will I enlarge on the matter
Not at all
Not only so
Not that I quarrel with
Nothing but the deepest sense
Nothing can be further from the truth
Nothing could be clearer
Nothing could be more striking
Nothing is more common in the world
Nothing that you can do
Notwithstanding all that has been said
Notwithstanding all this, I hold
Now, bear with me when I say
Now comes the question
Now, comparing these instances together
Now, from these instances it is plain
Now, having spoken of
Now, I admit
Now, I am far from denying
Now, I am far from undervaluing
Now, I am justified in calling this
Now, I am obliged to say
Now, I do not wish you to believe
Now, I have a closing sentence or two
Now, I pass on to consider

Now, I shall not occupy your time
Now, I understand the argument
Now, I will undertake to say
Now, I wish to call your attention
Now, if you will clearly understand
Now, is there any ground or basis for
Now, it is an undoubted fact
Now, it is evident
Now, it is not at all strange
Now, it is unquestioned
Now, let me speak with the greatest care
Now, let me stop a moment
Now, let us consider
Now, observe, my drift
Now, sir, I am truly horrified
Now, the answer we should give
Now, the question here at issue
Now, the world will say
Now, there is a close alliance between
Now, this is precisely the danger
Now, this is to some extent
Now, understand me definitely
Now, we do not maintain
Now, we will inquire
Now, what I want you to realize
Now, with regard to
Now, you will allow me to state
Now, you will understand from this

O
Observe again
Occasionally you ought to read
Of course I am aware
Of course I am putting an impossible
case
Of course I can not be taken to mean
Of course I do not maintain
Of course I do not stop here
Of course I would not allow
Of course much may be said
Of course these remarks hold good
Of course we may, if we please
Of course you will sympathize
Of one thing, however, I am certain
Of this briefly
Of this statement I will only say
Of this truth I shall convince you by

On a review of the whole subject
On occasions of this kind
On such a day as this
On the contrary, I am assuming
On the occasion to which I refer
On the other hand, it is clear
On the whole, then, I observe
On this auspicious occasion
On this point I do not mean to dwell
On this subject you need not suspect
Once again, there are those
Once more I emphasize
Once more let me try to put into words
One additional remark
One almost wishes
One can not decline to note
One concluding remark has to be made

One fact is clear and indisputable
One further word
One important topic remains
One is fairly tempted to wish
One lesson history may be said to repeat
One might be challenged to produce
One of the ancients said
One of the most commonly known
One of the most extraordinary incidents
One of the things I recollect with most pride
One of these signs is the fact
One or two points are made clear
One other circumstance
One other remark suggests itself
One remark I will make

One thing more will complete this question
One thing which always impressed me
One very striking tendency
One word in courtesy I must say
One word more in a serious vein
One would naturally suppose
Only so much do I know
Opinions are divided as to whether
Or to come nearer home
Or to take but one other example
Ordinarily speaking, such deductions
Others may hold other opinions
Ought we not to think
Our thoughts wander back
Over and above all this

## P

Pardon me if
Perhaps another reason why
Perhaps, however, in speaking to you
Perhaps, however, some among you will be
Perhaps I may be best able to illustrate
Perhaps I ought to say

Perhaps it may be doubted
Perhaps, sir, I am mistaken in
Permit me frankly to say
Permit me to add another circumstance
Permit me to bring home to you
Personally, I am far too firm a believer
Pray, sir, let me say

## R

Read but your history aright
Recollect, sir
Reflections such as these
Rely upon it

Remember, I do not seek to
Remembering some past occurrences
Returning, then, to the consideration

## S

Seriously, then, do I beg you
Shall I tell you
Shall we complain
Should there be objection, I answer
Since, then, it is provided
Since, then, this is the case
Sir, with all my heart, I respond
So accustomed are we
So at least it seems to me
So far as I know
So far as my observation and experience goes
So far in general
So I say to you

So it comes to pass
So long as we continue to love truth and duty
So men are asking
So much at first sight
So much on this subject
So that I may venture to say
So that if you were persuaded
So then ought we also
So, to add one other example
So, too, I may go on to speak
So when I hear people say
Some have insisted
Some of you can recall the time

Some of you may think this visionary
Some of you will remember
Some one will perhaps object
Some prejudice is attached
Some writer has said
Sometimes I venture to think
Sometimes it may happen
Speaking in this place
Startling as this may appear to you
Stating only the truth, I affirm
Still another encouraging fact
Still further
Still I can not part from my subject
Still I have generally found
Still I imagine you would consider it
Still I know what answer I can make to
Still it may with justice be said
Still one thing more
Still we ought to be grateful
Strange as it may seem
Strictly in confidence, I do not think
Strictly speaking, there is no such thing
Such a doctrine is essentially superficial

T
Take another instance
Take one of the most recent cases
Take the simple fact
Take this example
Taking a broader view
Taking the facts by themselves
That is a further point
That is a natural boast
That is a pure assumption
That is all that it seems necessary to me
That is all very good
That is far from my thoughts
That is final and conclusive
That is the lesson of history
That is the question of questions
That you may conceive the force of
The answer is easy to find
The answer is ready
The belief is born of the wish
The broad principle which I would lay
down
The circumstances under which we meet

Such are the rather tolerant ideas
Such considerations as these
Such, I believe, would be the
consequences
Such illustrations are not frequent
Such, in brief, is the story
Such is steadfastly my opinion
Such is the deep prejudice now existing
Such is the intellectual view we take
Such is the lesson which I am taught
Such is the progress
Such is the truth
Such, sir, I conceive to be
Such, then, is the true idea
Such, too, is the characteristic of
Suffer me to point out
Suffice it to say here
Summing up what I have said
Suppose we turn our eyes to
Surely I do not misinterpret
Surely it is a paradox
Surely it is not too much for me to say

The climax of my purpose in this address
The common consent of civilized
mankind
The conclusion is irresistible
The confusing assertion is sometimes
made
The day is at hand
The decided objection is raised
The doctrine I am combating
The doctrine is admirable
The effect too often is
The evolution of events has brought
The fact has made a deep impression on
me
The fact has often been insisted
The fact to be particularly noted
The facts are clear and unequivocal
The facts may be strung together
The first business of every man
The first counsel I would offer
The first great fact to remember is
The first point to be ascertained

The first practical thought is
The first remarkable instance was
The first thing I wish to note
The first thing that we have to consider
The future historian will, no doubt
The generous feeling that has promoted you
The great mass of the people
The hour is at hand
The illustration is analogous
The important thing is
The instance I shall choose
The irresistible tendency of
The kindness with which I have been received
The last and distinguishing feature is
The latest inclination I have seen
The lesson which we should take most to heart
The main cause of all this
The more you examine this matter
The most concise tribute paid
The most reasonable anticipation
The most remarkable step forward
The most striking characteristic
The most sublime instance that I know
The next point is
The next question to be considered is
The next thing I consider indispensable
The occasion that calls us together
The one central difference between
The only course that remains open
The only plea to be offered
The other day I observed
The paramount consideration is
The perils that beset us here
The pleasing duty is assigned me
The point I have urged upon you is
The point I wish a little further to speak of
The point to which I shall call your attention
The popular notion is
The practical inference from all this
The presence of this brilliant assemblage
The pressing question is
The prevalent opinion, no doubt

The proof of this statement is to be found
The question is deeply involved
The question, then, recurs
The remedy I believe to be
The result, I fancy, has been
The result of the whole
The rule will always hold good
The sacred voice of inspiration
The same is true in respect of
The scene all comes back
The sentiment to which I am to respond
The sentiment which you have expressed
The simple rule and test
The simple truth is
The soundness of this doctrine depends
The strongest proof I have
The subject of the evening's address
The subject which has been assigned to me
The task has been placed in my hands
The testimony of history is
The theory seems at first sight
The thought with which I shall close
The time has manifestly now arrived
The time is not far distant
The time is now come for me
The times are full of signs and warnings
The toast I am about to propose to you
The vain wish has sometimes been indulged
The view I have been enforcing
The view is more misleading
The warmth and kindness of your reception
The welcome that has been extended to me
The whole story of civilization
Then again, in corroboration
Then again, when men say
Then take the other side of the argument
Then the question arises
Then there is another story
Then, too, it must be remembered
There are certain old truths
There are few spectacles
There are hopeful signs of
There are, I believe, many who think

There are, indeed, exceptions
There are, indeed, persons who profess
There are many educated and intelligent people
There are people in every community
There are several reasons why
There are some slight modifications
There are some who are fond of looking at
There are some who have an idea
There are those of us who can remember
There are those who wish
There are two conflicting theories
There can be but one answer
There can be no doubt
There has been a great deal of discussion lately
There has been no period of time
There have been differences of opinion
There is a characteristic saying
There is a class of person
There is a common saying
There is a conviction
There is a degree of evidence
There is a genuine grief
There is a great deal of rash talking
There is a growing disposition
There is a large class of thinkers
There is a lesson of profound interest
There is a more important question
There is a most serious lesson
There is a multitude of facts
There is a question of vital importance
There is a very common tendency
There is a vital difference of opinion
There is an analogy in this respect
There is an ancient story to the effect
There is an eternal controversy
There is another class of men
There is another factor
There is another object equally important
There is another point of view
There is another remarkable analogy
There is another sense in which
There is, at any rate, to be said
There is but one consideration

There is certainly no reason
There is hardly any limit
There is, however, another opinion
There is, however, one caution
There is little truth in
There is no field of human activity
There is no good reason
There is no justification for
There is no mistaking the purpose
There is no more insidious peril
There is no more striking exemplification
There is no occasion to exaggerate
There is no page of history
There is no sense in saying
There is no worse perversion
There is not a shadow of evidence
There is nothing more repulsive
There is nothing overstated in this description
There is nothing to show
There is one story which it is said
There is only one sense in which
There is some difference of opinion
There is something strangely interesting
There is yet another distinction
There is yet one other remark
There ought certainly to be
There was but one alternative
There was one remarkable incident
There will always be a number of men
There will be no difficulty
There yet remains
Therefore, there is no possibility of a doubt
Therein lies your responsibility
These alone would not be sufficient
These are enough to refute the opinion
These are general counsels
These are generalizations
These are my reasons for
These are points for consideration
These considerations have great weight with me
These exceptions do not hold in the case of
These ideas naturally present themselves

These instances are far from common
These instances are indications
These last words lead me to say
These objections only go to show
These questions I shall examine
These various partial views
They mistake the intelligence
They would persuade you to
Think for a moment
Think of the cool disregard
This absurdity arises
This appeal to the common sense
This argument is especially cogent
[cogent = powerfully persuasive]
This, at least, is sure
This being the case
This being true
This being undeniable, it is plain
This being understood, I ask
This brings me to a single remark
This brings us to a subject
This episode goes to prove
This fact was soon made manifest
This from the nature of the case
This I conceive to be the business
This I consider to be my own case
This I have told you
This is a general statement
This is a very one-sided conception
This is a very serious situation
This is an astonishing announcement
This is conceded by
This is contrary to all argument
This is doubtless the truth
This is especially the case
This is essentially an age of
This is in the main just
This is like saying
This is not all
This is not the main point of objection
This is not the occasion or the place
This is obvious
This is on the whole reasonable
This is only another illustration of
This is owing in great measure to
This is precisely what we ought to do
This is said in no spirit of

This is suggested to us
This is the design and intention
This is the great fact
This is the main point on which the
inquiry turns
This is the meaning of
This is the obvious answer
This is the point I want to impress upon
you
This is the point of view
This is the position of our minds
This is the radical question
This is the sentiment of mankind
This is the starting-point
This is the sum
This is to be found in the fact
This is what I am led to say
This is what may be objected
This is why I take the liberty
This language is plain
This leads me to the question
This leads us to inquire
This may be said without prejudice
This might be illustrated at length
This much is certain
This sentiment was well-nigh universal
This, surely, is the conclusion
This, then, is the answer
This, then, is the drift of my illustration
This, then, is what I mean by saying
This will be evident at once
This you can not deny
Those who have watched the tendencies
Thus a great deal may be done
Thus analogy suggests
Thus far, I willingly admit
Thus I am led on to another remark
Thus if you look into
Thus instances occur now and then
Thus it comes to pass
Thus my imagination tells me
Thus much, however, I may say
Thus much I may be allowed to say
Thus much may be sufficient to recall
Thus we see
Time would not permit me
To a man of the highest public spirit

To avoid all possibility of being
misunderstood
To be more explicit
To be sure, we sometimes hear
To bring the matter nearer home
To convince them of this
To feel the true force of this argument
To illustrate
To make my story quite complete
To me, however, it would appear
To my way of conceiving such matters
To prevent misapprehension
To some it may sound like a paradox
To sum up all that has been said
To sum up in one word

U
Under all the circumstances
Under these favoring conditions
Under this head
Undoubtedly we may find

V
Very strange is this indeed

W
We all agree as to
We all feel the force of the maxim
We all in equal sincerity profess
We almost shudder when we see
We are accustomed to lay stress upon
We are all familiar with
We are approaching an era
We are apt to forget
We are assembled here to-day
We are beginning to realize
We are bound to give heed
We are constantly being told
We are fulfilling what I believe to be
We are in the habit of saying
We are met to-night
We are not able to prove
We are not disinterested
We are quite unable to speculate
We are told emphatically
We are tolerably certain
We believe with a sincere belief

To take a very different instance
To the conclusion thus drawn
To the enormous majority of persons
To these general considerations
To this I answer
To this it will be replied
To what other cause can you ascribe
To-day, as never before
Treading close upon the heels
Tried by this standard
True it is
True, there are difficulties
Truly it is a subject for astonishment
Two things are made very clear

Unfortunately it is a truth
Unless I could be sure
Up to this moment I have stated

We can but pause to contemplate
We can imagine the amazement of
We can not but be struck with
We can not escape the truth
We can not have this too deeply fixed
We can not too highly honor the temper
of
We can not wonder
We can only applaud the sentiment
We can only bow with awe
We can presume
We can remember with pride
We can see to some extent
We continually hear nowadays
We deeply appreciate the circumstances
of
We do not quarrel with those
We do not question the reality
We do well to recall
We easily persuade ourselves
We feel keenly about such things

We grope blindly along
We have a firm assurance
We have a right to claim
We have an overpowering sense
We have been accustomed to
We have been told by more than one
We have come together to-night
We have great reason to be thankful
We have heard lately
We have here plain proof
We have need to examine
We have no means of knowing
We have no other alternative
We have not yet solved the problem
We have sought on this occasion
We have the evidence of this
We have the good fortune to-night
We have to admit
We have witnessed on many occasions
We hear it is said sometimes
We hear no complaint
We heartily wish and mean
We hold fast to the principle
We laugh to scorn the idea
We may all of us agree
We may be permitted to remember
We may contemplate with satisfaction
We may have a deep consciousness
We may indeed consider
We may not know precisely how
We must also look
We must constantly direct our purpose
We must not be deceived
We must not mistake
We must realize conscientiously
We must remember
We need no proof to assure us
We need not look far for reasons
We need not trouble ourselves
We of this generation
We often hear persons say
We ought in strict propriety
We pride ourselves upon the fact
We rightly pay all honor
We see in a variety of ways
We shall all doubtless concede
We shall be blind not to perceive

We shall do well to remember
We shall have no difficulty in
determining
We should be convinced
We should contemplate and compare
We should dread nothing so much
We should lend our influence
We should not question for a moment
We should not, therefore, question
We stand astonished at
We stumble and falter and fall
We take it for granted
We will not stop to inquire
Weighty as these conditions are
Well, gentlemen, it must be confessed
Well may we explain
Well, now, let us propose
Well, that being the case, I say
Were I to enter into a detailed
description
Were I to speculate
What are the precise characteristics
What are we to think of
What are you going to do
What can avail
What can be more intelligible
What can be more monstrous than
What can I say better
What commonly happens is this
What could be more captivating
What could be more true
What do we gain by
What do we understand to have been
What I mean is this
What I now say is
What I object to is
What I propose to do is
What I shall actually attempt to show
here
What I suggest is
What is more important
What is more remarkable
What is the pretext
What is this but to say
What more shall I say
What remains but to wish you
What strikes the mind so forcibly

What, then, are we to believe
What, then, can be the reason
What, then, I may be asked
What, then, is the use
What, then, was the nature of
What was the consequence of
What we are concerned to know is
What we have most to complain of
What would you say
Whatever a man thinks
Whatever difference of opinion may exist
Whatever opinion I may express
Whatever the truth may be
When I am told
When I hear it said
When I remember the history
When I review these circumstances
When I speak of this question
When I thus profess myself
When one remembers
When we consider the vastness
When we contemplate
When we get so far as this
When we look closely at
When will men understand
When you are assured
When you did me the honor to invite me
Whence it is, I say

Whence was the proof to come
While acknowledging the great value
While I feel most keenly the honor
While I have hinted to you
Whilst I am on this matter
Who can deny the effect
Who can say in a word
Who does not like to see
Who has not felt the contrast
Who that reads does not see
Who will accuse me
Why, again, should I take notice
Why need you seek to disprove
Will any gentleman say
Will anyone answer
Will it be whispered
Will it not be well for us
Will you allow me to present to you
Will you bear with me
Will you mistake this
Will you permit me to thank you
With all my heart I share
With possibly a single exception
With respect to what has been said
With this ideal clearly before us
With whatever opinions we come here
Without going into any details
Without my saying a word more

Y
Yet I am convinced
Yet I am willing to admit
Yet I am willing to conclude
Yet I feel quite free to say
Yet I, for one, do not hesitate to admit
Yet I have never been thoroughly satisfied
Yet I suppose it is worth while
Yet I would have to think
Yet if you were to ask the question
Yet it is instructive and interesting
Yet it is no less true
Yet it is perfectly plain
Yet let me consider what consequences must
Yet may I not remind you

You all know the history of
You and I are always contrasting
You are at a parting of the ways
You are now invited to do honor
You can never forget
You can not assert
You do not need to be told
You have all read the story
You have been gracious enough to assign to me
You have been mindful
You have been pleased to confer upon me
You have but to observe
You have done me great honor
You have no right

You have not forgotten
You have often pondered over
You have sometimes been astonished
You know that it is impossible to
You know the legend which has grown up
You know very well
You may also be assured
You may be acquainted with
You may be sure
You may depend upon it
You may remember
You may well be proud
You may well study the example
You might apply to yourselves
You must not forget
You must understand I do not mean to claim
You ought not to disregard what I say

You remember how
You will allow me to say with becoming brevity
You will be pleased to hear
You will bear me out when I say
You will clearly understand
You will expect me to say something about
You will forgive me
You will join with me, I trust
You will observe
You will pardon me, I am sure
You will scarcely be surprised
You would never dream of urging
You yourselves are the evidence
Your friendly and generous words
Your good sense must tell you
Your presence seems to say

# SECTION 11
# MISCELLANEOUS PHRASES

A
A bewildering labyrinth of facts
A blank absence of interest or sympathy
A bloodless diplomatist
A breach of confidence
A brilliant and paradoxical talker
A burning sense of shame and horror
A century of disillusionment
A certain catholicity of taste [catholicity = universality]
A cheap and coarse cynicism
A civilizing agency of conspicuous value
A cleanness and probity of life [probity = integrity; uprightness]
A commendable restraint
A condescending and patronizing spirit
A confused and troublesome time
A conscientious anxiety to do the right thing
A conspicuous and crowning service
A constant source of surprise and delight
A contemptible species of mockery
A convenient makeshift
A copious torrent of pleasantry
A course of arrogant obstinacy
A crumb of consolation
A crystallized embodiment of the age
A cynical and selfish hedonist
A dangerous varnish of refinement
A dead theological dogma
A decorous and well-intentioned person
A deep and most impressive solemnity
A deep and strange suggestiveness
A deep authentic impression of disinterestedness
A dereliction of duty
A disaster of the first magnitude
A distorted and pessimistic view of life
A dogmatic and self-righteous spirit
A duel of brains
A dull collocation of words
A fastidious sense of fitness

A fatal moral hollowness
A feeling of lofty remoteness
A feminine excess of inconsequence
A final and irrevocable settlement
A firmness tempered by the most scrupulous courtesy
A fitting interval for penitence
A flippant rejoinder
A flood of external impressions
A flourish of rhetoric
A fund of curious information
A furtive groping after knowledge
A gambler's desperate chance
A ghastly mixture of defiance and conceit
A glaring example of rapacity [rapacity = plundering]
A graceful nonentity
A great and many-sided personality
A great capacity for generous indignation
A great source of confusion
A gross piece of stupidity
A habit of riding a theory too hard
A habit of rigorous definition
A happy and compensating experience
A haughty self-assertion of equality
A hideous absurdity
A hideous orgy of massacre and outrage
A high pitch of eloquence
A homelike and festive aspect
A hopeless enigma
A hotbed of disturbance
A hushed rustle of applause testified to a widespread approbation [approbation = warm approval; praise]
A keenly receptive and intensely sensitive temperament
A kind of fantastic patchwork
A kind of surly reluctance
A laudable stimulus

A law of retributive justice
A less revolutionary innovation
A life of studious contemplation
A limpidity and lucidity of style
[limpidity = transparent clearity; easily intelligible]
A lingering tinge of admiration
A lively sense of what is dishonorable
A long accumulating store of discontent and unrest
A long tangle of unavoidable detail
A look threatening and peremptory
[peremptory = ending all debate or action]
A many-sided and far-reaching enthusiasm
A marvelous sharpener of the faculties
A melancholy preponderance of mischief
A memory-haunting phrase
A mercenary marriage
A mere conjectural estimate
A microscopic care in the search of words
A misconception which is singularly prevalent
A mixture of malignancy and madness
A modicum of truth
A monstrous travesty
A mood of hard skepticism
A more than ordinary share of baseness and depravity
A most laudable zeal
A most repulsive and incomprehensible idiom
A most unseasonable piece of impertinence
A multitude of groundless alarms
A murderous tenacity about trifles
A mysterious and an intractable pestilence
A mysterious and inscrutable power
A narrow and superficial survey
A nature somewhat frivolous and irresolute
A needlessly offensive manner
A nimble interchange of uninteresting gossip

A noble and puissant nation [puissant = with power, might]
A novel and perplexing course
A numerous company
A painful and disconcerting deformity
A partial disenchantment
A passage of extraordinary daring
A patchwork of compromises
A permanent and habitual state of mind
A pernicious and growing tendency
A perversion of judgment
A phantom of the brain
A piece of grotesque stupidity
A pleasant flow of appropriate language
A pompous failure
A potential menace to life
A powerful and persuasive orator
A prevalent characteristic of her nature
A prey to the tongue of the public
A pristine vigor of style
A profusion of compliments
A proposition inherently vicious
A puerile illusion [puerile = immature; childish]
A quenchless thirst for expression
A rage akin to frenzy
A rare precision of insight
A rather desperate procedure
A reckless fashion
A recrudescence of superstition
[recrudescence = recurrence of a pathological symptoms after a period of improvement]
A relish for the sublime
A reversion to the boldest paganism
A rigid avoidance of extravagance and excess
A ripple of applause
A restraining and conservative force
A robust and consistent application
A sacred and indissoluble union
A sane philosophy of life
A secluded dreamer of dreams
A secret and wistful charm
A sense of deepening discouragement
A sense of indescribable reverence
A series of brief and irritating hopes

A settled conviction of success
A sharp difference of opinion
A sharp pang of regretful surprise
A shrewd eye to the main chance
A signal deed of justice
A skeptical suspension of judgment
A slight and superficial tribute
A slowly subsiding frenzy
A snare and a delusion
A somewhat complicated and abstruse calculation [abstruse = difficult to understand]
A sordid and detestable motive
A sort of incredulous stupefaction
A source of unfailing delight and wonder
A species of moral usurpation
A spirit inimical to learning
A spirit of complacent pessimism
A startling and unfortunate digression
A state of scarcely veiled insurrection
A state of urgent necessity
A stern decree of fate
A stern foe of snobbishness
A storm of public indignation
A strange mixture of carelessness, generosity, and caprice
A strangely perverse and poverty stricken imagination
A strong assumption of superiority
A subjugated and sullen population
A sudden revulsion
A supposed ground of affinity
A synonym for retrogression
A taunting accusation of falsehood
A tedious and needless drudgery
A temper which brooked no resistance
A temporary expedient
A tender tone of remonstrance
A theme of endless meditation
A thing of moods and moments
A thoroughly sincere and unaffected effort
A thousand mangled delusions
A tissue of dull excuses
A tone of exaggerated solicitude
A touch of exquisite pathos
A trace of obvious sarcasm

A transcript of the common conscience
A trifle prim and puritanic
A truth begirt with fire
A unique and overwhelming charm
A vague aversion
A variety of conflicting and profound emotions
A variety of enfeebling amendments
A vast multitude of facts
A vastly extended vision of opportunity
A vehement and direct attack
A very elusive and delicate thought
A very formidable problem
A vigilant reserve
A violent and base calumniator [calumniator = makes malicious or knowingly false statements]
A voice of matchless compass and eloquence
A warmth of seemingly generous indignations
A wealth of resource that seemed inexhaustible
A welcome release from besetting difficulties
A whole catalog of disastrous blunders
A whole whirlpool of various emotions
Abounding bodily vigor
Above and beyond and before all else
Absurd and inconsequential career
Abundant and congenial employment
Accidental rather than intentional
Accustomed to ascribe to chance
Acquired sentiments of propriety
Activities of the discursive intellect
Actuated by an unduly anxious desire
Acute sensibility coupled with quickness of intellect
Adhere too tenaciously to forms and modes
Admirable mastery of technique
Admit the soft impeachment
Admitted with a childlike cheerfulness
Advance by leaps and bounds
Advancing to dignity and honor
Adventitious aids to memory [adventitious = Not inherent; added

extrinsically]
Affectation and superfluous ornament
Aggravated to an unspeakable degree
Agitated and perplexed by a dozen cross-currents of conflicting tendency
Agreeable and humanizing intercourse
Aided by strong mental endowments
Airy swiftness of treatment
Alien to the purpose
All sorts of petty tyrannies
All the resources of a burnished rhetoric
Allied by taste and circumstances
Allied with a marked imperiousness [imperious = arrogantly overbearing]
Almost incredible obtuseness
Altogether monstrous and unnatural
Always observant and discriminating
Amaze and confound the imagination
Amiable and indulgent hostess
Amid many and pressing avocations
Amid the homeliest details of daily life
Amid the rush and roar of life
Ample scope for the exercise of his astonishing gifts
An abandoned and exaggerated grief
An accidental encounter
An act of folly amounting to wickedness
An afternoon of painfully constrained behavior
An agreeable image of serene dignity
An air of artificial constraint
An air of round-eyed profundity
An alarmed sense of strange responsibilities
An almost excessive exactness
An almost sepulchral regularity and seclusion
An ample and imposing structure
An apostle of unworldly ardor
An appreciable menace
An ardent and gifted youth
An arid dictum
An artful and malignant enemy
An assumption entirely gratuitous
An assumption which proved erroneous
An atmosphere of sunny gaiety
An attitude of passive impartiality

An authoritative and conclusive inquiry
An egregious assumption [egregious = outrageously reprehensible]
An elaborate assumption of indifference
An endless field for discussion
An enervating and emasculating form of indulgence
An ennobling and invigorating influence
An entirely negligible quantity
An essentially grotesque and commonplace thing
An eternal and imperishable example
An exalted and chimerical sense of honor [chimerical = highly improbable]
An excess of unadulterated praise
An excessive refinement of feeling
An expression at once confident and appealing
An extensive and populous country
An habitual steadiness and coolness of reflection
An honest and unquestioning pride
An icy indifference
An idle and unworthy action
An ill-assorted vocabulary
An immeasurable advantage
An imminent and overmastering peril
An imperturbable demeanor and steadiness of mind
An implacable foe
An inborn and irresistible impulse
An incongruous spectacle
An incredible mental agility
An indefinable taint of priggishness [priggishness = exaggerated propriety]
An indescribable frankness and simplicity of character
An indolent surrender to mere sensuous experience
An indomitable and unselfish soul
An ineradicable love of fun and mystification
An inevitable factor of human conduct
An inexhaustible copiousness and readiness of speech
An insatiable appetite for trifles
An insatiable voracity

An inscrutable mystery
An intentional breach of politeness
An interchange of civilities
An intolerable deal of guesswork
An involuntary gesture of remonstrance
An irrelevant bit of magniloquence
[magniloquence = extravagant in speech]
An irrepressible and impassioned hopefulness
An irritating and dangerous treatment
An itching propensity for argument
An object of indestructible interest
An obnoxious member of society
An ominous lull and silence
An open and violent rupture
An outburst of impassioned eloquence
An unaccountable feeling of antipathy
An unbecoming vehemence
An undisciplined state of feeling
An unerring sense of humor
An unparalleled and almost miraculous growth
An unparalleled atrocity
An unpatriotic and ignoble act
An unreasoning form of coercion
An utterly vile and detestable spirit
And now I address myself to my task
And the like
Announced in a tone of pious satisfaction
Another thought importuned him

B

Bandied to and fro
Based on a fundamental error
Beguile the tedium of the journey
Bemoaning and bewailing his sad fortune
Beset with external dangers
Betrayed into deplorable error
Bewildering multiplication of details
Beyond the dreams of avarice
Blended with courage and devotion
Blind leaders of the blind
Blunt the finer sensibilities
Blustering desire for publicity
Bound up with impossibilities and

[importuned = insistent or repeated requests]
Anticipated with lively expectation
Apparent rather than real
Appeal to a tardy justice
Appreciably above the level of mediocrity
Arbitrary assumption of power
Ardently and enthusiastically convinced
Argued with immense force and feeling
Arrayed with scrupulous neatness
Arrogance and untutored haughtiness
As an impartial bystander
As belated as they are fallacious
As by a secret of freemasonry
As odious as it is absurd
As ridiculous as it was unnecessary
As we scan the vague unknown
Assailed by poignant doubts
Assume a menacing attitude
Assumed almost heroic proportions
At once epigrammatic and arresting
[epigrammatic = terse and witty]
At once misleading and infelicitous
At the mercy of small prejudices
Attained by rigorous self-restraint
Attended by insuperable difficulties
Averted by some happy stroke of fortune
Await the sentence of impartial posterity
Awaited with feverish anxiety

absurdities
Breathed an almost exaggerated humility
Bred in the tepid reticence of propriety
Brief ventures of kindliness
Brilliant display of ingenious argument
Bring odium upon the individual
Brisk directness of speech
Brutal recognition of failure
Bursts of unpremeditated frankness
But delusions and phantasmagoria
But that is beside the mark
But this is a digression
By a curious perversity of fate
By a happy turn of thinking

By a whimsical diversion
By common consent
By means of crafty insinuations
By no means inconsolable
By temperament incompatible
By the common judgment of the thinking
world
By the sheer centripetal force of sympathy
By virtue of a common understanding
By way of rejoinder

## C

Calculated to create disgust
Calm strength and constancy
Capable of a severe scientific treatment
Capacity for urbanity and moderation
Carried into port by fair winds
Caught unawares by a base impulse
Ceaseless tramp of humanity
Censured for his negligence
Championing the cause of religious education
Chastened and refined by experience
Checked by the voice of authority
Cherished the amiable illusion
Cherishing a huge fallacy
Childishly inaccurate and absurd
Chivalrous loyalty and high forbearance
Clever and captivating eloquence
Coarse and glittering ostentation
Coherent and continuous trend of thought
Commended by perfect suavity
Common ground of agreement

Complicated and infinitely embittered
Conceded from a sense of justice
Conceived with imperfect knowledge
Concentrated and implacable resolve
Conditions of unspeakable humiliation
Conducive to well-being and efficiency
Confused rumblings presaging a different epoch
Constrained by the sober exercise of judgment
Consumed by a demon of activity
Continuous and stubborn disregard
Contrary to the clearest conviction of his judgment
Couched in terms of feigned devotion
Credulous and emotionally extravagant
Creed of incredulity and derision
Criticized with unsparing vigor
Crude undigested masses of suggestion
Cruel and baseless calumnies [calumnies = maliciously false statements; slander]
Cynically repudiate all obligations

## D

Daily usages and modes of thinking
Dangerously near snobbery
Darkly insinuating what may possibly happen
Dazzled by their novelty and brilliance
Debased by common use
Deep essentials of moral grandeur
Deeply engrossed in congenial work
Deeply moved as well as keenly stung
Deeply rooted in the heart of humanity
Defiant of analysis and rule
Degenerate into comparative feebleness
Degenerated into deadness and formality
Degrading and debasing curiosity
Deliberate and cautious reflection

Delicacy of perception and quick tact
Delude many minds into acquiescence
Dense to the point of stupidity
Descanting on them cursorily [descanting = discussion or discourse]
Devices generally held to be discreditable
Devious and perilous ways
Devoid of hysteria and extravagance
Dexterous modes of concealment
Dictated by an overweening partiality
Differ in degree only and not in kind
Difficult and abstruse questions [abstruse = incomprehensible ]
Diffidence overwhelmed him

221

Diffusing beneficent results
Dignified by deliberation and privacy
Dimly implying some sort of jest
Discreditable and insincere support
Disdaining the guidance of reason
Disenchanting effect of time and experience
Disfigured by glaring faults
Disguised in sentimental frippery
Dispel all anxious concern
Displayed enormous power and splendor
Distinguish themselves by their eccentricities
Distracted by contending desires
Diversity of mind and temperament

Divested of all personal feelings
Dogged and shameless beyond all precedent
Dominated by no prevailing taste or fashion
Doomed by inexorable fate
Doomed to impermanence and transiency
Draw back in distrust and misgiving
Dreaded and detested rival
Driven towards disaffection and violence
Due to historical perspective
Dull and trite commonplaces
Dwindled to alarmingly small dimensions

E

Easy-going to the point of lethargy
Elementary principles of right and wrong
Embittered and fanatical agitation
Encrusted with pedantry and prejudice [pedantry = attention to detail]
Endless and intricate technicalities
Endowed with undreamed-of powers
Enforced by coercive measures
Enormities of crime and anomalies of law
Entangled in theological controversy
Entirely futile and negligible
Erroneous assumptions and sophistries
Espoused with extraordinary ardor
Essentially one-sided and incomplete

Eternally fruitful and stimulating
Evidently malicious and adroit
Evinces a hardened conscience and an insensibility to shame
Exact and resolute allegiance
Examples of terrific and explosive energy
Exasperating to the last degree
Excruciating cruelty and injustice
Exposed to damaging criticism
Exposing his arrogance and folly to merited contempt
Expressions of unrestrained grief
Exquisite lucidity of statement
Extraordinarily subtle and penetrating analysis
Exuberant rush of words

F

Facile and fertile literary brains
Faithfully and religiously eschewed [eschew = avoid; shun]
Fallen into the convenient oblivion of the waste-basket
Fanatical and dangerous excesses
Far off and incredibly remote
Fastidious correctness of form
Fate had turned and twisted a thousand ways
Fed by many currents from the long stream of human experience

Feigning a virtuous indignation
Fertility of argumentative resource
Fictitious and adventitious aid
Finely touched to the fine issues
Fit to stand the gaze of millions
Fits and starts of generosity
Fixed convictions of mankind
Flouted as unpractical
Foolish and inflexible superstition
Fostering and preserving order
Free from all controversial pettifogging [pettifogging = quibbling over

insignificant details]
Freighted with the most precious cargoes
Frequently recurring forms of
awkwardness
Fresh and unsuspected loveliness
From the standpoint of expediency and
effectiveness
Full and tuneful diction

Full of ardent affection and gratitude
Full of presentiments of some evil
Full of singular freshness, insight and
power
Full of speculation and a deep restrained
excitement
Fumble and stumble in helpless
incapacity

G

Gain the applause of future ages
Generous to a pathetic and touching
degree
Give vent to his indignation
Giving an ear to a little neighborly gossip
Glances and smiles of tacit contempt
Gnawing at the vitals of society
Grace and gentleness of manner

Graceful succession of sentences
Gratuitous and arbitrary meddling
Greeted with unalloyed satisfaction
Grooves of intellectual habit
Growing sense of bewilderment and
dismay
Guilty and baffled antagonists

H

Habits of unintelligent routine
Habitual self-possession and self-respect
Happy and gracious willingness
Hard-souled and joyously joyous
Haunted by blank misgivings
He affected neither pomp nor grandeur
He became more blandly garrulous
[garrulous = excessive and trivial talk]
He declined the proffered hospitality
He dropped into an eloquent silence
He eludes analysis and baffles
description
He glanced at her indulgently
He had the habit of self-engrossed
silences
He harbored his misgivings in silence
He poured bitter and biting ridicule on
his discomfited opponents
He spoke with sledgehammer directness
He suffers nothing to draw him aside
He took his courage in both hands
He turned on me a glance of stored

intelligence
He was disheveled and untidy
He was inexhaustibly voluble
Heavily freighted with erudition
[erudition = extensive learning]
Heights of serene contemplation
Her voice had a wooden resonance and a
ghost of a lisp
Hidebound in official pedantry [pedantry
= attention to detail]
High and undiscouraged hope
High-handed indifference to all restraint
His chin had too vanishing an aspect
His first zeal was flagging
His general attitude suggested an idea
that he had an oration for you
His gestures and his gait were untidy
His mood was one of pure exaltation
His plea was irresistible
His tone verged on the ironical
His work was ludicrously perfunctory
Hopelessly belated in its appearance

I

I adjured him [adjured = command or
enjoin solemnly, as under oath]
I am not without a lurking suspicion

I bemoaned my unlucky fate
I could almost allege it as a supreme
example

223

I have somewhat overshot the mark
I lost myself in a reverie of gratitude
I made bold to retort
I must hazard the story
I was extremely perplexed
I will permit myself the liberty of saying
I would fain believe [fain = happily; gladly]
Illuminate with sinister effect
Immediate and effectual steps
Immense capacity for ceaseless progress
Immunity from criticism and control
Impartial and exacting judgment
Impatience of despotic influence
Impelled by strong conviction
Imperiled in a restless age
Imperious in its demands [imperious = arrogantly domineering]
Impotent outbreaks of unreasoning rage
Impromptu parades of noisy patriotism
In a diversity of application
In a fever of apprehension
In a frenzy of fussy excitement
In a frowning abstraction
In a great and fruitful way
In a high degree culpable
In a kind of confused astonishment
In a most commendable fashion
In a most impressive vein
In a position of undisputed supremacy
In a rapture of imagined ecstasy
In a secret and surreptitious way [surreptitious = done by clandestine or stealthy means]
In a spirit of friendliness and conciliation
In a state of mulish reluctance [mulish = stubborn and intractable]
In a state of nervous exacerbation
In a state of virtuous complacency
In a tone of uneasy interrogation
In a transport of ambitious vanity
In a whirlwind of feeling and memory
In accents embarrassed and hesitating
In alliance with steady clearness of intellect
In amazed ejaculation
In an eminent and unique sense

In an eminent degree
In deference to a unanimous sentiment
In extenuation of the past
In high good humor
In his customary sententious fashion [sententious = terse and energetic; pithy]
In its most odious and intolerable shape
In language terse yet familiar
In moments of the most imminent peril
In quite incredible confusion
In seasons of difficulty and trial
In spite of plausible arguments
In terms of imperishable beauty
In the dim procession of years
In the highest conceivable degree
In the local phrase
In the nature of things
In the ordinarily accepted sense
In the realm of conjecture
In the scheme of things
In the tone of one who moralizes
In the twinkling of an eye
In the world of letters
In tones of genuine admiration
Incapable of flashy make-believe
Incited by a lust for gain
Incomparable lucidity and penetrativeness
Inconceivable clumsiness of organization
Indulge a train of gentle recollection
Indulging a sickly and nauseating petulance
Ineffably dreary and unpicturesque
Infected with a feverish dissatisfaction
Infuse a wholesome terror
Inimical to true and determined principle [Inimical = harmful; adverse]
Inimitable grace and felicity [inimitable = defying imitation; matchless]
Injudicious and inelegant ostentation
Innumerable and incessant creations
Inordinate greed and love of wealth
Insatiably greedy of recognition
Insensibility to moral perspective and proportion
Insolent and riotous excess
Inspired by a vague malevolence

Inspirited by approval and applause
Instances might be multiplied
indefinitely
Instantly alive to the slightest breach of
decorum
Insufferable violence to the feelings
Intense and stubborn dogmatism
Intense sensitiveness to injustice
Intercourse with polished society
Intervals of respite and repose
Inveigh against established customs
[inveigh = angry disapproval; protest
vehemently]
Invested with a partial authority
Inveterate forces of opposition
Invincible jealousy and hate
Involuntary thrill of gratified vanity
Involved in profound uncertainty
Involving ourselves in embarrassments
Inward appraisal and self-renouncement
Irregulated and desultory education
[desultory = haphazard; random]
Irrelevant to the main issue
Irresistibly impelled by conscience
Irritable bitterness and angry suspicion
It assumes the shape of malignity
It betrays a great want of prudence and
discernment
It defies description
It dissipates every doubt and scruple
It enslaves the imagination
It extorted from him expressions of
irritability
It gives one a little grip at the throat

J
Jealous and formidable foes
Justifiable in certain exigencies

K
Keen power of calculation and
unhesitating audacity
Kindle the flames of genuine oratory

L
Labored and far-fetched elocution
Laid down in a most unflinching and

It has been stigmatized as irrelevant
It has more than passing interest
It has seldom been surpassed
It imposes no constraint
It is a capital blunder
It is a common error among ignorant
people
It is a consoling reflection
It is a mark of great instability
It is a staggering thought
It is always something vicious
It is an odd jealousy
It is an intolerable idea
It is impossible to resist acknowledging
this
It is little more than a platitude
It is not consistent with elevated and
dignified character
It is not wholly insignificant
It is notoriously easy to exaggerate
It is the common consent of men
It is unnecessary to multiply instances
It makes life insupportable
It must be a matter of conjecture
It occasions suspicion and discontent
It runs counter to all established customs
It was a matter of notoriety
It wears a ragged and dangerous front
It would be a fruitless and unthankful
task
It would be superfluous to say
It would not seem an improbable
conclusion
Its dominating and inspiring influence


[exigencies = urgent situations]


Knotty and subtle disquisitions
[disquisitions = formal discourse]


vigorous fashion
Lamentable instances of extravagance

Lash themselves into fury
Lax theories and corresponding practises
Lay hold of the affections
Leaden mood of dulness
Lend a critical ear
Lest the requirements of courtesy be disregarded
Links in the chain of reasoning
Little less than scandalous
Lofty and distinguished simplicity
Long-sighted continuity of thought and plan
Looking at the matter by and large
Looming large and ugly in the public view
Loose and otiose statement [otiose = lazy; indolent; of no use]
Lost in indolent content
Lovely beyond all words
Lucidity and argumentative vigor
Lulled into a sense of false satisfaction

M

Maddened by a jealous hate
Maintained with ingenuity and vigor
Manifestly harsh and barbarous
Marvelous copiousness of illustration
Marvelously suggestive and inspiring
Men of profound erudition [erudition = extensive learning]
Mere effects of negligence
Microscopic analysis of character
Mingled distrust and fear
Ministering to mere pleasure and indulgence
Minutely and rationally exposing their imperfections
Morbid and subjective brooding
More or less severe and prolonged
Moved to unaccustomed tears
My worst suspicions were confirmed
Mysterious and invincible darkness

N

Naked vigor of resolution
Naturally prone to believe
Necessity thus imposed by prudence
Nerveless and faithless folly
No more than brief palliatives or mitigations
Noble and sublime patience
Noisy torrent of talk
Not averse to a little gossip
Not so much polished as varnished
Noted for their quixotic love of adventure
Nothing could be more captious or unfair [captious = disposition to find and point out trivial faults]
Nothing remained but a graceful acquiescence
Notoriously distracted by internecine jealousies

O

Objects of general censure
Obscured beneath the rubbish of the age
Obsessed with an overweening pride
Obstacles that are difficult but not insuperable
Obviously at variance with facts
Occasioned by direct moral turpitude [turpitude = depravity; baseness]
Oddly amenable to the proposed innovations
Often employed promiscuously
Ominous and swift days
Omitting all compliments and commonplaces
On a noble and commanding scale
On sure ground of fact
On the edge of great irritability
On the horns of a dilemma
One of life's ironical adjustments
One of the foreseen and inevitable

results
One tissue of rashness, folly, ingratitude, and injustice
Openly flouted and disavowed
Oppressed by some vague dread
Organs of party rage and popular frenzy
Our opinions were diametrically opposed

Our vaunted civilization
Outward mark of obeisance and humiliation [obeisance = attitude of deference]
Overcome by an access of misery
Overshadowed by a fretful anxiety
Overwhelmed with reproach and popular indignation

## P

Painful and lamentable indifference
Palpably and unmistakably commonplace
Parading an exception to prove a rule
Paralyzed by infirmity of purpose
Paralyzing doubts and scruples
Paramount obligation and righteousness
Partial and fragmentary evidence
Passionately addicted to pleasure
Patently inimical to liberty
Patience under continual provocation
Peculiarly liable to misinterpretation
Peddling and pitiful compromises
Pelting one another with catchwords
Perfectly illustrated and exemplified
Perpetually excite our curiosity
Pierced to the quick
Pitiful shifts of policy
Plainly dictated by a lofty purpose
Pleading the exigencies of strategical interest [exigencies = urgent situations]
Plunged into tumultuous preoccupation

Pointed out with triumphant malice
Polished beauty of diction
Political storm and stress.
Position of titular command
Preached with a fierce unction [unction = exaggerated earnestness]
Precipitate and arbitrary changes
Predict the gloomiest consequences
Pregnant with a lesson of the deepest import
Presented with matchless vigor and courage
Princely generosity of praise
Prodigious and portentous events
Protracted to a vexatious length
Proud schemes for aggrandizement
Provocative of bitter hostility
Pruned of their excrescences and grotesque extremes [excrescences = abnormal growth, such as a wart]
Purged of glaringly offensive features
Pursued to a vicious extent

## Q

Questioned and tested in the crucible of experience
Quickened into a stabbing suspicion
Quickness to conceive and courage to

execute
Quite destitute of resources
Quixotically generous about money

## R

Radiantly and transparently happy
Railed at the world
Rare candor and flexibility of mind
Rare fidelity of purpose and achievement
Rarely brought to pass
Reeling headlong in luxury and sensuality

Regarded with sincere abhorrence
Regulated by the fixed rules of good-breeding
Religious rights and ceremonies
Reluctant to appear in so equivocal a character
Render null and void

Rent by internal contentions
Repugnant alike to reason and conscience
Resigned to growing infirmities
Resist a common adversary
Resting on some collateral circumstance

Rhetorical and ambitious diction
Rich and exuberant complexities
Rigid and exact boundaries
Rooted in immeasurable error and falsity
Roused to tumultuous activity
Rude and blind criticism

S
Sadly counterbalanced by numerous faults
Said with epigrammatic point [epigrammatic = terse and witty]
Salutary in the extreme
Salutary tonic of a free current of public criticism
Sanity and quietness of soul
Scorned as an impracticable theory
Scornful of petty calculations
Screen themselves from punishment
Scrupulous and chivalrous loyalty
See with eagle glance through conventionalisms
Seem to savor of paradox
Seize the auspicious moment
Self-centered anxiety and preoccupation
Self-command born of varied intercourse
Self-interest of the most compelling character
Selfish and uselessly recondite [recondite = not easily understood]
Selfishness pampered by abundance
Senses of marvelous acuteness
Sensible diminution of our comfort
Sensitive and apprehensive temperament
Sentimental wailings for the past
Serve the innocent purposes of life
Set down with meticulous care
Shames us out of our nonsense
Sharp outbursts of hatred and bitterness
Sharp restrictions of duty and opportunity
Sharply and definitely conceived
She had lost her way in a labyrinth of conjecture
She took refuge in a passionate exaggeration of her own insufficiency

Sheer midsummer madness
Silly displays of cheap animosity
Simple and obvious to a plain understanding
Sinister and fatal augury [augury = sign of something coming; omen]
Skulking beneath a high-sounding benevolence
Slack-minded skimming of newspapers
Slavish doctrines of sectarianism
Slow and resistless forces of conviction
Smug respectability and self-content
Snatch some advantage
Socialized and exacting studies
Some very undignified disclosures
Something essentially inexpressible
Something stifling and over-perfumed
Spinning a network of falsehoods
Spiritual and moral significance
Staring in helpless bewilderment
Stealthily escaping observation
Stern determination to inflict summary justice
Stigmatized as moral cowards
Stimulated to profitable industry
Stopped as if on the verge of profundities
Strange frankness of cynical brutality
Strange streak of melancholy
Strangled by a snare of words
Strenuous and conscientious endeavor
Stretched out in dreary monotony
Strict and unalloyed veracity
Struck incessantly and remorselessly
Stupendous and awe-inspiring spectacle
Subject to the vicissitudes of fortune [vicissitudes = sudden or unexpected changes]
Subjected to the grossest cruelties
Subordination to the common weal

Subservient to the ends of religion
Sudden and inexplicable changes of mood
Suddenly and imperatively summoned
Suddenly swelled to unprecedented magnitude
Sufficient to repel vulgar curiosity
Suggestive sagacity and penetration [sagacity = farsighted; wise]
Suit the means to the end
Sullen and widespread discontent

Superior in strength and prowess
Supported by a splendid fearlessness
Supremely and undeniably great
Susceptible to every impulse and stimulus
Sustained dignity and mellifluous precision [mellifluous = flowing with honey; smooth and sweet]
Swamping every aspiration and ambition
Swift and vehement outbursts of feeling

T

Take root in the heart
Take vengeance upon arrogant self-assertion
Taken in their totality
Tamed and wonted to a settled existence
Tempered by the emotional warmth of high moral ideals
That way madness lies
The abysmal depths of despair
The accumulated bitterness of failure
The agonies of conscious failure
The air was full of the cry and clamor
The animadversions of critics [animadversions = Strong criticism]
The applause was unbounded
The best proof of its timeliness and salutariness [salutariness = favorable]
The bewildered and tumultuous world
The blackest abyss of despair
The blemishes of an extraordinary reputation
The bluntness of a provincial
The bogey of bad luck [bogey = evil or mischievous spirit; hobgoblin]
The bounding pulse of youth
The brunt of life
The capacity for refined pursuits
The charming omniscience of youth
The cloak of cowardice
The collective life of humanity
The combined dictates of reason and experience
The companion of a noble and elevated spirit

The complaining gate swung open
The complex phenomena of life
The consequence of an agitated mind
The consequence of ignorance and childish assumption
The constant pressure of anxieties
The creature and tool of a party
The critical eyes of posterity
The dead and dusty past
The delimitation is sufficiently definite
The dictates of plain reason
The disjointed babble of the chronicler
The dull derision of the world
The dullest and most vacant minds
The dumb forces of brute nature
The dupe of some imposture
The eager pretentiousness of youth
The ebb and flow of events
The everlasting deluge of books
The evil was irremediable
The exchange of harmless amenities
The exertion of an inherent power
The expression was keenly intellectual
The facile conjectures of ignorant onlookers
The facts took him by the throat
The fitful swerving of passion
The flabbiness of our culture
The flaccid moods of prose
The flame of discord raged with redoubled fury
The flattest and most obvious truisms
The flippant insolence of a decadent skepticism

The foe of excess and immoderation
The fog of prejudice and ill-feeling
The frustration of their dearest hopes
The garb of civilization
The general infusion of wit
The gift of prophecy
The golden years of youth and maturity
The gratification of ambition
The grim reality of defeat
The hall-mark of a healthy humanity
The handmaid of tyranny
The hint of tranquillity and self-poise
The hints of an imaginable alliance
The hobgoblin of little minds
The holiest and most ennobling
sensations of the soul
The hollowest of hollow shams
The homely virtue of practical utility
The hubbub and turmoil of the great
world
The huge and thoughtful night
The hurly-burly of events
The idea was utterly hateful and
repugnant
The idle of all hobbledehoys
[hobbledehoys = gawky adolescent boy]
The ignoble exploitation of public
interests
The imminent fatality awaiting him
The impulse of prejudice or caprice
The incorrigibility of perverse human
nature
The incursions of a venomous rabble
The indulgence of an overweening self-
conceit
The inevitable climax and culmination
The inference is inescapable
The infirmity and fallibility of human
nature
The inflexible serenity of the wheeling
sun
The ingenuities of legal verbiage
The inmost recesses of the human heart
The insipidity of indifference
The insolence of power
The irony of circumstances
The jaded weariness of overstrained

living
The jargon of well-handled and voice-
worn phrases
The jostling and ugliness of life
The lawyer's habit of circumspection and
delay
The long-delayed hour of retribution
The lowest grade of precarious
mendacity [mendacity = untruthfulness]
The makeshifts of mediocrity
The malarious air of after-dinner gossip
The mazes of conflicting testimony
The mean and frivolous affections of the
idle
The menacing shadow of want
The mere fruit of his distempered
imagination
The mere reversal of the wheel of
fortune
The merest smattering of knowledge
The meticulous preciosity of the lawyer
and the logician [preciosity = extreme
overrefinement]
The most absurd elementary questions
The most amazing impudence
The most exacting and exciting business
The most fallacious of all fallacies
The most implacable logic
The most preposterous pride
The multitudinous tongue of the people
The outcome of unerring observation
The outraged conscience of mankind
The overpowering force of
circumstances and necessity
The overweening exercise of power
The panacea for the evils of society
The panorama of history
The pernicious doctrines of skeptics
The perpetrator of clumsy witticisms
The precarious tenure of fame
The precursor of violence
The pretty and delicate game of talk
The primitive instinct of self-
preservation
The property of little minds
The prophecies of visionaries and
enthusiasts

The proprieties of etiquette
The purse-proud inflation of the moneyed man
The question was disconcertingly frank
The ravening wolves of brute instinct
The remark was sternly uncompromising
The result of caprice
The rigor of the law
The sanction and authority of a great name
The severest shocks of adverse fate
The sharp and vehement assertion of authority
The sinister influence of unprincipled men
The speaker drew an indignant breath
The springs of human action
The staple of conversation
The stillness of finality
The stings of self-reproach
The straightforward path of inexorable logic
The strong hand of executive authority
The sum and fruit of experience
The sum total of her impressions was negative
The summit of excellence
The supernatural prescience of prophecy
The sweet indulgence of good-nature
The sycophants of the rich [sycophant = servile self-seeker attempting to win favor by flattery]
The taint of fretful ingratitude
The talk flowed
The target for ill-informed criticism
The tears welled up and flowed abundantly
The tediousness of inactivity
The tendency to evade implicit obligations
The ties of a common cause
The tranquil aspects of society
The tribute of affectionate applause
The ultimate verdict of mankind
The unbroken habit of a lifetime
The unimpeachable correctness of his demeanor

The unlicensed indulgence of curiosity
The unsophisticated period of youth
The utmost excitement and agitation
The vanishing thoughtlessness of youth
The vanity and conceit of insular self-satisfaction
The very texture of man's soul and life
The victim of an increasing irritability
The victorious assertion of personality
The virtue of taciturnity [taciturnity = habitually untalkative]
The voice was sharp and peremptory [peremptory = ending all debate or action]
The want of serious and sustained thinking
The widest compass of human life
The wonderful pageant of consciousness
The words stabbed him
Their authenticity may be greatly questioned
Their indignation waxed fast and furious
Themes of perennial interest
There was a blank silence
There was no sense of diminution
They affected the tone of an impartial observer
They rent the air with shouts and acclamations
Thoughts which mock at human life
Through ever-widening circles of devastation
Through the distortions of prejudice
Thwarted by seeming insuperable obstacles
Time was dissolving the circle of his friends
Times of unexampled difficulty
Tinseled over with a gaudy embellishment of words
To a practised eye
To be sedulously avoided [sedulously = persevering]
To prosecute a scheme of personal ambition
To state the case is to prove it
Too preposterous for belief

231

Too puerile to notice
Too sanguine a forecast [sanguine = cheerfully confident; optimistic]
Torn asunder by eternal strife
Totally detached from all factions
Touched with a sort of reverential gratitude
Transcend the bounds of human credulity

Transitory in its nature
Transparent and ridiculous self-importance
Treasured up with a timid and niggardly thrift
Treated the idea with lofty scorn
Tremendous exploits and thrilling escapades
True incentives to knowledge

U

Unamiable and envious attributes
Unbounded devotion and indulgence
Uncharted oceans of thought
Unconquerable fidelity to duty
Under all conceivable circumstances
Under the sway of arbitrary opinions
Undertaken under propitious circumstances [propitious = auspicious, favorable; kindly]
Uneasy sense of impending change
Unequaled simplicity and directness of purpose
Unexceptional in point of breeding
Unexpected obstacles and inextricable difficulties
Unfailing and miraculous foresight
Unfeigned astonishment and indignation
Unfounded and incredible calumnies [calumnies = maliciously false statements]
Unhampered by binding alliances
Universal in their signification

Unjust and unrighteous persecution
Unreasoning and unquestioning attachment
Unrivaled beauty and excellence
Unrivaled gift of succinct and trenchant speech [trenchant = forceful, effective, vigorous; incisive; distinct]
Unsparing industry and attention
Unspeakably alluring and satisfying
Unsurpassed in force and fitness
Unswerving and unselfish fidelity
Untiring enunciation of platitudes and fallacies
Unutterably trivial and paltry
Unwavering and unquestioning approbation [approbation = warm approval; praise]
Unworthy and ungenerous treatment
Upbraid ourselves with folly
Urgent warning and admonition
Utterly and essentially irreverent

V

Vast and vague aspirations
Vastly complex and far-reaching problems
Vehemently and indignantly repudiated
Venerable and dignified conservatism
Versatile and essentially original
Versed in the arts of exciting tumult and sedition [sedition = insurrection; rebellion]
Viewed in its general tenor and substance

Vigorous and well compacted
Violating all decency
Violent and unforeseen vicissitudes [vicissitudes = sudden or unexpected changes]
Vitiated by intolerance and shortsightedness [vitiated = reduce the value; corrupt morally; debase]
Vivid even to oppressiveness
Voracious and insatiable appetite
Vulgar eagerness for place

W

Warnings too pregnant to be disregarded
Warped by personal pretensions and self-consequence
We may parenthetically note
We must profoundly revere it
Weigh the merits and demerits
Welcomed at first with skeptical contempt
Well-concerted and well-timed stratagems

Whirled into rapid and ceaseless motion
Wholesale friction and discontent
Wholly devoid of public interest
Widely divergent social traits
Wield an unequaled and paramount authority
Wiser counsels prevailed
Withal decidedly handsome
Written in indelible characters upon his heart

Y

Yield to urgent representations

Z

Zealous in the cause he affected to serve
[Pencilled into the flyleaf: "A navy blue feeling where my heart used to be"]

Made in the USA
Lexington, KY
23 June 2010